AN
# AMERICAN FESTIVAL
OF
# WORLD CAPITALS

# AN
# AMERICAN FESTIVAL
## OF
# WORLD CAPITALS
## FROM GARLIC QUEENS
## TO CHERRY PARADES

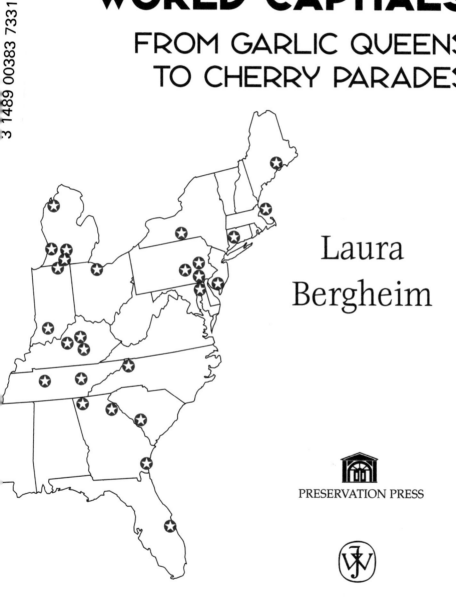

Laura

Bergheim

PRESERVATION PRESS

JOHN WILEY & SONS, INC.

New York • Chichester • Weinheim • Brisbane • Toronto • Singapore

*Library of Congress Cataloging-in-Publication Data*

Bergheim, Laura, 1962–
    An American festival of world capitals: from garlic queens to
cherry parades / Laura Bergheim.
        p.   cm.
    Includes bibliographical references (p.) and index.
    ISBN 0-471-14350-2 (pbk : alk. paper)
        1. United States—Guidebooks   I. Title
    E158.B457   1996
    917.304'929—DC20                                              96-27814

Printed in the United States of America
10 9 8 7 6 5 4 3 2 1

*For Jim, my husband, the world's most charming traveling companion — on the road and in life.*

# A CAPITAL COMMENT

This book offers a broad sampling of the myriad capital cities and towns across America. It is not a scientific survey nor a comprehensive directory of such places, but rather a sampling of Americana. If you know of, or live in, a capital that somehow slipped through the pages here, drop me a line, through the publisher, so I can write about your favorite capital community in the future!

# ACKNOWLEDGMENTS

This book would not have been possible without the help of many people from capital communities all across the country. They work in the chambers of commerce, the local historical societies, the tourism bureaus, the factories, the festival offices, the museums, and all the other places that make a capital community just that. My sincere thanks to all who provided information, photographs, interviews, and support for this book.

I also want to thank Jan Cigliano of Preservation Press, who climbed aboard this horse midstream and understood its temperament (and mine). My appreciation for her patience and affection for this project. And thanks to Ira Brodsky, my production editor at Wiley.

And, as always, I express my gratitude to my family, who always had great ideas, puns, and well wishes throughout this book. Special thanks to Beth Stephens, for her research help; and to Mel and Donna Bergheim, for their editorial efforts. And to my husband, Jim, without whom my happiness would not be possible.

*Laura Bergheim*

# CONTENTS

# INTRODUCTION

Who hasn't been on a road trip and cruised through a small Main Street community where billboards proudly proclaimed the town to be the Strawberry Capital of the World? Or maybe the Watermelon Capital, or the Bass Fishing Capital? Or even the Sock Capital?

It's as American as the Apple Pie Capital of the World: Homespun "sloganeering," the self-proclamation of local pride and productivity, is an endearing part of the national character. But this delightful tendency exhibited by even the smallest town to crown itself a world capital is more than sign-deep: It serves a real purpose, both economic and cultural, in the preservation of hometown heritage.

The history of individual American towns is often hidden, like clues in a picture puzzle, within the claims of a capital community. On the surface, you may see a seemingly silly slogan. But look more closely and you will discover an embedded code that identifies the roots of a place, the employment base, the hometown heros, and local legends that weave the unique patterns in the fabric of every town's everyday life.

Take Gilroy, California, for instance. It has gained quite a reputation with its title of Garlic Capital of the World. Though it's not the state's largest garlic producing area, it has made a name for itself with the Gilroy Garlic Festival, held every July, which attracts 130,000 visitors.

But beneath the hoopla you will find the agricultural legacy of how a particular crop — garlic — helped develop, influence, and ultimately alter the local economy and character. And behind the promotional facade of Gilroy's capital claim you find the secondary economic and cultural impact of tourism: As the Garlic Capital of the World, Gilroy attracts hordes of visitors who come not only for its festival, but also for its year-round attractions, including a colorful garlic mural and shops such as Garlic World and Garlic Grocery. Gilroy's crop was known long ago in kitchens worldwide; but its claim to the title of Garlic Capital of the World put the town itself on the map.

Such capitalism comes in myriad forms. Crop capitals are among the most common, with California, Michigan, and the southern states seeming to produce more fruit and vegetable capitals than other parts of the country. Though some of these green grocer communities have unique crops — Berrien Springs, Michigan, is the World's Christmas Pickle Capital — others have to stand in line for their titles. Watermelon capitals have sprouted from Pennsylvania to Oregon and Texas to Georgia. President Clinton, the man from Hope, Arkansas, was born in one of the many watermelon capitals of the world.

Most of these homegrown capitals celebrate the local crop with festivals featuring parades, beauty contests — Gilroy crowns a Garlic Queen, while wheat capital Wellington, Kansas, chooses a Little Miss Wheat Queen — cook-offs, eating contests, and dances (watermelon capital Hampton County, South Carolina, has a big Melon Ball). All of which bring tourists to town and ensure that the local farmer's markets and roadside stands have a steady stream of business. And, as in ancient times, there's nothing quite like a harvest festival to celebrate the labors of one's fruits.

Though crops are probably the most commonly capitalized community commodity, towns and cities create hometown titles to celebrate almost any feature special about their neck of the woods. Some celebrate animals — Haines, Alaska, is the Eagle Capital of America, home to one of the finest bald eagle refuges anywhere, while Columbia, Tennessee, is known as the Mule Capital of the World for its mule-trading heritage.

And fish capitals emerge all over the country. Most are devoted to recreational fishing — Stuart, Florida, is the Sailfish Capital of the World, and Eufala, Alabama, is one of several bass capitals of the world. But even the architecture of the sport gets celebrated in Mille Lacs, Minnesota, the Fish House Capital of the World, famous for its 5,000 ice fishing houses on the local lake. And several honor the local fish as dish — Breaux Bridge, Louisiana, the Crawfish Capital of the World, draws a crowd for its tasty Crawfish Festival the first weekend in May. And Madison, Minnesota, is known as the Lutefisk Capital, U.S.A. for its love of the traditional Norwegian dish of lye-soaked codfish. Madison even has a mascot, Lou T. Fisk, whose fishy figure can be seen throughout town.

Some towns put cooking and eating above all else, and so they celebrate their local cuisine with capital claims. Springfield, Illinois, calls itself the Chilli Capital of the World (they spell it with two *l*s there), while Battle Creek, Michigan, birthplace of the cold cereal business, is the Cereal Capital of the World. Some towns promote their foods without "capital"ization — Hershey, Pennsylvania, is known as both Chocolate Town, U.S.A., and the Sweetest Place on Earth — but with a flair for name-calling, nonetheless.

Recreation is another heavily promoted claim to fame for many communities. You'll find sporting capitals across the land, from the Learning to Ski Capital (Killington, Vermont) to the Snowshoe Baseball Capital of the World (Lake Tomahawk, Wisconsin). And less physical recreations get recognition as well — Reading and Berks County, Pennsylvania, is the Outlet Capital of the World, while Lincoln City, Oregon, is the Kite Capital of the World, and Sandusky, Ohio, is the Thrill Ride Capital of the World (thanks to Cedar Point Amusement Park).

Sometimes a town's foundation makes for a capital connection — from Wallace, Idaho, the Silver Capital of the World (it's home to four of the world's most productive silver mines), to the rock-solid claim of Bedford, Indiana, the Limestone Capital of the World.

And crafts and culture can give a town a title, too. The colorful windows created in the factories of Winona, Minnesota, have given the town the slogan of Stained Glass Capital of the United States, while Gallup, New Mexico, with its Native American crafters, has the nickname of Indian Jewelry Capital of the World.

If a town has a strong immigrant heritage, it may well be among the ranks of international capitals of America (or at least of their own states). You practically enter another country when you visit places like O'Neill, Nebraska, the Irish Capital of Nebraska, Yukon, Oklahoma, the Czech Capital of Oklahoma, and Solvang, California, the Danish Capital of America. In such towns, you'll find remarkable architecture reminiscent of European villages; and the local restaurants feature authentic dishes often made from recipes handed down from the homeland.

Some capitals are downright weird — they delight in their daffiness, exult in their eccentricity. Wisconsin has not one but two UFO Capitals of the World: Both Elmwood and Belleville got their alien appellations because of sightings of strange lights and objects in the sky. Willow Creek, California, perched at the edge of a wilderness area known for Sasquatch sightings, calls itself the Bigfoot Capital of the World, and even celebrates Bigfoot Days over Labor Day weekend. And holidays get their due as well — Anoka, Minnesota, is the Halloween Capital of the World, while Anthony Texas/New Mexico (its boundaries cross two states), is the Leap Year Capital of the World. Every four years, what a party!

The capital category that seems to have the deepest, most evocative sense of local history and development is that of manufacturing and industry. You can practically trace America's industrial heritage by examining the shift in capitals from the North to the South around the turn of the century, as cheaper labor below the Mason-Dixon line drained the North of its manufacturing base. New England and the Northeast are littered with former capitals and titleholders, from Lynn, Massachusetts, once fittingly called the Ladies Shoe Capital of the World, to Waterbury, Connecticut, once renowned as the Brass Capital of the World. Today, you'll find textile capitals in places like Fort Payne, Alabama, the Sock Capital of the World, and Dalton, Georgia, the Carpet Capital of the World.

The fascinating thing about industrial capitals is that once you begin digging, you can uncover the history of a community and its economic development. Take Elkhart, Indiana. This city and county, which share the same name, has the dual claim of Band Instrument and RV Capital of the World. The city was home to the father of American band instruments, C.G. Conn, and today it's still the headquarters for numerous instrument makers. But in 1935, it added a second industry, that of recreational vehicles and motor homes; today, the Elkhart area is home to more than a fourth of the nation's RV suppliers.

Every now and then, more than one town lays claim to a capital title. In some cases, as with the watermelon capitals, a taste-off or other competition is staged to prove the true capital. In others, as with the selection of barbecue capitals that stretch from Kansas City, Missouri, to Owensboro, Kentucky, and from Memphis, Tennessee, to Lexington, North Carolina, the differences in the local product are so great as to leave the competition relatively unfazed.

Of course, some towns are too modest to think the world of themselves; many will stake their capital claim only on America

(Boone, North Carolina, is the Firefly Capital of America), their region (Half Moon Bay, California, is the Pumpkin Capital of the West), or even just their own home state (Bonduel, Wisconsin, is the Spelling Capital of Wisconsin). And some have other nicknames that are similar, if not actually "capital"ized; Newton, Iowa, has often been called the Washing Machine Center of the World (the agitating cleanser was invented there).

And though most titled towns are self-proclaimed, quite a few go the extra step of having a state resolution or bill passed to officially bestow their status. Douglas, Wyoming's grip on the claim of Home of the Jackalope was precarious enough that the governor issued a proclamation warning off poachers to the town's tongue-in-cheek interest in the mythical antlered rabbit.

When you visit a capital community, you will find more than the local point of pride: You'll also often find treasure troves of architecture and landmarks that might in other towns have been torn down or left to decay. But as landmarks of a local industry or culture that gave the town its claim to fame, these structures are often beautifully preserved and restored. Visit Dalton, Georgia, the Carpet Capital of the World, and you can tour Crown Gardens, an early textile mill that has been turned into the local historical archives. And when you're in High Point, North Carolina — the Home Furnishings Capital of the World — you can visit the whimsical World's Largest Bureau, a building designed to resemble an antique dresser. Nearby Thomasville, North Carolina, the Chair Capital of the World, boasts the World's Largest Duncan Phyffe Chair. This local dedication to preserving the built environment makes such hometown capitals landmark communities in their own right.

So why do towns make such a fuss over their local crop or company, rock, or recreation? It's a complicated answer. On the surface, towns can reap real rewards from the tourism boost they gain by promoting their unique qualities. When one exit looks just like another to a passing driver, having a sign that says "Welcome to the Barbed Wire Capital of the World" (à la La Crosse, Kansas) can entice pass-through travelers to pull off and stay awhile. And the attendant festivals that accompany many capital claims have that mark-your-calendar appeal for day-trippers and family travelers.

In 1993, David Muench, a professor and community resource agent for the University of Wisconsin-Extension at Outagamie County, published the second edition of a fascinating study called "Wisconsin Community Slogans: Their Use and Local Impacts." Muench surveyed hundreds of Wisconsin communities about the development and impact of their slogans on local life. The study reported on some 225 places ranging from capitals such as Taycheedah, the Sheep Shearing Capital of the World, and Sparta, the Bicycling Capital of America, to communities with other unique nicknames such as Wonewoc, We Are User Friendly, and Lodi, Home of Susie the Duck.

The survey found that most communities experienced some form of economic benefit from their slogans. A few could even put a dollar amount on this impact. "Monroe, the Swiss Cheese Capital of the United States, estimates its Cheese Days celebration brings in $1 million during the three-day festival. Hunters in Park Falls — the Ruffed Grouse Capital of the World — bring in $12,300 per day during peak grouse hunting, according to chamber estimates (1989 estimates)," the study reports.

And since tourists translate into dollars, the study noted that "The bottom line on the economics of a community slogan program is tourism.... The key is to get...travelers to come to your community, either as a destination or as an unplanned trip stop. They may be attracted there to buy fresh bakery [goods] in the Kringle Capital of the World; take kids fishing at the Sunfish Capital of the World; have their picture taken next to a 16-foot-high loon at the Loon Capital of the World; eat ice cream at the Birthplace of the Ice Cream Sundae; or stand on the exact Center of the Northwestern World."

And the tourism numbers do add up, often drawing crowds that outnumber the local population: The study reported that "Over 20,000 people visit the Snowmobile Museum at its birthplace in Sayner (unincorporated); over 25,000 polka enthusiasts are drawn to Pulaski (population 2,100) for the Polka Fest; over 100,000 are drawn to the Bratwurst Capital — Sheboygan (population 48,000) for their annual three-day festival; and over 25,000 tour the First Kindergarten Building in Watertown (population 18,500)."

But towns with capital claims cling to more than just the almighty tourist dollar. They often exhibit a local pride and dedication that is as unconditional as a parent's love for a child. Towns that thus celebrate their own special niche are doing more than promoting their image; they're preserving a sense of communal character, of local devotion to the industries, events, and activities that have made their community what it is.

The Wisconsin study found just such local pride to be a major component in the reasons why communities have developed slogans and are pleased with their results. "One of those intangibles often mentioned in the [study] surveys and in conversation with communities was the pride exhibited by the residents over their community's recognition....Pride, however, is not restricted only to residents....The existence of business community pride and support for a slogan becomes evident when it is adopted in the business name, such as Circus City Cleaners (Baraboo) or Ranger City Restaurant (Wausaukee)."

What the Wisconsin study shows is that capital claims for communities are neither accidental nor casual; they hold both communal and economic power to enhance a town's reputation, attract tourists, and develop a sense of self for the citizens and their community at large.

Modern America looks more alike than ever, with the same fast food restaurants, video store chains, and banks sprawling through every region, transforming the once varied landscape of communities into an often monotonous litany of the same signs, the same services, the same tastes and sights and sounds.

In a nation where homogenization has become a potentially destructive force, towns that promote their own special contribution to the world through their capital claims are helping to maintain and protect the distinctive characteristics that make each town a hometown.

This book celebrates hundreds of capital communities, showcasing their unique histories, attractions, events, and style that make you want to take the next exit and spend a little time in a place you've never been before. Or maybe you have; like all great places, many of these towns seem unique and yet mysteriously familiar, for these Main Street capitals share that indefinable sense of community that revels in the power of place, in the meaning of home.

# CHAPTER 1

# INDUSTRIAL STRENGTHS

ip O'Neill once said that all politics is local; so, too, is all industry. Much of America's industrial heritage springs from the towns where products were first invented, first manufactured, or first used. And the communities where a business was born or flourished became company towns. Detroit is Motor City thanks to Ford and General Motors; Los Angeles is Tinsel Town because of the Hollywood dream factories; Pittsburgh is the Steel Capital, famous for the metals magnates who lived and operated there. But small towns also have a great stake in the industries that created, or at least strengthened, the local economy. And to promote these industries, many also proudly carry a capital claim.

You can trace America's industrial history in the ebb and flow of these hometown capitals. The great textile mills and factories of the North once gave communities such as Lynn, Massachusetts, the right to boast of being the Ladies Shoe Capital of the World. But that was before cheaper labor and manufacturing space in the South drained the North of much of its industry.

1

Lynn, Massachusetts, was once the Ladies Shoe Capital, with factories turning out many well-turned heels. *Courtesy Lynn Historical Society*

New England and the Mid-Atlantic states are littered with former world capitals. Cortland, New York, was once the Typewriter Capital of the World, home to Smith-Corona and other major typewriter makers; Danbury, Connecticut, was once the Hat Capital of the World; Lawrence, Massachusetts, was the Textiles Capital of the World; Paterson, New Jersey, was the Silk City.

Some have found other industries to fill the gap. Take **READING AND BERKS COUNTY, PENNSYLVANIA,** the Outlet Shopping Capital of the World. Reading used to be a hosiery manufacturing leader before the local textile companies headed for warmer, less-expensive climes. But those old factory buildings no longer stand vacant; one of Reading's great accomplishments in preservation has been its transformation of former warehouses and factories into shopping malls.

The North's loss was the South's gain, and you'll find the industries that relocated to the other side of the Mason-Dixon line early in this century have since taken root, giving rise to capital claims in their new hometowns.

The South is now rife with textile capitals. Ft. Payne, Alabama, for instance, is the Sock Capital of the World—a darned good title for a community with more than 150 hosiery mills producing more than a million pairs of socks a week. Ft. Payne's first knitting mill opened in

1907 and employed about 30 people; by 1915, it had 300 employees and was turning out about 500 dozen socks a day. Tube socks and cushion-soled socks were invented in Ft. Payne. Today, with more than 60 million pairs of socks streaming from Ft. Payne annually, every dryer in every laundromat in America would have to work year-round to lose even half the socks so proudly knit in this capital community.

**HIGH POINT, NORTH CAROLINA,** used to be the Furniture and Hosiery Capital of the World, though it has since dropped its stockings to become the Home Furnishings Capital of the World (more on that shortly). Winder, Georgia, meanwhile, works hard at being the Work Clothing Capital of the World; and Martinsville, Virginia, is the Sweatshirt Capital of the World, though labor disputes in recent years have focussed attention away from the products and onto the producers.

One note about labor problems: Sometimes one town's difficulty can become another's reason to crow. Take the case of Garfield, New Jersey. It dubbed itself the City of Industrial Peace to promote the fact that it did not suffer from the same labor troubles that hampered the nearby Silk City of Paterson, where textile workers frequently struck against management.

One of Dixieland's most famous capitals is **DALTON, GEORGIA,** the Carpet Capital of the World. Dalton's industry was born not of a northern exodus but rather of homespun ingenuity. Early in the century, local women began hand-tufting chenille bedspreads and rugs to earn extra income; by the Depression, it was a colorful local industry, and the roadside stands along U.S. Hwy. 41—a.k.a. Bedspread Alley near Dalton—were flapping with handmade chenille. During the 1940s, mechanical manufacturing methods came to Dalton, turning the homespun cottage business into a full-fledged carpeting industry. As the post-World War II era housing boom heated up, Dalton carpet companies were covering America's households wall-to-wall and coast-to-coast.

**DID YOU KNOW...**

**The Birth of Industry**
Paterson, N.J., the "Silk City," was founded in 1791 on the banks of the Passaic River as America's first planned industrial city. The city's fast-developing textile industries (the first cotton-spinning mill was established there) helped Paterson weave its fortune into the whole cloth of the northern manufacturing boom of the 19th century.

A cottage industry built by women who hand-tufted chenille was the impetus for Dalton, Georgia's reputation as the Carpet Capital of the World. *Courtesy Whitfield-Murray Historical Society*

The 1950's housing surge catapulted another southern capital into the economic stratosphere. **HIGH POINT, NORTH CAROLINA,** as already noted, is now known as the Home Furnishings Capital of the World. It began turning out furniture and textiles at a steady clip to fill new homes built during the postwar era. What began as a small local business at the turn of the century—crafting furniture from famous Carolina hardwoods—was transformed within 50 years into a multimillion dollar industry. Today, the International Home Furnishings Market, held twice a year in and around High Point, draws some 70,000 design professionals to see the fine furnishings for which the area is famous.

Another nearby town, Thomasville, North Carolina, has a more specific furniture claim. It's the Chair Capital of the World. If you don't believe it, visit the World's Largest Duncan Phyffe Chair, a local landmark. And to move all that furniture, you need a pretty big vehicle; hence, Henderson, North Carolina, was once the Corbitt Truck Capital of the World. Corbitt trucks and tractors are no longer manufactured, but the town still promotes its famous vehicles, which were built from 1911 until the early 1950s.

Another North Carolina community, Carborro, not far from Chapel Hill, also has a former capital claim; it was once the Railroad

Tie Capital of the World. Though textiles were Carborro's leading industry at the turn of the century, the cross tie market was a close second. Early in the century, the Southern Railway began buying railroad ties from Carborro farmers, who cut the wood from the plentiful white and red oaks on their land. The farmers hand-stripped the wood, and sold the best of the ties for about 50 cents apiece. By the 1920s, the town had become the main tie supplier to the East; but within a decade, as railroad construction plummeted, Carborro's capital tie status became undone.

The Carolina furniture and textile markets still boomed. America's mass-consumption culture spawned by the post-World War II era helped many an industry reach new heights of economic growth. New families, fresh as the coats of paint on their new houses, were bombarded with advertisements from the new medium of television as well as from the radio and print media urging them to spend ever more on life's luxuries, large and small.

Families trying to keep up with the Cleavers found they needed not just a new couch or dining table, but an entirely new living room or dining room set. And if before the war they needed a car, after the war they needed two. And perhaps a trailer for family vacations.

**ELKHART COUNTY, INDIANA,** with its unusual dual capital claim as the Band Instrument and RV Capital of the World, is home to the RV/MH (Recreational Vehicle/Motor Home) Heritage Foundation's Hall of Fame, Museum, and Library. Here, you can see the evolution of the Recreational Vehicle from its early, converted wagon stylings (Wilbur J. Shult's Elkhart factory was one of the first manufacturers), through the classic silver Air Stream era, on up to its modern rendition as a living room on wheels. To this day, the Elkhart area has dozens of companies manufacturing RVs, parts, or conversion vans.

The other half of Elkhart's equation reflects the flip side of the American consumer revolution: While Americans were trying to escape the bonds of their everyday lives through travel, they clung to hometown values. Which is why Elkhart, with its large ensemble of instrument manufacturers, is the Band Instrument Capital of the World. Its musical moniker dates back to the nineteenth century, when an eccentric Elkhart entrepreneur, C.G. Conn, founded the first major American band instrument manufacturing company. The city of Elkhart (in the county of the same name) has been playing along ever since.

In many ways, even as America's leisure time increased, the products that were once integral to a simpler way of life disappeared behind the smoke screen of mass marketing and manufacturing. Take the corn cob pipe; now, it's often thought of as a just a novelty item sold in souvenir shops. But in the nineteenth century, when the Missouri Meerschaum Pipe Company of **WASHINGTON, MISSOURI,** began manufacturing its newfangled invention, it was a huge hit with smokers who enjoyed the cool draw of the porous pipes.

That was before mass-produced cigarettes destroyed much of the market for pipe tobacco and, hence, pipes. But the Meerschaum Pipe Company still turns out its famous product, and its hometown still proudly calls itself the Corn Cob Pipe Capital of the World.

Some classics never go out of style. Take toys, for instance. Once just the playthings of childhood, toys are becoming more the objects of collectors' whims. And nowhere is this playful trend more evident than in **DYERSVILLE, IOWA,** the Farm Toy Capital of the World.

Dyersville is home to four major makers of farm toys and other die-cast miniatures. The big kid in town is Ertl, the world's largest manufacturer of farm toys and a leading maker of scale models, model kits, and other miniature collectibles. Dyersville is also home to the National Farm Toy Museum, which showcases the work of local toymakers.

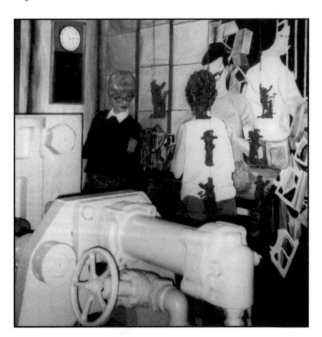

Dyersville, Iowa's National Farm Toy Museum features a manufacturing exhibit that shows how the toys are die-cast and painted.
*Laura Bergheim*

Chicago is not just another Midwestern town; along with its many nicknames, it has gained the title as Pinball Capital of the World because the Windy City region shoulders the headquarters for the four largest makers of arcade games—Bally, Williams, Data East, and Premier Technology. More than half of the pinball machines made in the world come from the Chicago area, and Chicagoan Steve Kordek is credited with reinventing the classic pinball machine in 1948 by adding flippers to the popular ball game, inserting an element of control, and therefore skill, with his wrist-flicking mechanism.

> ### CYBERSPACE CONTACTS
> # Toy Farmer Magazine
> **http://www.toyfarmer.com/html/home.html/**
>
> Farm toy collectors can check out the latest models, events schedules, and product updates at the bright, fun *Toy Farmer Magazine* home page, which features tiny truckloads of info on the Dyersville farm toy manufacturers, local events, and the National Farm Toy Museum.

Back in New England, some capital communities still thrive despite the twentieth-century industrial siphon southward. Take Hartford, Connecticut, the Insurance Capital of the World. The modern insurance industry was born in Hartford, and the Connecticut capital is still home to myriad insurance companies, including Aetna Life and Casualty, the Travelers, the Hartford Insurance Group, and Connecticut Mutual Life Insurance Company.

Another New England business community born and bred is the stationery staple of Holyoke, Massachusetts, referred to alternately as the Fine Writing Paper Capital of the World or as Paper City.

Other New England communities have lost their industries to the new technologies. Littleton, New Hampshire, used to be the Stereographic Production Capital of the World. That was then, this is now.

Others have held fast to their capital claims despite the loss of most, or all, of the industry that brought them glory. There's Westfield, Massachusetts, for instance. It's still called Whip City despite the serious drop in demand for buggy whips over the last century. And though Amesbury, Massachusetts, is no longer known as the Carriage Capital of the World—horse-drawn contraptions were a major industry there from 1894 to 1905—you can still see the local products on display at the Amesbury Carriage Museum.

And then there's **WATERBURY, CONNECTICUT,** formerly the Brass Capital of the World. Waterbury dominated the American brass industry during the nineteenth century, with dozens of factories turning out everything from brass buttons to cow bells. A one-two punch of conglomeratization and the Great Depression (exacerbated by a devastating flood in 1955) took the shine off the brass industry. Today, the town has polished off its classic buildings and redeveloped itself into a convention capital.

In the face of changes, some old-fashioned products and their capitals endure. If you visit the tiny town of Farmington, Maine, in early December, you may find yourself watching one of the nation's most unusual parades. Everyone and everything, from the cop cars and school buses to the horses and dogs, will proudly be sporting earmuffs. That's because Farmington is the Earmuff Capital of the World, thanks to its warmly remembered hometown inventor Chester Greenwood. Born December 4, 1858, Greenwood showed his genius early. He was a mere lad of 15 when a lobe-freezing pond skate inspired him to devise his Greenwood Ear Protectors. He patented his cozy invention in 1877, and for the rest of his life he ran Chester Greenwood & Co. as the country's leading earmuff manufacturer.

The ever-evolving landscape of twentieth-century technologies has spawned numerous capital communities, too. Alabama has a number of mechanical capitals. For twirly birds, visit Ozark, Alabama, the Helicopter Capital of the World. Mobile, Alabama, is another high-flying capital; it's the Piston Engine Manufacturing Capital of the World, thanks to Teledyne Continental Motors, which makes piston engines for non-turboprop planes there. The Mobile factory made the engine that flew around the world on Dick Ruttan's Voyager.

Greenville, Missouri, was once known as the Towboat Capital of the World. As Howard Brent of Brent Towing will tell you, that title was firmly in line until taxes put most of the independent towboat operators out of business. He's a chatty fellow and he'll tell you the history of the company his father Jesse Brent founded in 1956. He'll wax poetic about the good old days of independent towing—"They called it the Million Dollar Mile along Lake Ferguson back then," Brent notes. "Now, just a handful of boats are owned by individuals. Most are owned by big companies."

Alabama is also home to another capital born of modern necessity. Albertville is the Fire Hydrant Capital of the World. When the Mueller Co., which produces more than 40 percent of the world's fire hydrants, turned out its one millionth hydrant, a commemorative granite monument featuring a nickel-plated hydrant was erected to honor the achievement. Needless to say, the dogs went wild. And before we leave Alabama behind, let's not forget that Anniston, Alabama, is the Soil Pipe Capital of the World.

New England and the South are not the only manufacturing regions with plenty of industrial capitals lying around like spare parts. The Midwestern states have capitals for everything from timber (Saginaw, Michigan) to gunstock (Warsaw, Missouri). Some of the biggest industrial capitals are scattered throughout the Midwest. Akron, Ohio, is the Rubber Capital of the World, thanks to the Goodyear Tire & Rubber Co. Visitors can even bounce through the Goodyear World of Rubber exhibit at the corporate headquarters to learn about the history of rubber and about the life of company founder Charles Goodyear, who invented the vulcanization process that gives the natural material its elasticity.

And if you ever wondered where you were calling when you picked up the phone to dial a hotel chain's 800-number or to order something "As Seen on TV," chances are you were chatting with someone in Omaha, Nebraska, the 800-Number Capital of the World. Omaha's toll-free title comes, oddly enough, courtesy of the Cold War. Omaha was home to the Strategic Air Command (SAC), ground zero of the nation's airborne nuclear defense system. And because SAC needed the most sophisticated phone lines in the world, Omaha got wired in a big way. The area's central location, and naturally friendly, accent-free workforce also made the city a magnet for telemarketing ventures.

Telemarketing is one of Omaha's biggest businesses; indeed, the majority of toll-free calls resulting from TV infomercials and other advertising media end up at Omaha phone banks. Though the companies are proud of their industry, their cheerful operators may not always let on that you've reached someone in Nebraska. Stroll through the offices of telemarketers who are handling reservations lines for hotels or other travel destinations, for instance, and you'll notice that the computer screens often have pop-up information about the weather where the call is supposedly being routed to—just for that personal touch.

Toledo, Ohio, is another big city with a capital claim that many may not know about. It's the Glass Capital of the World. You can see right through some of the finest local products at the Toledo Art Museum, which has a large collection of fine glass objects.

You can also raise a glass in Milwaukee, Wisconsin, which many call the Brewing Capital of the World because of its beer-making heritage. Some people assume that Milwaukee's other nickname, Cream City, somehow relates to its location in the Dairy State; in fact, the moniker comes from the beige brick used in many a Milwaukee building.

Another Wisconsin city, Green Bay, is known worldwide for its meat packing industry. Oddly, however, another local industry has given the city its capital title. Though this claim is unlikely to wipe out the local packing fame, Green Bay is known as the Toilet Paper Capital of the World. The squeezably soft company now known as Charmin evolved there from the Holberg Paper Mill, founded in nearby Kaukana in 1892. The company started a trend, and other tissue makers, including Northern Paper (founded in 1911), Diana Manufacturing (also founded in 1911), and the Fort Howard Paper Co. (founded in 1920), soon followed. By 1920, Northern Paper was the world's largest toilet tissue maker, and by 1923, area factories were rolling out 200 tons of paper a day, making Green Bay the world's toilet paper manufacturing capital.

Another town up North with a capital claim that's kind of cute is Cedar Springs, Michigan. It's still called the Red Flannel Capital of the World, even though the flannel factory is now closed. That doesn't stop the locals from celebrating their snuggly industry with a Red Flannel Festival every year.

As for machinery, well, the Midwest seems to specialize in labor-saving devices. North Canton, Ohio, has the spotless reputation as Vacuum Cleaner Capital. The Hoover Co., which introduced its first product, the Electric Suction Sweeper, in 1908, was founded there by local tannery owner William H. Hoover. Exhibits at the Hoover Historical Center at the Hoover family homestead tell the story of the company's founding and showcase the sweeping history of mechanical cleaning machines.

The Jasper County Museum in Newton, Iowa, showcases historic washing machines, the town's capital claim to fame. *Laura Bergheim*

Then there's Newton, Iowa, the Washing Machine Capital (or sometimes Center) of the World. The washing machine was invented there in the 1890s by one Arthur Ogburn, who created a hand-cranked "Ratchet Slat" that twisted and squeezed clothes around wooden slats. Though Ogburn's machine didn't exactly clean up in the marketplace, it launched an industry for which Newton became the homebase. Many companies came and went, but one, Maytag, founded in 1909, stayed around and became a world leader.

The Jasper County Historical Society Museum in Newton reveals the agitating history behind the washing machine industry, an evolution that paralleled the emancipation of women from endless household drudgery as they moved from the home to the workplace. The museum's Maytag Exhibit is the largest and most complete collection of Maytag washers and dryers on public display, and this march of machines—including early models with attachments such as an ice cream churn and a meat grinder—is a product parade of the domestic sciences.

Newton has also been called the Advertising Specialties Capital of the World, for the souvenirs and premium advertising giveaways once produced by local manufacturers.

While in Iowa, if you're taking a capital cities tour, head east to Muscatine, the Pearl Button Capital of the World. Though pearl buttons are hardly in fashion anymore, it's yet another example of a quaint claim to fame preserved in the hearts of the locals, sometimes as proof that times may change yet hometown products last forever.

All that machinery needs something to run it with. That's where the Western states' capitals plug into the picture. Tulsa, Oklahoma, may be the Oil Capital of the World, but did you know that little ole Duncan, Texas, is the Oil Well Cementing Capital of the World? Drumright, Oklahoma, meanwhile, is the Pipeline Capital of the World, while Hugoton, Kansas, is the Gas Capital of the World.

And what those westerners wear on their feet while digging for fossil fuels comes out of Olathe, Oklahoma, a.k.a., the Cowboy Boot Capital of the World, thanks to major bootmakers cobbling away in town. El Paso, Texas, also calls itself the Boot Capital of the World.

Another well-shod town, or one that used to be, is Haverhill, Massachusetts, once the Queen Shoe City of the World. That was back when royalty was revered, and before the shoe industry, like so many others, headed south.

America's material culture is as much about the products we make and the places that make them as it is about the ways we use them every day. The towns that today call themselves capitals of the world might, tomorrow, be harboring little more than the ghosts of their former industrial giants. Will today's Silicon Valley be tomorrow's computer chip graveyard? It's hard to know. But manufacturing has grown up since the early days of mom-and-pop sweatshops, so today's capitals are perhaps more protected from the march of progress.

Then again, sad to say, as industry has matured it has sometimes lost touch with the hometowns that once provided the cradle-to-grave workers upon whom it depended, and who depended upon it. Times have changed, business has changed. But as long as there are sock capitals and boot capitals, toilet paper capitals, and washing machine capitals, a bit of that manufacturing heritage will be preserved, if not in production then at least in pride of place.

## ✪ Elkhart County, Indiana

BAND INSTRUMENT CAPITAL OF THE WORLD AND
RECREATIONAL VEHICLE CAPITAL OF THE WORLD

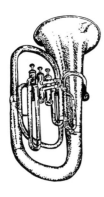

One of the wonders of American business is the diversity of industry you can find even within a small section of a state. Take Elkhart County, Indiana, for instance. This Amish country county in northern Indiana has two industrial strengths that are seemingly disparate yet intriguingly linked, both by proximity and culture.

As the Recreational Vehicle (RV) Capital of the World, the county is home to dozens of mobile home, RV, and RV parts manufacturers. As the

Elkhart's municipal band has long included many local instrument factory workers, playing their own handiwork. *Courtesy Elkhart County Convention & Visitors Bureau*

Band Instrument Capital of the World, the county's namesake city, Elkhart, is home to a finely tuned collection of musical instrument makers.

The RV industry is a modern one, born of leisure time, good roads, and evolving automotive manufacturing standards. The band instrument business dates back to the last century, providing the paraphernalia for many towns' only built-in entertainment—the community band.

And though these industries serve seemingly disparate purposes—the RV whisks the family away from home in an insular traveling environment, while band instruments equip hometown gatherings such as football games and summer concerts in the park—they both supply the basic tools for leisure-time pursuits.

Elkhart County comprises two cities, Elkhart and Goshen (the county seat), and six towns, Bristol, Middlebury, Millersburg, Nappanee, New Paris, and Wakarusa. It also has a large Amish population, and the Amish lifestyle predominates at many local events and festivals, creating a large tourism base.

But industrially, Elkhart's instruments and RVs have brought big business to this county of 157,000. The second largest employer in

CYBERSPACE CONTACTS

## Dr. Margaret Downie Banks Home Page

http://www.usd.edu/~mbanks/

Dr. Margaret Downie Banks, curator of the Shrine to Music Museum and Center for Study of the History of Musical Instruments at the University of South Dakota at Vermillion, uses the Web to showcase her research on the C.G. Conn Musical Instrument Manufacturing Company; included are a 1911 factory postcard and product list.

the area is RV manufacturer Coachmen Industries, Inc., which employs some 1,425 people. The largest of the instrument manufacturers, L.P. Selmer Co., employs 720.

Elkhart's musical legacy was composed by Col. C.G. Conn, a flamboyant former military officer who played the cornet in the local band. In 1873, Conn earned a badly split lip in a fist fight. He created a special mouthpiece so he could play despite his injured mouth, and soon he was designing special equipment for other musicians. In 1875, after a visit from a French horn manufacturer, Conn realized he could also make instruments himself, and that same year he created the first American-made cornet.

By 1880, the C.G. Conn Factory employed more than 80 workers turning out cornets and other instruments; three years later—on Conn's 39th birthday—his factory burnt to the ground. So he built another, larger, factory, and made even more instruments. Conn became a powerful citizen, publishing the local newspaper and serving as Elkhart's mayor before winning a seat in Congress in 1892. When he moved to Washington, D.C., in 1893, he bought and ran the *Washington Times,* one of the city's major dailies; but he served only one term before selling the paper and returning to his instrumental roots.

By the time Mr. Conn went to Washington, his business had spread beyond Elkhart. In 1887, he opened a branch plant in Massachusetts, and by 1893, his company had more than 300 employees, many with specialized skills. Conn instruments were considered among the world's finest, and many American musicians swore by them. John Philip Sousa, who led the U.S. Marine Band and penned some of the greatest marches ever written, loved Conn instruments. One of the factory's workers, Ted Pounder, even invented a special, low-pitch brass instrument designed for marching musicians. Built to Sousa's specifications, the Sousaphone went into production at the Conn factory in

1898. Pounder stayed with the company for more than a half-century.

Drawn by Conn's success and the workforce he had helped train, other music makers picked up the beat, making Elkhart a major manufacturing center for band instruments. By 1915, Conn was ready to retire; he sold his factory (a newer one, built after another fire in 1910) to C.D. Greenleaf. Conn scandalized Elkhart by leaving his wife and daughter behind when he retired to California. He got a divorce, remarried, and fathered a son at age 70. He died 16 years later, in 1931.

Though the Conn factory is no longer in business, to this day, famous makers such as Selmer, Bach, Armstrong, Blessing, and Gemeinhardt are still making band instruments and accessories in the Elkhart area. "Seventy-six trombones," as the tune from the Broadway band musical *The Music Man* (set in Indiana) sings out, might be just another week's output in Elkhart. For accompaniment, Elkhart has the Charles R. Walter Co., which manufactures high-quality pianos.

Despite modern amusements, most communities maintain their commitment to the high-school or college band, so the amateur as well as commercial market still exists for quality instruments. And Elkhart plays along with its capital claim, especially during the Elkhart Jazz Festival, held in mid-June. Visitors can get a firsthand look at some of the locally produced instruments, which are often played by the world-class talents who come to perform. And the town's longstanding municipal band still plays on, its players frequently drawn from the instrument factories, and using the instruments their companies make.

But Elkhart County continued to evolve beyond its musical roots; in 1935, it added the RV industry to its business profile. That was the year that Wilbur J. Shult opened his first trailer factory in a small wooden building. There, his staff of 20 carpenters built a trailer a day, and customers lined up to buy the trailers at a price tag of $198. Within a year, Shult's trailers—little camper-type models towed behind cars—were so popular he had moved to new quarters in a former carriage factory and was producing 1,000 trailers a year. In 1937, his production was up to 1,500 trailers, and his company had become one of the country's leading producers of leisure trailers.

As with myriad instrument makers who jumped on the bandwagon, Shult may have been the first trailer maker in the state, but he certainly wasn't the last: By 1969, the Elkhart area alone boasted more than 80 mobile home manufacturers.

Today, according to Mark Doud, research manager of the Greater Elkhart Chamber of Commerce, "Of the 176 companies reporting RV shipments, 43 are located in Elkhart County. Over one-fourth of the RV suppliers are in Elkhart. Additionally, many of the big names in van converters can be found in Elkhart County." Statistically speaking, nearly one in three of the RVs you see traveling down the highway was probably shipped from or equipped in Elkhart. And since RV purchases skyrocketed by 44 percent from 1992 to 1995, according to the Recreational Vehicle Industry Association, Elkhart is rolling merrily along.

Elkhart has become both an industrial and historical center for those in the MH (Mobile Home) and RV world. To preserve and promote the industry, the RV/MH Heritage Foundation Inc. has a spacious complex featuring a Hall of Fame, Museum, Library, and Exhibition Hall devoted to highlighting the history and culture of these homes away from home.

The facility was opened in 1990 in a custom-built, 15,000-square-foot complex designed to house the organization's archival and historical collections and artifacts. The museum shows early RV and MH models and traces their evolution, while the Hall of Fame honors more than 140 inductees who have shaped and changed the industry—including, naturally, Wilbur Shult.

If you want to see for yourself how RVs and their ilk are built, a number of local manufacturers offer regularly scheduled tours of their facilities; many have showrooms for browsing as well. Among those with scheduled tours are Coachmen, Carriage, Barth, Firan Motor Coach, Diversified Mobile Products, Dutchman Mfg., Estate Manufacturing, Holiday Rambler Corp., International Vehicles, Jayco, Journey Motor Homes, Layton Travel Trailers, Newmar RV, Rockwood, Shasta Industries, Sun-Lite, Travel Supreme, and Wells Cargo. Other manufacturers offer tours by appointment only. The Elkhart County Convention and Visitors Bureau distributes a list of manufacturers' tours.

Whether you're an RV'er or an instrumentalist, Elkhart County's companies probably make a difference in your life. Old-fashioned business and newfangled technology alike have given the county its leisurely working pace.

## For Further Information

### General Information

**Elkhart County Convention and Visitors Bureau**
219 Caravan Dr.
Elkhart, IN 46514
(219) 262-8161 or (800) 262-8161

### Attractions and Events

**Elkhart Jazz Festival**
Elkhart Centre
P.O. Box 1284
Elkhart, IN 46515
(219) 295-8701 or (800) 597-7627

**RV/MH Heritage Foundation Museum and Hall of Fame**
801 Benham Ave.
Elkhart, IN 46516
(219) 293-2344

**RV Factory Tours**
For a list, contact the Elkhart County Convention and Visitors Bureau

# ❂ Waterbury, Connecticut

FORMER BRASS CAPITAL OF THE WORLD

In a perfect world, the industries that brought fame and fortune to communities would last forever, or at least stay put in their hometowns. But as the Industrial Age has given way to the postmodern world, society's needs have evolved, companies have moved, and the American corporate landscape looks very different from the way it did a century ago.

Such is the case with Waterbury, Connecticut. Once known as the Brass Capital of the World, and the Brass City, Waterbury is still proud of that legacy, though the brass industry is but a shimmering memory. But in the late nineteenth and early twentieth centuries, Waterbury, thanks to the

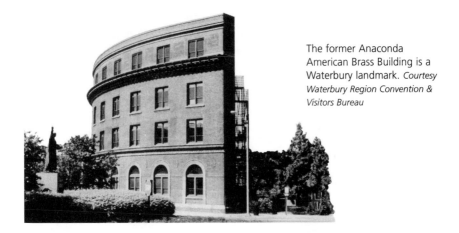

The former Anaconda American Brass Building is a Waterbury landmark. *Courtesy Waterbury Region Convention & Visitors Bureau*

American Brass Company and a number of smaller manufacturers, was the world's largest producer of shiny brass buttons, pins, shell cases, kerosene lamps, and just about anything else made from this highly polished metal. Its products were so far-reaching that the city had another nickname: The City That Had Something on Everyone—meaning that almost everyone wore garments with Waterbury-made brass buttons or other accessories.

Waterbury is still home to a major button manufacturer, the Waterbury Companies, Inc., but brass buttons make up only a small portion of its output. Plastics, as in many an industry, have replaced fine metals for most button products.

Situated 26 miles southwest of Hartford, Waterbury, which today has a population of around 110,000, got its start as a metallic metropolis during the War of 1812, when the usual flow of brass goods from England dried up because of the conflict between the two countries. Locals began rolling their own brass for buttons to fill the hole left by the war. The Benedict and Burnham Manufacturing Co. (which would later merge with other brass makers into the American Brass Company) went into the business of brass, and soon a new industry was born stateside.

In 1817, another local company, Abel and Porter, had the cheek to sneak a master brass craftsman out of England; this began a slow leak of trained talent from British factories. One legend, as recalled in Charles Monagan's *Greater Waterbury: A Region Reborn* (Windsor Publications, 1989), involves a crafty Waterburian named Israel Holmes, who "ran an excellent trade by smuggling skilled English metalworkers and toolmakers in casks out of England (where the government was trying to prevent the loss of skilled craftsmen) and through the Port of New York."

The metals industry grew so quickly in Waterbury that, by the middle of the nineteenth century, immigrants from all over Europe were recruited to work in the city's flourishing plants. More than a dozen metal-working companies were operating in the city by then. Some, such as the American Pin Company and Waterbury Buckle, specialized in certain products, while others produced a variety of items large and small.

The button (brass, ivory, and cloth-covered) business was particularly strong. And though brass was the leading metal, local factories also turned out items made from copper and steel. From powder flasks to cow bells, valves to rivets, Waterbury manufacturers were leading the way; seemingly every new invention or product had parts made in Waterbury, and by the turn of the century, it was one of America's richest industrial cities.

The new century brought more growth to the region; factory owners were so well off they built grand mansions for themselves, and decent housing for their workers. And World War I brought even greater rewards, thanks to the industrial demand for small metal parts. But the brass industry was tarnishing.

In the 1920s, smaller companies began to merge into larger concerns, and not all of them were local. The American Brass Co. merged with Anaconda Copper Mining Co. in 1922; Chase Brass merged with Kennecott Copper in 1929. These and other mergers polished off the smaller companies, which either joined the conglomerates or were forced to close because they couldn't compete. Some companies, now lacking local ties to Waterbury, felt no compunctions about moving their factories to less-expensive areas. Others brought in efficiency experts to trim the workforce and increase profits. The community began to suffer.

---

**CYBERSPACE CONTACTS**

## The TIMEX Museum

**http://www.timex.com/museum.htm**

Though the museum is scheduled to open in late 1997, cybertourists can turn the clock ahead for an advance glance at the TIMEX Museum in Waterbury. The site features a TIMEX Timeline and the Curator's Wishlist of wanted items, such as Ingersoll comic character watches.

The final blow to Waterbury's brass industry was a wet one: A devastating flood in 1955 that killed 87 people in the valley, including 24 in Waterbury, also damaged or destroyed most of the area's remaining factories. The brass industry never recovered; by the mid-1970s, the city was in a bitter depression. Waterbury, whose self-assured city motto was *Quid Area Perennius*—What Is So Lasting as Brass?—had lost more than its livelihood; it had lost its sheen.

An urban renaissance in the 1980s, fueled by a burgeoning convention base, helped give the city a newly polished look and an old-fashioned sense of pride. And a few glimmers of the brassy past remain. The American Brass Company building, a magnificent four-story brick structure at 414 Meadow St., still stands. Built in 1913, it was recently sold and renovated as an office building; like much of downtown Waterbury, it has been restored as part of an impressive rehabilitation project that is preserving within the city core a solid collection of fine old buildings. Many, like the Republican and American Building, a newspaper publishing plant housed in the former Union Waterbury Station (a grand 1909 railroad station), were built for other purposes than those for which they are now used.

The city's most famous landmark, the Waterbury Clock, is attached to the former train station; its 240-foot-tall tower is New England's highest clock tower. It stands in remembrance of another industry that brought the city fame: clock making. TIMEX was born here as the Waterbury Clock Co. But that hand-crafted industry, like the brass biz, disappeared into the mists of the mid-twentieth century (though TIMEX remains).

*The town's famous Waterbury Clock tower is the tallest in New England and recalls the city's other famous business, clock making. Courtesy Waterbury Region Convention & Visitors Bureau*

To learn more about Waterbury's history, visit the Mattatuck Museum, a local historical collection that features an exhibit called Brass Roots; there, you'll hear the re-created voices of nineteenth-century brass factory workers describing their lives, and see displays of brass buttons and other products.

If the phrase "button, button, who's got the button?" keeps running through your mind, head for the Waterbury Button Museum. Owned by the button manufacturing Waterbury Companies, Inc., the collection dates back to the 1930s. It was started by Warren F. Kaynor, then the company's president, who attended a button society meeting and was hooked on button collecting. The museum does more than display company products: It showcases buttons throughout history and from around the world. Perhaps its most treasured holding is a collection of fasteners from George Washington's military uniforms.

Waterbury is old, even by New England standards; it predates Washington and the Revolution by a century. As a granite memorial in downtown Waterbury explains, "The present site of Waterbury was made on land in this region. The original settlement [in 1674], known as Town Plot, was abandoned during King Phillip's War and the town site changed to this location in 1677."

Much has changed since Waterbury was the Brass City; now its largest growth industry is the convention business, which has helped expand the city's hospitality industry. Today, Waterbury has one of the highest concentrations of hotel rooms in Connecticut.

So although Waterbury is no longer home to the top brass, it still shines in its own right, casting a glow to light the way for business travelers and convention planners. All of which gives the locals a reason to smile as they continue to polish the city's image.

## FOR FURTHER INFORMATION

### *General Information*

**Waterbury Region Convention & Visitors Bureau**
83 Bank St.
P.O. Box 1469
Waterbury, CT 06721
(203) 597-9527

*Attractions*

Mattatuck Museum
144 W. Main St.
Waterbury, CT 06702
(203) 753-0381

**Waterbury Button Museum**
Waterbury Companies, Inc.
32 Mattatuck Heights Rd.
Waterbury, CT 06705
(203) 597-1812

# ✿ Dalton, Georgia

CARPET CAPITAL OF THE WORLD

Workers at Cabin Craft Co. turned out Dalton chenille bedspreads in the 1930s. *Courtesy Whitfield-Murray Historical Society*

In Dalton, Georgia, the Carpet Capital of the World, people come just to tread on the local industrial base. Dalton is one of the nation's most prominent world capitals. It promotes the local carpet-manufacturing and carpet outlet industries heavily, drawing in thousands of bargain-conscious tourists as well as design professionals who travel the southern home furnishings circuit that also includes the furniture and textile manufacturing areas of the Carolinas.

It was one of Dalton's young ladies who helped create the carpet industry. In 1900, Catherine Evans Whitener, a farm girl, took up the old-fashioned art of hand-tufting. She sold her first piece, a chenille bedspread, for $2.50. She began teaching others the skill and soon many women in the area were tufting to help make ends meet; when the Depression struck, it was common to see chenille bedspreads flapping in the wind at roadside stands along U.S. Hwy. 41 between Dalton and Cartersville. The section of the highway even gained the nicknames of Bedspread Alley and Peacock Alley (for a popular spread design of a peacock in full-feathered glory).

The chenille industry spread first into other handmade products—robes and throw rugs—but then grew beyond the local crafters for whom it had become a livelihood. Factories with automated tufting machines began producing for the mass market, transforming the industry of carpet weaving into one of 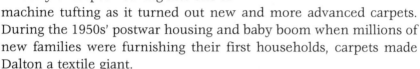 machine tufting as it turned out new and more advanced carpets. During the 1950s' postwar housing and baby boom when millions of new families were furnishing their first households, carpets made Dalton a textile giant.

Today, the Dalton area produces 65 to 70 percent of America's carpeting, with more than 150 textile plants, including such major makers as Shaw Industries, Beaulieu of America, and Mohawk/Galaxy Carpet Mills. And the stats (from data compiled by the Dalton Chamber of Commerce) are simply sweeping: Dalton produces 1.1 billion square yards of carpet annually (of that, 70 percent is replacement carpet). Its use breaks down into 55 percent residential, 25 percent commercial, 14 percent residential contract, and 6 percent transport/outdoor. The largest local carpet manufacturer uses two million pounds of fiber a day; of that fiber, 73.4 percent is nylon, 31.5 percent is polypropylene (olefin), 5.8 percent is polyester, and .4 percent is wool. And the dollar value of this local industry's products? In 1995, it was a whopping $6.9 billion at mill level and $12 billion at retail level. That's some magic carpet.

Not that visitors to Dalton have to pay retail. Dalton boasts more than 100 outlet stores selling carpets at discounts of 30 to 70 percent. The outlet stores dot the landscape no matter where you travel; Dalton is practically wall-to-wall carpet outlets.

Despite the competition, Dalton's carpet companies work together as part of a national organization; the Carpet and Rug Institute (also in Dalton) promotes the industry and furthers public education about carpet purchasing and care. The outlet stores also have an organization, the Dalton Carpet and Rug Outlet Council. A program of the Dalton-Whitfield Chamber of Commerce, its membership includes carpet and floor-covering industry wholesalers and retailers.

But Dalton was important long before its textile industry unfurled. The area was originally Cherokee land, and Dalton served as the gateway to the 150-mile Chieftains' Trail (travelers now use it to trace a path through a number of Northwest Georgia Native

Dalton's Crown Gardens Archives is housed in a building that was once part of one of the area's oldest textile mills. *Courtesy Whitfield-Murray Historical Society*

American sites). The infamous Trail of Tears—over which Andrew Jackson forced the Cherokees to march from their homeland—began at the Red Clay Council Grounds in Whitfield County, where Dalton is situated. This was the last capital of the Cherokee Nation.

Dalton itself was founded in 1847; it gained another place in the history books in May 1864, when General Sherman's Union troops battled Johnson's Confederates at Tunnel Hill, Dug Gap, and along Rocky Face Ridge. The Confederate breastworks and cemetery of Dug Gap have been preserved as the Dug Gap Battle Park.

Much of this often bitter history is explored at the Crown Gardens and Archives, a local historical collection housed at one of the area's first textile mills. The museum includes exhibits on the chenille bedspread makers and the evolution into the carpet manufacturing industry, as well as displays on the region's Civil War history and Native American heritage.

Though Dalton's high-tech carpet industry has left the chenille hand-tufters far behind, a few locals still practice the craft. You'll find them selling their soft and cozy wares at the Prater's Mill Country Fair, held Mother's Day weekend at a restored gristmill just outside Dalton.

Now when you come home from a hard day at the office, take off your shoes, and dig your toes into that deep pile, consider that you may well be walking all over Dalton—and leaving nothing but a smile on the faces of folks of this rugged Georgia community.

## FOR FURTHER INFORMATION

### *General Information*

**Dalton Convention & Visitors' Bureau**
Northwest Georgia Trade & Convention Center
2211 Dug Gap Battle Rd.
Dalton, GA 30722
(706) 272-7676

**Dalton-Whitfield Chamber of Commerce**
524 Holiday Ave.
Dalton, GA 30720
(706) 278-7373

### *Attractions and Events*

**Carpet and Rug Institute**
310 Holiday Ave.
Dalton, GA 30720
(706) 278-3176

**Dalton Carpet and Rug Outlet Council**
c/o Dalton-Whitfield Chamber of Commerce
524 Holiday Ave.
Dalton, GA 30720
(706) 278-7373

**Crown Gardens and Archives**
715 Chattanooga Ave.
Dalton, GA 30720
(706) 278-0217

**Prater's Mill Country Fair**
The Prater's Mill Foundation
848 Shugart Rd.
Dalton, GA 30720
(706) 275-MILL

## ✿ Washington, Missouri

CORN COB PIPE CAPITAL OF THE WORLD

When was the last time you saw someone walking down the street with a corn cob pipe jutting jauntily out of the side of his (or her) mouth? Well, if you lived in Washington, Missouri, it might have happened yesterday. Or today. Because there's still one place left that makes old-fashioned corn cob pipes—the Missouri Meerschaum Company. And its presence has given Washington the bragging rights as the Corn Cob Pipe Capital of the World.

Washington is a comfortable riverfront town with a population of about 15,000—the kind of place where quaint shops and a waterfront park attract visitors, who stroll along the banks of the Missouri River and take in the atmosphere. It promotes itself as "Located In the Heart of Missouri's Wine Country"—a surprise for many out-of-staters who didn't know Missouri even had a wine country. But the town's most unique appeal, its corn cob capital claim, is more than just a smokescreen. Washington is home to the first, and now last, corn cob pipe factory.

The Missouri Meerschaum Co. has been manufacturing corn cob pipes for more than a century. *Courtesy Missouri Meerschaum Co.*

The local history of corn cob pipes involves not only manufacturing but also, as the legend goes, invention. As company literature tells it, in 1869 a Dutch immigrant named Henry Tibbe was asked by a local farmer to try turning a corn cob on his lathe. It seems the farmer had whittled the thing into a pipe and liked the draw so much he wanted Tibbe to

do a few more for him on real machinery. Soon, Tibbe was turning corn cob pipes for everyone, producing more pipes than woodwork for his clients. From that kernel of an idea was born an industry.

In 1872, Tibbe established his company, and went into full-scale pipe production. And the more he made, the more he improved on his product. Tibbe and a chemist friend created a method to preserve and refine the pipes through plastering and sanding, using a process they patented in 1894.

In 1907, the H. Tibbe & Son Co. changed its name to the Missouri Meerschaum Company—from the German word for seafoam, *meerschaum,* which reminded Tibbe of the porous, cool-drawing quality of his pipes. By then, imitators were already at work. During the first 25 years of the new century, a dozen or so corn cob pipe manufacturers went into business in Franklin County, where Washington is situated, many along the same Missouri River banks where Missouri Meerschaum was making its pipes.

But Tibbe's company outlasted the others; today, operating in the same brick building on Front St., the Missouri Meerschaum Factory is now the world's only mass manufacturer of corn cob pipes. The factory's 50 employees turn out about 7,000 pipes a day, which are shipped worldwide, using a production process similar to that of a century ago—with a little automation thrown in.

It's a simple, efficient process: Corn cobs are stripped of their remaining kernels, sawed to uniform length, then bored with tobacco holes. Most go on to turning machines to be shaped, though larger cobs are still hand-turned. After a white plaster coating is applied to the bowls, they dry for a day before being sanded for smoothness.

The next stop is the finishing room, where stem holes are bored, the bowls are varnished, and the wooden stem is glued into the bowl. After the mouthpiece is added, the pipes are ready for packing and shipping.

Today, the pipes are still primarily used for tobacco smoking—many connoisseurs cherish the uniquely smooth, cool draw from the naturally porous corn cob—though the souvenir market is also strong. The company produces 18 different styles of pipes, the main variation being in the shape of the bowl and the angle (bent or straight) of the stem.

Washington is proud of its corn cob pipe heritage, though neither it nor the company does much to promote its capital claim. No pipe festivals, for instance, or smoke-ins are held here, though once upon a time, a former pipe manufacturer, Buesher's Corn Cob Pipes, sponsored a pipe-smoking contest at the Washington Town and Country Fair. Still, continuing public curiosity about this homegrown industry led the Missouri Meerschaum Company to open a visitors center in 1993, where folks can see how these homespun pipes are made and learn a little bit more about their history and use.

## For Further Information

**Washington Area Chamber of Commerce**
323 W. Main St.
Washington, MO 63090
(314) 239-2715


**Missouri Meerschaum Corn Cob Pipes**
400 W. Front St.
P.O. Box 226
Washington, MO 63090
(314) 239-2109

# ⊙ Dyersville, Iowa

FARM TOY CAPITAL OF THE WORLD

Most tourists come to Dyersville, Iowa, as baseball film buffs, to step up to the plate or explore the corn field from the movie *Field of Dreams*. After they've pitched a few or purchased souvenirs, they may wander back into town and then discover that Dyersville has another claim to fame. It's also the Farm Toy Capital of the World.

Long before the film made the fields famous, Dyersville, a town not far from the Illinois border, was on the map for many kids, whose favorite toy cars, buses, trucks, and farm equipment were produced by the Ertl Co. Today, you can still tour the factory (now owned by U.S. Industries) and buy Ertl products at the factory outlet. But Ertl isn't the only game in town. Dyersville is also home to Scale Models and Spec-Cast, which also make farm toys and other small-scale cast models.

If you want to see the microscopic view of farm toy history, make tracks (albeit tiny ones) to the National Farm Toy Museum. Opened in Dyersville in 1986, it's home to a collection of more than 25,000 tiny tractors, puny ploughs, itsy-bitsy backhoes, and other minuscule machines. Housed in a spacious modern facility that could just as easily be a fine art gallery, this marvelous museum offers visitors a chance to rediscover the toys of their youth. And today's kids, though perhaps overstimulated by video and computer games, still delight in the back-to-basics joys of these low-tech toys.

The museum is part collector's gallery, part educational exhibit. It showcases early, rare,

For Ertl's 50th anniversary, it produced a special commemorative line, including this Dyersville farm toy keepsake.
*Courtesy the Ertl Company*

## CYBERSPACE CONTACTS

# Left and Center Field of Dreams

**http://199.120.110.2/dreams/**

Dream online at the official Web site of the Left and Center Field of Dreams (the Right Field portion is separately owned and operated). The site features pages about the annual Field of Dreams Festival (held in August), a souvenir catalog, Dyersville maps, and photos of the homegrown Ghost Players who play at the magical movie field.

and modern masterpieces of the model vehicle (not just farm toys here, despite the museum name), and its factory diorama shows how workers cast and paint the miniature vehicles.

But if you think that this is just a hometown salute to local industry, think again: Farm toys and other miniature vehicles are highly collectible. The museum hosts the annual National Farm Toy Show in November, which draws some 15,000 collectors from around the country to this community of 4,000. Other major collectibles events held in Dyersville include the Summer Toy Show (June), the Railroad Memorabilia & Model Show (April), and the Toy Truck and Construction Show (every other August, in odd years).

To raise money to support the museum, every year its gift shop offers a new, limited-edition Farm Toy Museum tractor model made by Ertl. Though the original sticker price is usually just a few dollars, the models quickly become collector's items.

The Ertl Co. got its start in 1945 when, after losing his job as a journeyman molder, Fred Ertl, Sr. started making model farm tractors for sale as toys. Working from his basement in Dubuque, Iowa, Ertl melted down war surplus aluminum aircraft pistons in the furnace and enlisted his wife and six kids to help sand-cast, paint, and package his creations. They sold so well that within four years Ertl had a contract with the John Deere Co. to make model tractors, and his basement business became a full-fledged factory, which was turning out some 5,000 toys a day. Ertl gained licenses to make models based on other companies' products as well, and the business branched out into model cars and other machinery.

When it was time to expand again, Ertl moved the business to a larger facility in Dyersville in 1959, transforming the small farming community into the Farm Toy Capital of the World. Eight years later, the company was sold to the Victor Comptometer Corp. (though the family was still involved; Fred Ertl, Jr. became president in 1967). Victor merged with Kidde, Inc. in 1977. Ertl is now owned by U.S. Industries.

Today, Ertl is the world's largest manufacturer of farm toys and one of the world's largest makers of scale models, model kits, custom imprints, and premium toys. But not all of its products are vehicular: One of Ertl's latest lines, in conjunction with the National Trust for Historic Preservation's Barn Again! project, is the Ertl Collectibles American Country Barn Series honoring the nation's most famous and important barn structures. And to commemorate the company's 50th anniversary, Ertl has released a limited-edition collection reproducing some of its original models, as well as a special Dyersville keepsake.

The other three Dyersville toymakers, Scale Models, Spec-Cast, and the Toy Factory by Dyersville, Inc., also produce farm toys and other miniature models, though neither offers factory tours. Scale Models was founded by Joseph L. Ertl in 1977, evolving from a foundry and toolshop business he started in 1970. The company makes toy tractors, replicas of antique farm toys, metal car kits, and other toys and parts. Scale Models has its own museum, attached to its gift shop, and sells its products through a mail-order catalog.

In contrast, Spec-Cast took a winding road to Dyersville. Founded in Rockford, Illinois, in 1974, its first products were brass and lead belt buckles. After being sold in 1977, the company added replica machines to its product line, taking on major clients such as International Harvester. It also expanded its buckle business, making ornate molded buckles for specialty markets. Ken and Dave Bell bought Spec-Cast in 1986 and moved it to Dyersville the following year. The company still specializes in scale model machinery; one of its latest lines features painted pewter scale models.

The latest addition to the local cottage industry is The Toy Factory of Dyersville, Inc., opened in May 1996 by Roger and Claudia Slade. Roger learned all the tiny details of the trade during his ten years with Ertl and three years with Scale Models. Visitors are encouraged to drop by for tours.

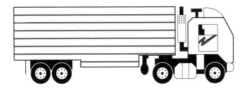

The National Farm Toy Museum gift shop, as well as such stores as the Toy Farmer Country Store and the Toy Collectors Club of America store (both of which are situated just east of the Farm Toy Museum), sells products made by all four companies.

And speaking of toys—for those who still see children in shades of pink and blue and think their daughters may be bored by the "boy toys" at the Farm Toy Museum, Dyersville also has the Dyer/Botsford Doll Museum, an impressive private collection of rare and special dolls.

The Field of Dreams may draw visitors like a mythopoetic magnet, but once out of the cornfield, it's the tiny toys that keep them touring about for at least a few hours. Though they may never plough a real field, these tiny machines boast the horsepower of imagination and childhood memories.

## FOR FURTHER INFORMATION

### General Information

**Dyersville Area Chamber of Commerce**
Hwy. 136
P.O. Box 187
Dyersville, IA 52040
(319) 875-2311

### Attractions and Events

**Dyer/Botsford Doll Museum**
331 E. First St.
Dyersville, IA 52040
(319) 875-2414

**Ertl Toy Co.**
Hwys. 136 and 20
P.O. Box 500
Dyersville, IA 52040
(319) 875-5613 (outlet store); (319) 875-5699 (factory tours)

**Field of Dreams**
28963 Lansing Rd.
Dyersville, IA 52040
(319) 875-8404

**Left and Center Field of Dreams**
29001 Lansing Rd.
Dyersville, IA 52040
(319) 875-7985

**National Farm Toy Museum**
1110 16th Ave. S.E.
Dyersville, IA 52040
(319) 875-2727

**Scale Models Museum and Outlet Store**
Hwy. 136
P.O. Box 327
Dyersville, IA 52040
(319) 875-8625

**Spec-Cast**
P.O. Box 324
Dyersville, IA 52040
(319) 875-8706

**The Toy Factory of Dyersville, Inc.**
P.O. Box 204
204 5th St. N.W.
Dyersville, IA 52040
(319) 875-6000

**Toy Collectors Club of America**
1235 16th Ave. S.E.
Dyersville, IA 52040
(319) 875-7444

**Toy Farmer Country Store**
1161 16th Ave. S.E.
Dyersville, IA 52040
(319) 875-8850

**Toy Shows (throughout year)**
Contact the Dyersville Area Chamber
of Commerce or the National Farm
Toy Museum

# ❁ High Point, North Carolina

HOME FURNISHINGS CAPITAL OF THE WORLD

The craftspeople, woodworkers, designers, and decorators of North Carolina have long been recognized as among America's finest, and nowhere is the art of domestic design more apparent, abundant, or absolute than in High Point, North Carolina, the Home Furnishings Capital of the World. This is the latest in an evolutionary chain of capitals claims for the community—past incarnations have included such titles as the Furniture and Hosiery Capital of the World, and then just Furniture Capital of the World. But home furnishings best describes what comes out of High Point now, and that's where the claim is currently staked.

In truth, the whole region around High Point—encompassing much of central and western North Carolina along the I-40 and I-85 corridors—is part of this capital area. Towns from Hickory to Thomasville, Lexington to Charlotte, are home to dozens of furniture manufacturers and textile makers. But High Point is the center of this universe.

High Point's Showplace on the Park is one of the many venues that spotlight the region's fine furnishings. *Courtesy High Point Convention & Visitors Bureau*

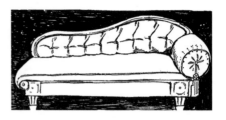

High Point's reputation is international; when people want home furnishings at discounted retail prices, they go to the source. The area is home to more than 140 furniture plants (15 of which are world leaders in production) as well as more than 85 retail showroom stores and outlets.

But High Point's international appeal extends beyond its collection of manufacturers. Twice a year it hosts the International Home Furnishings Market, which sprawls throughout High Point and neighboring Thomasville (the Chair Capital of the World).

The Market is a major event for the home furnishings professionals attending this world's fair of fine furnishings. Held for nine days in April and October, the event dates back to 1909, when it was known as the Southern Furniture Market. That name stuck until 1989, when it was changed to reflect the event's international reputation.

More than the name had changed by then: The event saw exponential growth during the high-design explosion of the 1980s—38,500 attendees came to the Market in 1983. A decade later, attendance had nearly doubled, with some 67,500 visitors moving through the exhibition areas.

Today's International Home Furnishings Market takes up more than 7 million square feet of exhibit space, with more than 150 buildings in High Point and Thomasville devoted to the display of home furnishings. Some 2,300 manufacturers (about 10 percent of whom are foreign) showcase their latest offerings at the event, which draws close to 70,000 attendees from the United States and 93 other countries.

The event is open only to industry professionals, but the public sees the results soon enough in showrooms and designer houses as the latest in domestic decor trickles down to the retail level. Non-industry visitors can, however, get a glimpse of this world by arranging for group tours of the showroom buildings. These must be arranged in advance and are offered only for groups of 15 or more (organized bus trips into the area often feature such tours). But don't plan on touring during the six weeks surrounding the Market in April and October, when the showrooms are off-limits to outsiders.

To complement the furnishings (not to mention the textile manufacturers), High Point hosts another big event of note: The twice-

Furniture showrooms display the area's design offerings during High Point's International Home Furnishings Market. *Courtesy High Point Convention & Visitors Bureau*

yearly Showtime International Fabric Show takes place in January and July. Like its larger sibling, this show is for industry professionals only.

The North Carolina furniture business began its ascendancy around the turn of the century. As the northern industrial cities began losing their hold on the furniture manufacturing base—Boston had 28 furniture plants in 1875, a number that had dwindled to six by 1900—the South began to rise again, this time as a furnishings leader, and North Carolina led the way. Textiles also moved to the South around this time.

It was a slow but steady progression; though the North Carolina makers traveled to exhibit their wares at northern furniture markets in Chicago and New York, they felt secure enough in their status to create their own market. By 1909, the Southern Furniture Market was established as an annual event.

Furniture and textile manufacturers remain sprinkled throughout North Carolina, but High Point's concentration grew out of its location near the railroad and the hardwood forests of central and western North Carolina. Manufacturers clustered together, drawn to the area by the number of other manufacturers already established there. Since traveling salespeople couldn't easily take their wares on the road—although a miniature furniture collectibles market has developed for the tiny samples salesmen once carried—buyers routinely traveled to the factories to see the products. Thus the competition also attracted new factories, drawn to High Point by the number of buyers who visited the area. Another major North Carolina furniture city, Hickory, developed from this same formula of manufacturing magnetism.

The Depression put a dent in furniture sales. But the 300 percent increase in home building after World War II created a home furnishings boom as families bought furniture for their new homes. This postwar buying binge cemented North Carolina as the nation's premier furnishings manufacturing state. Today, more than 35 percent of the furniture manufactured in the U.S. was made in North Carolina, mainly in the High Point area. Considering that Americans spend some $47 billion a year on furniture, it's an industry that could make even a lazy boy sit up and take notice.

But if you don't know your Hepplewhite from your Hitchcock, or think Duncan Phyffe is the brother of Andy Griffith's deputy, Barney, you can polish your furniture knowledge with a visit to the Furniture Library on Main Street. Established in 1970, it has the world's most comprehensive collection of books on the history of furniture, with some 7,000 volumes on home furnishings back to Ancient Egypt. Library literature notes that the collection "encompasses all significant volumes published since 1640, and includes America's only complete collection of the original works of eighteenth-century furniture masters Chippendale, Sheraton, and Hepplewhite, as well as a complete set of Diderot's *Encyclopedia.*"

And if the Furniture Library whets your appetite for information, pay a visit to the Furniture Discovery Center, a museum that replicates a furniture factory. Highlights include a talking tree that describes how wood gets from forest to furniture, a collection of miniature bedroom furnishings, and a furniture industry hall of fame. Another furniture museum can be found in Hickory (just off I-40, exit 125), at the Hickory Furniture Mart; this one tells the story of the North Carolina furniture industry.

Another High Point landmark worth investigating is the World's Largest Bureau, at 508 Hamilton Street. It's actually a building, constructed in 1926 to promote High Point's capital claim; it has recently been restored to its original, nineteenth-century dresser appearance. Then you can hit the road to Thomasville, home to the World's Largest Duncan Phyffe Chair.

Even if you can't get to High Point yourself, you can pay a visit via the information superhighway: The community's World Wide Web site has information on everything from local schools and cultural pursuits to area furniture makers, the Furniture Library, and other local resources. It also has a link to the World Furniture Network (WFN), a Web site where manufacturers promote their products and history.

High Point's furnishings and textiles can be found around the world, but those in the know know there's only one place to buy the best for less.

## FOR FURTHER INFORMATION

### General Information

**High Point Convention
and Visitors Bureau**
300 South Main St.
P.O. Box 2273
High Point, NC 27261
(910) 884-5255

### Attractions and Events

**Furniture Discovery Center**
101 W. Green Drive
High Point, NC 27260
(910) 887-3876

**The Furniture Library**
1009 North Main St.
High Point, NC 27262
(910) 883-4011

**The Furniture Museum**
Hickory Furniture Mart
2220 Hwy. 70 East
Hickory, NC 28602
(800) 462-MART

**Showroom Tours**
Contact: Group Tour Manager
High Point Convention and Visitors Bureau

## TRADE-ONLY MARKET INFORMATION

**International Home Furnishings Marketing Association, Inc.**
300 South Main St.
P.O. Box 5687
High Point, NC 27262
(910) 889-0203

CHAPTER **2**

# THE BIRDS
# AND THE
# BEASTS

 ven before Walt Disney made movie stars of ducks, mice, and other unlikely critters, Americans have had a vast and often edible appreciation for the furry and the feathered. From the house pets who are beloved companions to the wild birds who flock to popular wilderness areas, the creatures with which we share the land, water, and sky are an integral part of our lives.

And sometimes when a place is intimately connected with its local livestock or wildlife, it finds the link worthy of honor — of festivals and parades, billboards, and souvenirs. Many a town or city stakes a "capital of the world" claim to a particular bird or beast as a point of local pride, heritage, and tradition. It's a nice way to attract tourists, to promote the area's unique charms, and to generate a sense of creature comfort for community cohesiveness.

It's not hard to find such places. Is a region known for its watchable wildlife or great hunting? Chances are, there's a world capital in its midst. Are there meat packaging plants, or animal breeders associated with a particular area? Look for capitals there, too.

Many towns honor their favorite four-legged creatures. High on the list are mules, and the towns that honor them are particularly stubborn in their loyalty. Both **COLUMBIA, TENNESSEE,** and Bishop, California, call themselves the Mule Capital of the World. And these, as well as a number of noncapitalized communities, celebrate Mule Days, a tradition that usually dates from nineteenth-century mule-trading market days.

Horses also trot out town spirit in some places. **LEXINGTON, KENTUCKY,** understandably, is renowned as the Horse Capital of the World for its famous purebred horse farms. Visitors can revel in this horse sense at Lexington's Kentucky Horse Park, an equine paradise of museums, galleries, race courses, and farms. Northridge, California, also calls itself the world's horse capital, while breeds apart are Goodwell, Texas (the Saddle Bronc Capital of the World), Shelbyville, Tennessee (the Walking Horse Capital of the World), and Mexico, Missouri (the Saddle Horse Capital of the World). Horses even get capital claims on a state level: Purcell, Oklahoma, calls itself the Horse Capital of Oklahoma.

Smaller mammals also win points with small-town America. Kenton, Tennessee, proudly proclaims itself Home of the White Squirrel, because of its peculiar population of albino nut-munchers. Meanwhile, the entire state of Minnesota is known as the Only

Lexington's Thoroughbred horse farms are world-renowned. *Courtesy Greater Lexington Convention & Visitors Bureau*

Gopher State in the World. And two towns honor the venerable woodchuck weatherman: Both Punxsutawney, Pennsylvania, and Sun Prairie, Wisconsin, celebrate their local spring-predicting varmints, though each takes a different claim for the same fame. Sun Prairie goes by Groundhog Capital of the World, while Punxsutawney calls itself the Weather Capital of the World. And both stage groundhog prediction ceremonies and festivals (see Chapter 10 for more on this competition).

Continuing in this critterly tradition, Rhonesboro, Texas, is the Possum Capital of the World—actually, that should be the Dead Possum Capital of the World, since it has gained its reputation as a roadkill record-holder thanks to all the big rigs tooling down the highway that runs past town. Presumably, critters with longer legs would have a better shot at making it across the road. A visit to Rayne, Louisiana, the Frog Capital of the World, could put the theory to the test—though Rayners have a talent for making the most of a frog and a frying pan (frog fritters anyone?), so those frogs can't be *that* fast.

Turtles crossing the road wouldn't do much better than possums, but they might have a fighting chance if they'd been training in Longville, Minnesota, the Turtle Racing Capital of the World (no hares allowed). In Jensen Beach, Florida, Sea Turtle Capital of the World, it's the humans who try to stay out of the way of this endangered species, although visitors are encouraged to study the animals in controlled viewing areas.

Bird watchers can set their sights on a number of towns around the country. **MERCER, WISCONSIN**—a.k.a., the Loon Capital—attracts visitors with its 2,000-pound fiberglass loon statue (said to be the world's largest), as well as its local loon nesting areas, which draw thousands of common loons and tourists (in that order) during the spring and summer. Mercer has some competition from another loony locale, Nisswa, Minnesota, which calls itself the world's loon capital.

And though it's not easy to get to, eagle fanciers find it worth the trip to the Alaska Chilkat Bald Eagle Preserve near **HAINES,** the Eagle Capital of America, where the birds nest and feed in a photographer's dream setting. And long-legged bird lovers can swoop down on Coteau Holmes, Louisiana, the Heron Capital of the World.

More common birds of a feather flock to towns such as Bickleton, Washington, the Bluebird Capital of the World, and Griggsville,

**Flying North**

Though the U.S. has a flock of species-specific bird capitals, the town of McClennan in Alberta, Canada, puts all its eggs in one basket. As the Bird Capital of Canada, McClennan's fowl features include the Kimiwan Lake Birdwalk and Interpretive Centre — the lake is at the intersection of three major North American migration paths.

Illinois, the Purple Martin Capital of the World; in these communities, the citizens are such avid fans of their avian friends that they have built numerous birdhouses to keep their birds well fed. In the Hummingbird Capital of the World, Swainton, New Jersey, visitors can stroll through Leaming's Gardens and watch the happy hummers drinking their fill at a variety of bird-feeders.

For some people, however, birds are more sporting to hunt than to watch. Bird hunters flock to towns such as Sumner, Missouri (the Wild Goose Capital of the World), and Fulda, Minnesota (the Wood Duck Capital of the World). Hunters in search of a pheasant afternoon head for Winner, South Dakota; Norton, Kansas; or Sherman County, Nebraska, each of which calls itself the Pheasant Capital of the World.

One of the fowlest fests is the Wings over the Prairie Festival in Stuttgart, Arkansas, the Rice and Duck Capital of the World, home of the World Championship Duck Calling Competition. A local museum even gives festival-goers a shot at a simulated duck hunt.

Bird hunters in search of the real decoy head north, to Havre de Grace, Maryland, to buy the fabulous fakes carved in the Decoy Capital of the World. And hunting dogs get their due in Waynesboro, Georgia, Bird Dog Capital of the World, where some of the country's finest birders are bred.

For those who prefer their birds processed by someone else, a number of towns package their pride. Gainesville, Georgia, the Poultry Capital of the World, has one of the country's largest poultry processing plants. It's also home to Poultry Park, a peaceful place dotted with fowl statuary. But don't buy a bucket of fried chicken in Gainesville unless you plan to use your hands. A peculiar and funny town ordinance bans the eating of fried chicken with fork and knife. You might even be given a silly citation by a local cop if caught in the utensilitarian act.

And come Thanksgiving, both Worthington, Minnesota (the Turkey Capital of the World), and Oxford, Nebraska (which sets its sights at a less loftier goal as Turkey Capital of Nebraska), work overtime to fill the nation's holiday meal zeal.

For meat on the hoof, America has a large herd of cowtowns (a term applied to many cattle industry communities). From Woodstown, New Jersey, to Ellsworth, Nebraska, communities that have served up red meat remain proud of their beefy backgrounds. You could call the entire Lone Star state a Cowtown Capital, since Texas has more Cowtowns per square mile than anywhere in the world: Ft. Worth, San Antonio, Burleson, Colleyville, Arlington, Athens, Crowley, and Aledo are among the longhorn state's collection of Cowtowns. Alliance, Nebraska, is both a Cowtown and the Cattle Capital of the World; Kansas City, Missouri, is both a Cowtown and a Barbecue Capital of the World (a tasty combo, though it has a lot of competition for both claims).

Some towns even honor what their cows produce. Russell Springs, Kansas, tossed its name in the ring as Cow Chip Capital of the World.

When it comes to fishing and seafood, there are so many capitals that this book has a chapter devoted to such fishy places. You can play Jacques Cousteau for an afternoon if you visit **CAPE ANN, MASSACHUSETTS,** the Whale Watching Capital of the World, where tourists sail out from the famous fishing port of Gloucester to gasp in awe as these graceful sea creatures leap into the air or show off with a watery spout-blowing exhibition.

If you thought that only those with fur, fins, or feathers can elicit civic pride, think again: The buzz is out on bugs as well. Lepidopterists long for Pacific Grove, California, sometimes called Butterfly Town, U.S.A., because of its yearly influx of monarchs, while Selma, Alabama, calls itself the Butterfly Capital of Alabama for its preponderance of beautiful bugs. And light and lively **BOONE, NORTH CAROLINA**—the Firefly Capital of America—has a glow-in-the-dark festival to celebrate its claim.

Every creature featured by a town or city is somehow connected to that place, through work or play, industry or recreation. And in coming together to honor these beasts and birds, the communities celebrate their heritage as well as the ageless interdependence of man and beast in this extended Garden of Eden called Earth.

## ✪ Haines, Alaska

EAGLE CAPITAL OF AMERICA

Alaska remains the United States' final frontier, a place of majesty and open space, wilderness and wildlife, relatively untouched by modern civilization. What better place to find the symbol of American freedom? The bald eagle, once near extinction, thrives in this vast state.

The world's largest concentration of bald eagles can be found at the Alaska Chilkat Bald Eagle Preserve, just outside the city of Haines. The preserve was created June 15, 1982, by order of Alaska's governor, Jay Hammond, to commemorate the bicentennial of the bird's selection as the national symbol. Once the eagle had officially landed in Haines, so too did Haines' claim as Eagle Capital of America.

The closest civilization to the Chilkat Preserve is the Tlingit Indian Village of Klukwan, near the eagle nesting grounds. Haines is about 20 miles from the main viewing area; the 43,000-acre preserve sprawls between mile 10 and mile 26 of the Haines Highway. But as the largest community nearby, situated at the top of Alaska's Inside Passage, Haines is the base for eagle watchers and is a popular stop-over for tourists and adventure-seekers.

During the summer and early fall, float trips take eagle-eyers to see the birds in their nesting and feeding areas; the fall is the highlight of the year, as thousands of bald eagles gather to feast on spawning salmon in an unusually wide area called the "flats," at the meeting place of the Chilkat, Tsirku, and Klehini Rivers.

Even amateur photographers often return from

**DID YOU KNOW...**

**Tours for any Taste**
A variety of special tour companies offer unique excursions into the wilderness areas around Haines. Among them: Chilkat Guides, which offers rafting trips through the bald eagle preserve (907/766-2491); Chilkoot Sled Dog Adventures, which offers Alaskan husky sled dog shows, rides, and winter tours (907/767-5667); and Haines Airways, one of several "flightseeing" companies that offer flights over Glacier Bay (907/766-2646).

The Chilkat Preserve is one of the world's best places for spotting our national bird, the bald eagle. *Alaska Division of Tourism*

float trips with images of hundreds of eagles. Water-wary sightseers can take the Haines Highway and stop at various viewing areas that also provide amazingly close proximity to these rare raptors.

The creation of the Chilkat Bald Eagle Preserve was merely a formality, for birdwatchers have long flocked to this fascinating feeding ground. Indeed, Chilkat Valley has often been called the Valley of the Eagles, and one of the most active eagle areas is known as Eagle Council Grounds.

Though the eagle population peaks during the fall, the birds begin arriving in the springtime to nest in a stand of black cottonwood along the Haines Highway. Their first meals consist of spring smelt runs—mere appetizers for the Chinook, sockeye, pink, chum, and coho salmon soon to be flopping about in the river flats.

By summer, the eagles are feeding and breeding by the hundreds; as the autumn salmon spawn draws near, more eagles appear in the Chilkat Valley. By autumn, some 3,000 to 3,500 bald eagles can be found around the river flats, plucking squirming salmon from the water and ripping them apart in a feeding frenzy. Hundreds of eagles stay on through the winter months, feasting on remaining spawned-out salmon and trout in these placid waters.

The Haines Highway traces roughly the same path as the famed Dalton Trail, once the main supply route to the Klondike. Though now a bird-lovers city, Haines was once a gold-obsessed town. Settled by Native Americans, its population exploded with the onslaught of miners who sought their fortune during the Klondike Gold Rush of 1896–1899.

Evidence of Haines' intriguing heritage—native, gold, and eagle—can be found throughout the city. Numerous galleries specialize in Native American art, and Alaska Indian Arts at Ft. Seward (decommissioned after World War II) has native artisans in residence, including totem carvers and jewelry makers. Visitors can see a local melodrama depicting the Klondike gold fever, "Lust for Dust," performed twice a week at the Chilkat Center for the Arts. And, of course, a variety of tour operators offer float and road trips to the eagle preserve. Fishing lodges and outfitters—the eagles aren't the only ones catching salmon and trout, though only eagles may fish in the preserve—also are popular.

Photographers usually come to capture images of eagles, but another of nature's most magnificent spectacles is also on display here: The aurora borealis (the northern lights) is visible from fall through spring.

From the dancing lights to the soaring eagles, Haines is a treat for lens or the naked eye; it's an American capital treasure to be prized and preserved as a rarity more precious than gold.

## FOR FURTHER INFORMATION

**Haines Visitors Bureau**
P.O. Box 530
Haines, AK 99827
(907) 766-2234

**Alaska Chilkat Bald Eagle Preserve**
c/o Alaska State Parks
Dept. of Natural Resources
Division of Parks and Outdoor Resources
400 Willoughby
Juneau, AK 99801
(907) 456-4563 (Main)
(907) 766-2292 (Haines District)

# ✪ Boone, North Carolina

## FIREFLY CAPITAL OF AMERICA

Remember what it felt like to roam through the backyard in the shadow of night, breathlessly anticipating that brief glow of light that gave you a glimmer of guidance? Catching fireflies is as common a childhood ritual as playing marbles or climbing trees. And when it comes to this beloved pastime, one town has its name in flickering lights: Boone, North Carolina, the Firefly Capital of America. It also has America's only Firefly Festival. Though barely a twinkle in the town's eye when planners organized the first festival in 1993, after 3,000 people showed up that year, it was clear the Firefly Festival would become a Boone tradition.

Even before lights-out in Boone, in mid-June, the firefly fun has begun. Lightning bug lovers head over to the Horn in the West grounds (home to an outdoor drama by the same name), where they delight in such glow-in-the-dark gaiety as a firefly hunt (no keeping) and a street dance.

Boone's Firefly Festival at the Horn in the West grounds draws visitors for the flying light show. *Photo by Judi Scharns, copyright 1990, courtesy Boone Convention and Visitors Bureau*

The town's claim to glow-bug fame is young—and, unlike most places whose capital status is self-proclaimed, Boone's nickname was bestowed by the *Southern Farmer's Almanac*. The 1994 *Almanac* dubbed Boone "Lightning Bug Capital of America" (locals shortened it to Firefly Capital).

The *Southern Farmer's Almanac* had a vested interest in highlighting Boone's newfound flame: It has been campaigning for the firefly to be named America's official national insect. Boone enthusiastically threw itself into the effort; the Firefly Festival was in part a response to the *Almanac's* call to action.

But Boone was not necessarily assured of its title. Indeed, the *Almanac* had Dr. James Lloyd, a "nationally renowned lightning bug expert," draw up a short list of U.S. towns worthy of the title, based on their firefly populations. The radiant runners-up included Lake City, Florida; Oxford, Mississippi; Tallulah, Louisiana; Monck's Corner, South Carolina; and Blakely, Georgia.

In the end, the title went to Boone, not only because of the Firefly Festival, but also because the area has more than 30 different species of lightning bugs. That's a lot of wattage, especially for a town with a population that hovers around the 13,000 mark. Both the town and its festival earned the *Southern Farmer's Almanac's* well-deserved and glowing endorsement.

## FOR FURTHER INFORMATION

Firefly Festival Association and
Boone Convention and Visitors Bureau
208 Howard St.
Boone, NC 28607
(800) 852-9506
(704) 262-3516

# ❀ Lexington, Kentucky

HORSE CAPITAL OF THE WORLD

You can almost hear the whinnying when you turn off the interstate and drive past the bluegrass pastures, toward Lexington's Kentucky Horse Park. This is the mane mecca for the equine set, the

The Kentucky Horse Park is an equine dream, with farms and horses dotting the blue-grass landscape. *Courtesy Lexington Convention & Visitors Bureau*

horsey heartland's stomping ground, where visitors from around the globe come to learn about the frisky fillies and sterling stallions bred and raced here.

Lexington's status as the Horse Capital of the World comes from more than two centuries of world-class horse breeding. Today, some 450 horse farms—many of them for Thoroughbreds—grace this lush landscape known as Bluegrass Country. And Lexington is its fulcrum. Farms breeding standardbreds (used in harness racing) and saddlebreds (show horses) also dot this area. Blend in the myriad races, shows, and other horse-related attractions, and you have the ingredients that make Lexington a breed apart.

The lexicon of Lexington's legacy is enough to make the eyes of a horse-lover turn misty. The manifest of famous names—whether of farms such as Calumet (home of Triple Crown winners Whirlaway and Citation) or of horses such as Man O' War, Secretariat, and Seattle Slew—hangs in the air like a horse's breath after a hard run.

Visitors to Lexington often start their touring with a day at the Kentucky Horse Park, a multiuse complex that sprawls over 1,032 acres. Horse farms can be seen on the perimeters (more than 40 different breeds are represented at the Horse Park), and as you drive onto the property you pass acres of race and show grounds.

The park's admission fee includes sites such as the International Museum of the Horse, the William G. Kenton Gallery (of equestrian art), and the Man O' War Memorial. Walking tours of the Horse Park are also available.

For a seat-of-the-pants experience (not included in the park admission price), visitors ride everything from ponies to horse-drawn carriages.

Visit the International Museum of the Horse for an overview of 50 million years of horse history and culture, then tour the American Saddle Horse Museum (not affiliated with the Horse Park except as a tenant) for a delightful look at Kentucky's only native breed of horse. From battlefield (General R.E. Lee's famous gray charger Traveler) to boob tube (Mr. Ed, as portrayed by a finicky golden palomino named Bamboo Harvester), saddle horses have played significant roles in American culture, both pop and circumstance.

The Horse Park's most famous site is the memorial to the great race horse Man O' War, which also serves as his tomb. He was embalmed and later moved to the Horse Park to be buried beneath his statue.

Lexington's historic Keeneland Race Course is one of the nation's most esteemed Thoroughbred tracks. *Courtesy Lexington Convention & Visitors Bureau*

Though the Kentucky Horse Park is the ultimate horse-lover's experience, Lexington offers other equestrian excursions. If you're in a contemplative mood, visit Thoroughbred Park on Main St., with its bronze memorials honoring great horses and jockeys. If you're curious about training, arrange a tour of the Kentucky Horse Center, the world's largest Thoroughbred training center, where you'll see the horses going through their paces.

Those champing at the bit for action can visit some of the area's renowned racing venues, including the Red Mile Harness Track, which dates back to 1875; it's Kentucky's oldest harness racing track and still hosts the Kentucky Futurity, the third leg of trotting's triple crown, held the first week in October.

Keeneland Race Course (6 miles west of downtown on Versailles Road) is the area's top Thoroughbred race course. Founded in 1936 on a farm land-granted to the Keene family by Patrick Henry in 1783 (Henry was a Keene cousin), the park has an international reputation and royal fans. Queen Elizabeth II was there to see the inaugural running of the Queen Elizabeth II Challenge Cup on October 11, 1984. Horse shows and sales are also conducted at the Keeneland facility. Keeneland races are traditionally held during three weeks in April and three weeks in October.

As a community, Lexington has horsepower to spare—there's even a Toyota plant for those more enamored of mechanical movement. But no matter what your equestrian acumen, Lexington is a destination worth taking at a relaxed walk, not a gallop.

## FOR FURTHER INFORMATION

### General Information

**Lexington Convention and Visitors Bureau**
301 E. Vine St.
Lexington, KY 40507
(606) 233-7299 or (800) 845-3959

*Attractions and Events*

**American Saddle Horse Museum**
4093 Iron Works Pike
Lexington, KY 40511
(606) 259-2746

**Keeneland Race Course**
4201 Versailles Rd.
P.O. Box 1690
Lexington, KY 40592
(606) 254-3412  or (800) 456-3412

**Kentucky Horse Center**
3380 Paris Pike
Lexington, KY  40511
(606) 293-1853

**Kentucky Horse Park**
4089 Iron Works Pike
Lexington, KY 40511
(606) 233-4303

**Red Mile Harness Track**
1200 Red Mile Rd.
P.O. Box 420
Lexington, KY 40585
(606) 255-0752

# ✿ Mercer, Wisconsin

THE LOON CAPITAL

Wisconsin has its share of oddities and wonders, from the giant fiberglass fish of the National Freshwater Fishing Hall of Fame in Hayward to the eclectic collections of the House on the Rock in Spring Green. But there's only one really big loon, and it's in Mercer, Wisconsin, which calls itself the Loon Capital (period; no world, no America).

The 2,000-pound fiberglass loon, which looms 16 feet high, was built in 1981, the same year Mercer received its official capital des-

Mercer's giant loon statue attracts flocks of tourists. *Courtesy Mercer Chamber of Commerce*

ignation from the state. The statue, financed with $10,000 raised by the chamber of commerce, honors the graceful, long-necked waterbird that has made Mercer a loon-lover's paradise.

The common loon migrates north from the Gulf of Mexico and the Florida coast to nest in the Mercer area during warm months before heading south again at the first sign of ice. Area university groups lead birdwatchers to the nesting areas; and on Loon Day, the first Wednesday in August, some 9,000 people descend on this town of 1,342 to engage in a variety of loony activities. The biggest event is the Loon Calling Contest (hey, what do you call a loon, anyway?); the event also boasts a crafts fair, where more than 250 artisans show their often loony work.

Mercer is situated in the Northwoods region of Wisconsin, an area once popular with Chicago gangsters in search of a nearby getaway. In fact, Al Capone's less-than-infamous little brother, Ralph "Bottles" Capone, moved to Mercer in 1945 and bought the Rex Hotel (legend has it he operated illegal slot machines there); he sold the Rex in 1955, but supposedly also had an interest in another Mercer retreat, the Beaver Lodge. An avid fisherman, Ralph took full advantage of the area's recreational opportunities; and, after an active life, he died in a nursing home in nearby Hurley in 1974 at the age of 81.

These days, the gangland goons have long since given way to the graceful loons, who attract a decidedly less dangerous element of

vacationer. But even if you don't get to see many of the real loons, there's always the big loon. Maureen Leibach, the Mercer Chamber of Commerce's office manager and executive secretary of the board, claims it's "the world's largest loon statue." When asked if she knows of any other loon statues, she admits she has never heard of any. "But I do know ours is the largest."

As it happens, at least one other loon statue does exist: Virginia, Minnesota, has a lake-mounted statue, which it calls the World's Largest Floating Loon Statue. Mercer isn't even the only loon capital. The town of Nisswa, Minnesota, in another major loon-spotting area, claims that status, too. But the competition doesn't seem to be hurting Mercer. Leibach says: "It has helped with tourism and recreation. We get people who are interested in the birds, and they come and just fall in love with our loons, and they decide to come back for vacation. Then, some of those people come for vacation and they decide they want to move here." So thanks to the lure of the loons, there's a lot more nesting going on in Mercer these days.

## For Further Information

**Mercer Chamber of Commerce**
P.O. Box 368
Mercer, WI 54547
(715) 476-2389

# ✹ Columbia, Tennessee

MULE CAPITAL OF THE WORLD

Just 40 miles south of Nashville, there's a town that takes stubborn pride in its heritage: Columbia, Tennessee, calls itself the Mule Capital of the World, a title not to be taken lightly. Other towns may try to lay claim to it—Bishop, California, also dubs itself the world's mule capital, and Muleshoe, Texas, even has a statue honoring the beasts of burden—but Columbia's slogan was hard-earned, thanks to the town's nineteenth-century role as a mule-trading center and its twentieth-century tradition of Mule Day.

Mule dealing became a major industry in Columbia in the 1840s, when the town's central location made it a mule-trading crossroads. Young mules from Missouri were shipped to Columbia, where street traders bartered them off or sold them to southern cotton and sugar plantations.

The town's major Market Day, the first Monday in April, took on such significance that, in 1934, the event became a full-fledged celebration. That day, "1,000 girls on 1,000 mules," as posters promised, paraded through town—the first official Mule Day—and a new tradition was launched.

Mule Day faded from sight during the middle part of the century, but in 1974, the Maury County Bridle and Saddle Club gave Columbia the kick in the pants it needed to revive the tradition. Today's Mule Day—now actually four days over the first weekend

Columbia's Mule Day features a beauty-on-a-beast parade and other celebrations. *Courtesy Maury County Convention and Visitors Bureau*

in April—still includes the beloved Mule Parade, wherein mule lovers show off their often elaborately dressed animals.

Other Mule Day festivities include a Liar's Contest, Flea Market, Pancake Breakfast, Old Time Fiddler's Contest, and—at Columbia's Reese Horse and Mule Co., which still deals in mules — the traditional Mule Sale.

The town does have another claim to fame: The eleventh president of the United States, James K. Polk, hailed from Columbia. Visitors can see his restored ancestral family home, built by his father in 1816, on W. 7th St. in downtown Columbia. Polk also had his first law practice in Columbia.

If you've not yet had your fill of capitals while in Maury County —which itself holds the title of Antebellum Homes Capital of Tennessee—not far from Columbia you'll find the town of Mt. Pleasant, a.k.a. the Phosphate Capital of the World. The town was once a major player in the phosphate industry; locals are presently rebuilding the Phosphate Museum, which burned down in 1993.

But before you depart from Columbia, here's one more mule morsel: The great cowboy comedian, Will Rogers, once declared, "What the thoroughfare of Wall Street will do to you if you don't know a stock, Columbia will do to you if you don't know a mule."

## FOR FURTHER INFORMATION

### General Information

**Maury County Convention and Visitors Bureau**
# 8 Public Square
308 W. 7th St.
Columbia, TN 38402
(615) 381-7176

### Attractions and Events

**Mule Day Office**
P.O. Box 66
Columbia, TN 38402
(615) 381-9557

**James Polk House**
301 W. 7th St.
P.O. Box 741
Columbia, TN 38402
(615) 388-2354

# ❂ Cape Ann, Massachusetts

WHALE WATCHING CAPITAL OF THE WORLD

Cape Ann, the "other Cape" in Massachusetts, was once known primarily for the fishing vessels that sailed from Gloucester and its other coastal towns, while the fishermen's wives nervously paced their widow's walks, gazing out at the empty waters in hopes of sighting their husbands' returning ships.

Though fishing vessels still sail from Cape Ann, another kind of ship also leaves its harbors, decks crowded with tourists seeking a chance to sight the marvelous mammals of the deep. Cape Ann calls itself the Whale Watching Capital of the World.

The Cape Ann Chamber of Commerce adopted the slogan in 1984 after realizing the tourism potential of the then-budding industry. Now, dozens of whale watch expeditions set sail weekly from Gloucester and Rockport, the Cape's two major coastal towns. A trip to Gloucester's docks reveals an array of whale watch boats bobbing at anchor, enticing tourists aboard. Two of the largest companies, Capt. Bill's Whale Watch and Yankee Whale Watch, also offer deep sea fishing excursions. Rockport, known more for its art galleries and lobster boats than for its whale watching, has been a little late in joining the act.

CYBERSPACE CONTACTS

## Whale Watching Web

http://www.physics.helsinki.fi.whale/

The Helsinki-based Whale Watching Web is a must-surf for whale watching buffs and newcomers alike. It features pages of whale photos and sounds, a Cetacean Encyclopaedia, and links to a variety of Massachusetts whale watch operators and information sites.

Similar whale expeditions depart from other Massachusetts ports—notably from Boston and a few Cape Cod locations. And Pacific whale watchers can sail from major West Coast ports as well; but Cape Ann's claim remains strong, as its fleet was one of the first to capitalize on this growing tourism trend.

Cape Ann is known for its commercial fishing. It is home to Gorton's of Gloucester, one of the world's largest packagers of frozen fish. And the famous statue of the fisherman at his ship's wheel, the image of which is Gorton's logo, is a landmark of the Gloucester waterfront.

But as times change, so too must industries. Searching for ways to stay afloat in the face of declining fish populations and heightened regulations on over-fishing, local boat owners realized that the abundance of whales off the coast could be a natural draw for Cape Ann's summer visitors.

Whale watchers are usually guaranteed at least one whale sighting, and with their sophisticated sonar and tracking equipment, as well as the help of friendly dolphins (and other boats) that lead the way, most trips meet that guarantee; if not, a rain check is given for another excursion.

Most companies offer morning and afternoon trips. The whales can be found about 10 to 12 miles out, and after motoring out to sea, the boat begins searching for signs of whales. When one or more are sighted, the vessel creeps to the viewing area; lucky tourists may see anything from a single waterspout to a family of leaping humpback whales. But no matter the extent of the sighting, this proximity to the world's largest animals can catch the breath of even the most jaded tourist.

Another spectacle is the congestion of the whale watch vessels once there has been a sighting. You can be sure that if yours is the first boat to spot a spout or tail, others are sure to follow. Often, three or more tourist-laden boats from competing outfits bob about together, waiting for the whales to show themselves. Most people will see far more whale watchers than whales.

In the past few years, environmentalists have begun noting the negative impact of whale watch expeditions around the world. The whales are sometimes wounded by tourist vessels venturing too close, though no such incident has ever been reported off Cape Ann. Indeed, much of the Cape Ann fleet works for the good of the

whales. Some vessels gather information for the Atlantic Cetacean Research Center in Gloucester, which sends researchers on whale watching expeditions. They study, count, and follow the whale populations in the region, and often engage tourists in conservation and research efforts.

Whale watch expeditions don't appear to be damaging the local whale population; indeed, in the early 1990s, researchers began noting record numbers of humpback whales, including newborn calves. Other whale breeds have also thrived, notably minke whales, which are small and swift, and finback whales, which are second in size only to blue whales. And members of one of the rarest breeds, the right whale—once popular with whalers because of its buoyancy after being killed—have been showing up more frequently as well.

The Cape Ann whale watch season stretches from May through late October. Three-hour expeditions cost around $21 for adults and $12 for kids, with discounts for senior citizens and large groups. Those prone to motion sickness should be forewarned, though; these are relatively small boats sailing into the open sea, and there can be a lot of rocking and rolling. One unlucky lady was overheard describing her expedition as a "pail watch," because she'd spent most of the voyage with her head in a bucket.

Cape Ann, which consists of the communities of Gloucester, Rockport, Manchester-by-the-Sea, and Essex (which calls itself America's Antique Capital) is one of the gems of New England. Far less crowded than Cape Cod, its rocky shores and quiet villages remain one of the region's best-kept secrets. Though no festivals directly celebrate the whale watching fleet, several events do highlight the Cape's maritime history. Among these are the annual Schooner Festival, held in early September (featuring the race for the Esperanto Cup), and the Waterfront Festival, held the third week in August; both take place in Gloucester.

Likewise, several local attractions highlight Cape Ann's seafaring heritage. Visit the Essex Shipbuilding Museum for a glimpse of the craft of crafts; and tour the collections of the Cape Ann Historical Association, which include a local art and history museum as well as several restored vessels.

## For Further Information

### General Information

**Cape Ann Chamber of Commerce**
33 Commercial St.
Gloucester, MA 01930
(508) 283-1601

**Atlantic Cetacean Research Center**
P.O. Box 1413
Gloucester, MA 01930
(508) 283-3296

### Attractions and Events

**Cape Ann Historical Association**
27 Pleasant St.
Gloucester, MA 01930
(508) 283-0455

**Capt. Bill's Whale Watch**
9 Traverse St.
Gloucester, MA 01930
(508) 283-6995 or (800) 33-WHALE
[Location: 33 Harbor Loop]

**Essex Shipbuilding Museum**
28 Main St.
Essex, MA 01929
(508) 768-7541

**Schooner Festival and Waterfront Festival**
Contact the Cape Ann Chamber of Commerce

**Yankee Whale Watch**
75 Essex Ave.
Route 133 at Gloucester Harbor
Gloucester, MA 01931
(508) 283-0313 or (800) WHALING

CHAPTER 3

# HOMEGROWN

 merica is the world's fruit bowl and salad bar, its granary and nursery, and many a community's claim to fame grows from the soil of its local fields or gardens. **GILROY, CALIFORNIA,** is perhaps America's most famous world capital. The Garlic Capital of the World honors its bounty with everything from a Garlic Festival to a number of year-round garlic markets, including the aptly named Garlic World. Gilroy is even planning a garlic theme park, presumably with plenty of minty mouthwash on sale at the concession stands.

But Gilroy is just one of many places that call themselves world or state capitals for their favorite fruits and veggies, flowers and plants. They celebrate out of local pride, but also for real gain: Agricultural festivals can bring thousands of tourists and their dollars to town, and the attendant fame of a capital claim can help build business for mail-order companies and establishments that serve up the local specialties.

California has a particularly rich field of contenders—from A to Z (or T, anyway). Name a plant and there's a California crop capital to honor it. Castroville is the Artichoke Center of the World (its giant artichoke was recently featured in a national phone company ad), Stockton is the Asparagus Capital of the World, Sacramento is the Almond Capital of the World (the world's largest almond processing plant is there), and Fallbrook is the Avocado Capital of the World.

The brussels sprout capital is in Santa Cruz (which is also a surfing capital; go figure), while George Bush's least favorite vegetable is celebrated in Greenfield, the Broccoli Capital of the World.

Sweet treats abound in California as well. Linden, California, calls itself the Cherry Capital of the World—though it's pitted against the better known Traverse City, Michigan, for that title. Likewise, Watsonville isn't alone in its claim as the Strawberry Capital of the World. Contenders coast to coast vie for that slogan. McCloud, California, is the Blackberry Capital of the World, and Half Moon Bay is the Pumpkin Capital of the West. And Lodi is the Tokay Grape Capital of the World (it's also known as America's Sherryland, so we know what happens to those grapes).

Salad eaters head for John Steinbeck country. The author's hometown of Salinas, California, is the Lettuce Capital of the World, and driving through the area you can view acres of lettuce fields as far as the eye can see. And to add to your salad, hop over to Holtville, the Carrot Capital of America, or to Lindsey, the Olive Capital of the World.

Castroville, California, welcomes you to the Artichoke Center of the World. *Laura Bergheim*

California raisins have several capitals clamoring for their wrinkled attention; both Selma and Fresno call themselves the Raisin Capital of the World, while Dinuba calls itself Raisinland, U.S.A.

You don't have to leave California to let your tastebuds travel the world. Enjoy the down-under flavors of Gridley, the Kiwi Fruit Capital of the World; or visit **INDIO,** the Date Capital of the World, where the annual Arabian Nights' themed Date Festival is a desert delight.

California is as famous for its flowers as for its edibles. Sacramento, in addition to its almond fame, is also known as the Camellia Capital of the World; Smith River is the Lily Growing Capital of the World; and Wasco is the Rose Growing Capital of the World. Encinitas Leucadia goes for the more generic title of Flower Capital of the World, but where would it be without Lompoc, the Flower Seed Capital of the World?

California may revel in its homegrown heritage, but all across the country, towns celebrate their crops and flowers, though sometimes it seems there aren't enough fruits and vegetables to go around. Many crops have multiple capitals. Popeye's favorite, spinach, has been caught in a battle between two towns, Alma, Arkansas, and Crystal City, Texas, both of which have statues to the stalwart cartoon sailor and call themselves Spinach Capital of the World. Three towns work for peanuts: Dothan, Alabama; Sylvester, Georgia; and Blakely, Georgia, all call themselves peanut capitals.

And don't even think of spitting out the phrase "Watermelon Capital of the World" without knowing whereof you speak, because there are several of these, from President Clinton's hometown of Hope, Arkansas, to Luling, Texas (home of the famous Luling Watermelon Thump festival), as well as numerous other melon capitals (Chapter 10 has more on these competitive titleholders).

There's even competition for plants you wouldn't expect to have a champion in the world. Take the ramp, for instance. It's a pungent but surprisingly sweet wild leek, and several towns claim it as their own. Cosby, Tennessee, calls itself the Ramp Capital of the World and hosts the Cosby Ramp Festival, while Flanagan Hill, West Virginia, vies for the same honor, with its own festival and capital claim (the towns of Waynesville, North Carolina, and Franklin, North Carolina, also hold ramp festivals).

Flower power has turned plenty of towns into petal pushers. **PEKIN, ILLINOIS**—Marigold Capital of the World—honors the flower as well as the man who put the town on the map. The late Senate Minority Leader Everett M. Dirksen (R-IL) was a Pekin native who fought unsuccessfully to have the marigold named the nation's official flower. Pekin still honors its flower and its favorite son with the Marigold Festival held in August.

Flower capitals grow all across the country, and all have festivals or garden shows to share their good fortune. Among these are Wheatridge, Colorado, just outside Denver, which has the title of Carnation Capital of the World; Dixon, Illinois, the Petunia Capital of the World; Ft. Myers, Florida, the Gladiola Capital of the World; Mackinac Island, Michigan, the Lilac Capital of the World; and Rhinebeck, New York, the Violet Capital of the World.

Anchorage, Alaska, gets its fame, in part, for its arrangements. Garden writers have dubbed the city the Hanging Basket Capital of the World because of the more than 100,000 flower-filled baskets that grace the city. To see the basket capital in all its glory, visit 2nd, 3rd, and 4th Streets in downtown, which in warm months are aglow with 320 trailing sapphire lobelia and gold triploid marigold baskets. The color scheme is no accident: Blue and gold are the colors of the Municipality of Anchorage and the State of Alaska.

Even that flowery weed so disdained by gardeners has a champion in the town of **VINELAND, NEW JERSEY,** the Dandelion Capital of the World, which hosts an annual festival serving dandelion delicacies. And if you want your sinuses cleared, visit Eau Claire, Wisconsin, the Horseradish Capital of the World, home of Silver Spring Gardens, the world's largest horseradish grower and packager.

Berries are hand-picked by numerous towns as their favorite fruits. Blueberries have several title contenders, ranging from **SOUTH HAVEN, MICHIGAN,** to Hammonton, New Jersey. The towns of Ponchatoula, Louisiana, and Watsonville, California, are in a jam over which is the real Strawberry Capital of the World, while Plant City, Florida, takes the more distinct title of Winter Strawberry Capital of the World; and Anita Bryant's favorite squeeze is capitalized in towns ranging from Eusha, Florida, the Orange Capital of the World, to Winter Haven, Florida, the Citrus Capital of the World.

As for apples: Wenatchee, Washington, and Winchester, Virginia, both have impressive orchard outputs and harvest festivals to support their self-proclaimed Apple Capital of the World status, but since they're on opposite sides of the country, little conflict has arisen from their dual claims.

The legume competition starts in **THE PALOUSE** region that straddles Washington and Idaho. Known as the Dry Pea and Lentil Capital of the Nation, it includes Pullman, Washington, which hosts the National Lentil Festival to highlight the benefits of this high-protein dish. Beans of a different breed are honored in two towns: Dove Creek, Colorado, and Leoti, Kansas, both of which call themselves the Pinto Bean Capital of the World. And even the little-known vetch—described in Webster's as an "herbaceous twining leguminous plant"—has wrapped itself around the town of Elgin, Nebraska, the Vetch Capital of the Nation. They'd go for Vetch Capital of the World but it's a title that's already taken by Cooper, Texas.

When it comes to vegetables (or is it a fruit?) the tomato is championed in **BRADLEY COUNTY, ARKANSAS,** the Pink Tomato Capital of the World, and home of the Pink Tomato Festival, one of the state's largest agricultural fairs, while Dania, Florida, goes for the more generic title of Tomato Capital of the World. Also in Florida, Sanford used to be known as Celery City, though the celery fields have long since disappeared; now its claim to fame is as the end of the line for the Amtrak AutoTrain that takes families and their vehicles down the East Coast to Disney World. Hence, Kalamazoo, Michigan, now has the Celery City title all to itself—though you never know where another contender might crop up.

And lest we forget the amber fields of grain, there's another rich harvest of communities that honor their farmland traditions. **WELLINGTON, KANSAS,** the Wheat Capital of the World, hosts an annual wheat fest where even the littlest of

## DID YOU KNOW...

**Wild About Native Flowers**
Though local blooms have given many a town capital claims, there's a place in Austin, Texas, devoted to planting the seeds of preservation for the native wildflowers of the entire nation. The National Wildflower Research Center is a nonprofit organization "committed to the preservation and reestablishment of native North American wildflowers, grasses, trees, shrubs, and vines in planned landscapes."

local lovelies can vie for the crown of Little Miss Wheat Queen.

Corn and its processing show up in several capital claims: Hoopeston, Illinois' water tower still proclaims the town's title of Sweet Corn Capital of the World, but the Stokely U.S.A. cannery closed in 1993, ending Hoopeston's 114-year tradition as one of the country's largest sweet corn canners. But Hoopeston still hosts its annual Sweet Corn Festival, proving it still has that can-do attitude. The colonel of corn, King Niblet himself, stands guard as a huge statue overlooking his hometown of Le Sueur, Minnesota, the Green Giant Capital of the World (there's even a museum in town with Green Giant artifacts).

North Loup, Nebraska, butters up its visitors with its title of the Popcorn Capital of Nebraska, though Marion, Ohio, is a contender, with its Popcorn Museum and September Popcorn Festival—complete with a "tri-ear-thalon" race.

Another claque of competitors have vied over the years for the name of Broom Corn Capital of the World, among them McPherson, Kansas; Walsh City, Connecticut; Elk City, Oklahoma; and Arcola, Illinois. Arcola may sweep the title, if for no other reason than that it also boasts (as far as we know) the world's only broom and brush museum: The Louis P. Klein Broom & Brush Museum, housed at the town's railroad depot. And the Arcola Broom Corn Festival in mid-September is a crowd-pleasing event that features silly entertainment such as a precision drill team, the Lawn Rangers, which performs routines while marching with lawn mowers and brooms.

The "fabric of our lives" (and the softest of crops) is honored in Greenwood, Mississippi, Cotton Capital of the World, where visitors can tour the U.S. Cotton Row, now listed on the National Register of Historic Places. It still serves as a spot cotton market (one of only nine in the country), operating 24 of its original 97 cotton companies. Greenwood is also home to the Cottonlandia Museum, a regional history museum that relates the area's culture and development, including the legacy of the cotton industry.

With the plethora of vegetables and fruits produced in this country, the farms and villages that grow and package them have every reason to parade and party in the name of their local crops. They crown their garlic queens while they may, for tomorrow they rise again to till the fields and plant the seeds for the next harvest.

# ✪ South Haven, Michigan

## BLUEBERRY CAPITAL OF THE WORLD

I f you've read Roald Dahl's classic children's book *Charlie and the Chocolate Factory* or seen the movie based on it, you know the weird fate of a naughty girl who samples some forbidden food-flavored gum: She is transformed into a giant blueberry and then rolled away for juicing. You know what that feels like if you visit South Haven, Michigan, the Blueberry Capital of the World, during the National Blueberry Festival.

Held in mid-August, it's a true-blue gathering of blueberry growers and lovers from all around the country. Though it lasts only two days, you may never want to see another blueberry again—at least until the next morning, when you awaken to the aroma of hot blueberry pancakes at one of the local inns.

When they're not crowning Little Miss Blueberry or marching in the blueberry parade, the people of South Haven are growing blueberries, or at least making things from them.

Blueberry pies are a part of the de rigueur dress code at South Haven's National Blueberry Festival. *Photo by Lynn Kelly, courtesy National Blueberry Festival*

The blueberry farmers in southwestern Michigan compete mainly with those in New Jersey to produce the bulk of the nation's blueberry crop. But most of the berries grown in Michigan won't show up in your produce section; three quarters of the crop are grown for processors who use them in packaged yogurts, frozen pies, muffin mixes, and a variety of other blueberry products. When you bite into a Sara Lee blueberry coffeecake, you're probably savoring those Michigan blues.

New Jersey has its own Blueberry Capital of the World—Hammonton—which celebrates its claim with an all-American Red, White, and Blueberry Festival, held the last weekend in June. The blueberries grown in the Hammonton area are more likely to show up in the produce section, especially in the eastern United States.

Meanwhile, back in Michigan, South Haven's fair is a major midwestern event. But even if you miss the festival, you can still sample the crop at the Blueberry Store, run by the area blueberry cooperative, where you'll find a variety of sweet goodies and gifts, from exotic edibles such as blueberry fettucini and blueberry wine to inedible delights such as blueberry scented soap and potpourri.

If all this makes you feel a little blue, don't worry. Soon that sweet flavor will roll across your tongue and trickle down your throat. Before long, you'll understand why that little girl in the candy factory was so tempted: There's nothing some people won't do for a blueberry thrill.

## FOR FURTHER INFORMATION

### General Information

**South Haven Chamber of Commerce**
300 Broadway
South Haven, MI 49090
(616) 637-5171

### Attractions and Events

**National Blueberry Festival**
P.O. Box 469
South Haven, MI 49090
(616) 434-6791

**The Blueberry Store**
525 Phoenix St.
South Haven, MI 49090
(616) 637-6322

**Red, White and Blueberry Festival**
c/o: Greater Hammonton Chamber of Commerce
10 S. Egg Harbor Rd.
P.O. Box 554
Hammonton, NJ 08037
(609) 561-9080

# ❁ Traverse City, Michigan

CHERRY CAPITAL OF THE WORLD

I f you happen to be traveling through the Great Lakes region this summer, there's no sweeter pit stop to make than Traverse City, Michigan, where a multimillion dollar cherry crop has given the city its reputation as the Cherry Capital of the World.

For anyone who loves cherries, this is truly a mecca, for nearly half of America's cherry crop comes from the area. The major crops grown in this area are more sour than sweet, including bing (those pop-in-your-mouth yummies); Montmorency (pucker-up treats); and Queen Annes (yellow, waxy-looking fruits used to make maraschino cherries; they're dyed that eye-popping maraschino red, not grown that way, although they are now gaining popularity in their own natural state and hue).

The famed National Cherry Festival, one of the Midwest's largest events, takes place in early July, and from the pit-spitting competitions to the crowning of the Cherry Queen, it's truly a cherry jubilee. Some of the competitions are messier than others. The pie eating contest, for instance, pits kids and their mouths (no hands allowed) against each other in a face-first match that leaves parents awestruck at the skin-staining quotient of cherry filling.

Then there's the Very Cherry Luncheon, one of the festival highlights, where anything and everything cherry, from soup to sauce, salads to sausages, is dished out to eager eaters. For those who like to see where their next meal is coming from, tours are available at Amon Orchards to give visitors a taste of the cherry-grower's life. By the end of the festival, even the sourest of cherry aficionados will leave with a hot-pink grin.

The festival dates back to 1926, making it one of the region's oldest ongoing events. And it just keeps getting bigger and bigger: In 1985, attendance topped 200,000, and by 1995, it was at least 500,000.

Cherries are a livelihood for many farmers in this Lake Michigan peninsula area called the Grand Traverse region, which incorporates five counties (Grand Traverse, Leelanau, Antrim, Benzie, and Kalkaska), and Traverse City is the area's cherry center. But throughout the region, orchards and packagers, mail-order companies and mom-and-pop fruit stands spread the rewards out beyond Traverse City.

The summer cherry season is short but sweet, but with such popular nouveau treats as dried cherries being packaged in this area, you can buy a bag of summer and nibble on it all year. Life may not be a bowl of cherries, but in Traverse City, it sure tastes like one.

Downtown Traverse City celebrates its favorite fruit with a parade and other events during the National Cherry Festival. *Courtesy National Cherry Festival*

## For Further Information

Traverse City Convention and Visitor's Bureau
101 W. Grandview Pkwy.
Traverse City, MI 49684
(800) TRAVERS

National Cherry Festival
108 W. Grandview Pkwy.
Traverse City, MI 49684
(616) 947-4230

# ❂ Vineland, New Jersey

DANDELION CAPITAL OF THE WORLD

One man's weed is another man's wine. That's the lesson to be learned from a visit to the community of Vineland, New Jersey, the Dandelion Capital of the World.

It may seem odd for a town to take as its mascot the bane of backyard gardeners—to most of the potting and planting set, a dandelion is as welcome as root rot—but this weed has a real following as both a personal and commercial crop in Vineland. So, in 1977, the town's then-mayor, the late Patrick Fiorelli, decided to make it official: He dubbed Vineland the Dandelion Capital.

Good things have happened since. This community of 54,000, which was not known for much of anything (except for having the state's widest Main Street) suddenly got worldwide publicity for its tongue-in-cheek dande-lion doings. Even *National Geographic* sent in a photographer to

## DID YOU KNOW...

**Egging 'em on**
Vineland may now be the Dandelion Capital, but before the weed came the egg. Established in 1931, the Vineland Egg Auction garnered the city the title of "Egg Capital of the East." That title later scrambled when production costs and competition from the South hatched a decline in local egg farming; in 1973, the Vineland Egg Auction closed for good.

document the town's story. When folks stopped laughing and started listening, they discovered that Vinelanders were on to something. The dandelion is, in fact, as healthy a food as anything you'd spend money on at a farmer's market. It's a surprisingly rich source of protein, fiber, iron, potassium, and Vitamin C. And, as many a gardener will tell you, it's an easy plant to grow.

No doubt, you may have heard of dandelion wine—you can pick up various recipes and sample some yourself at the town's Dandelion Festival in April—but imbibing the fermented flower is just one way to enjoy it. How about dandelion tempura? Some Asian cultures have long nibbled on the flower of the plant, batter-dipped and deep-fried. Or why not munch on a dandelion salad? Local cooks serve up these and other recipes.

Vineland's dandelion crop is worth its weight in gold as well as vitamins. The dandelion farms scattered around the area bring in at least $500,000 annually, and it's a growing market as Americans become more familiar with nontraditional greens. We have the yuppie salad bar culture to thank for the rising profile of this formerly disdained weed.

Every April the town hosts the Dandelion Festival, where folks share their favorite recipes and dishes; and those who have never tasted dandelions but are drawn by the quirky nature of the event often leave as converts to the myriad uses of this versatile plant.

Folks here are known for pulling out the grass and leaving the dandelions to grow undisturbed. It's a nice metaphor for finding balance in life: Good can be found in the most mundane of places, and we shouldn't overlook the hidden assets of even the most common of nuisances.

## FOR FURTHER INFORMATION

Greater Vineland Chamber
of Commerce
City Hall
7th and Wood Sts.
P.O. Box 489
Vineland, NJ 08360
(609) 691-7400 or (800) 309-0019

# ✪ Indio, California

DATE CAPITAL OF THE WORLD

S o you've come to the desert town of Indio, California, in search
of a date, eh? Well, you're in the right place—if your type is
plump, juicy, and grows on a palm tree. Russ Waters, former marketing director of the Indio Chamber of Commerce, quips: "If you
can't get a date in Indio, you're in big trouble," for Indio is the Date
Capital of the World.

The Coachella Valley, where Indio is situated, grows 95 percent
of America's dates. Locals fete their fruit for 10 days in February
during the National Date Festival, an event that began in the 1920s.
In its early days, the festival had a decidedly Arabian theme—

Hollywood set and costume
designers even motored out
to give it some pizazz—and
included events such as the
crowning of Queen Scheherazade and her comely court.
But over the years the festival's Middle Eastern theme
faded away as the event
evolved into a more generic
harvest celebration. In 1938,
it became the county fair. In
1948, the festival's manager,
R.M.C. Fullenwider, uncov-
ered the event's exotic roots
and decided to bring back
the foreign fun.

Royalty at the National Date Festival
contribute beautifully to the Arabian
Nights theme by wearing appropriate
costumes. *Courtesy National Date Festival,
copyright 1996*

Today, the National Date Festival, held at the 130-acre Desert Expo Center, is a blend of county fair and Arabian flare. Festival-goers can enjoy date-related doings such as cooking demonstrations, competitions, and tastings. And Queen Scheherazade and her court once again reign supreme, while camel and ostrich races and entertainments on the Arabian Night & Fantasy Stage make it a date to remember. The festival even has its own Arabian Nights parade.

The valley's primary date crop is Deglet Noor, though other varieties, such as Medjool, also are grown in the area. The date crop came to Indio early in the century, brought first by the federal government, which planted experimental date gardens, and then introduced as a commercial crop by an Eastern European immigrant, Bernard Johnson. Having seen other date-growing areas across the ocean, he recognized the Coachella Valley's fertile potential. Johnson and other local growers founded the Coachella Valley Date Growers Association to import their own offshoots in 1913—and thus the date industry was firmly planted in this sandy soil.

Even if you get the dates wrong for the festival, you can still get a taste of the Indio area crop, as several date gardens in the area allow visitors. One of the best public facilities is the Oasis Date Gardens in Thermal, California, 10 minutes southeast of Indio on Highway 111. Open since 1912, this 230-acre date garden would inspire even a restless nomad to stop and stay awhile. Those curious about the date in history can watch a video documentary, or just enjoy the Unique Palm Arboretum, with its unusual palm varieties. And naturally there's a large and luscious gift shop chockful of dates, dried fruits, and other treats. Another great date place is Shields Date Gardens in Indio, which also has a visitors center, gift shop, and tour areas for viewing the date-growing palms.

Indio is indeed a desert dream come true for those who enjoy this savory, succulent fruit of the palm. But it soon may have a new date with destiny. Russ Waters, until recently at the chamber of commerce, reports that Indio's International Tamale Festival, held in early December, has grown from its small start in 1991 as a local Hispanic holiday event into a major festival. So, Waters informs, "We may soon be calling Indio the Tamale Capital of the World, too!" Hot tamales *and* hot dates? What an oasis.

## FOR FURTHER INFORMATION

### General Information

**Indio Chamber of Commerce**
82-503 Hwy. 111
Indio, CA 92201
[Mail only: P.O. Drawer TTT, Indio, CA 92202]
(619) 347-0676 or (800) 44-INDIO

### Attractions and Events

**Riverside County Fair and National Date Festival**
Riverside County Fair Grounds
46-350 Arabia St.
Indio, CA 92201
(619) 863-8247

**Oasis Date Gardens**
59-111 Hwy. 111
P.O. Box 757
Thermal, CA 92274
(619) 399-5665 or 1(800) 827-8017

**Shields Date Gardens**
80-225 Hwy. 111
Indio, CA 92201
(619) 347-0996

# ✿ The Palouse, Idaho/Washington

DRY PEA AND LENTIL CAPITAL
OF THE NATION

You know legumes are good for you. But somehow you never remember to eat enough (or any) of nature's little protein packs. But if you lived on the Palouse, a region that spans the Idaho–Washington border, it would be hard to forget your legumes. You might even make your living from them. The Palouse is the Dry Pea and Lentil Capital of the Nation.

CYBERSPACE CONTACTS

## Pullman Community Bulletin Board

http://www.pullman.com/

## Welcome to Moscow

http://www.moscow.com/

Planning a visit to dry pea and lentil country? Stop by the home pages for the communities of Pullman, Washington, and Moscow, Idaho, for info on local events, lodging, and attractions. Both offer a taste of the area's culture, weather, and news.

A country of rolling hills named for the Palouse River, which runs through it, the Palouse is about an hour south of Spokane. Here, some 500 million pounds of dry peas and lentils are produced annually. Moscow, Idaho, is home to the U.S.A. Dry Pea and Lentil Industry, which trades internationally. The Palouse also is a major wheat-growing area.

Among the richest sources of protein and fiber found in grown foods, dry peas and lentils are a staple of many national diets. And though our own fatty, fast-food habit has erased legumes from many American menus, enter any natural food store and you'll find bins and bags of beans and their ilk.

Once a year, the people of the Palouse honor their growth industry with the National Lentil Festival. Held in the town of Pullman, Washington (named for George Pullman, inventor of the Pullman Sleeping Car), the festival takes place the weekend before Labor Day, the harvesttime for lentils.

The festival starts out with a lentil pancake breakfast, but that's just an appetizer to the goodies that await on Lentil Lane, a concession area featuring a surprising array of dishes, from lentil lasagna and tacos to lentil brownies and ice cream.

If the name Palouse sounds familiar to your ear, it may be because of a horse: The Appaloosa is the region's nonlegume claim to fame. So if you find yourself lentiled-out, take a break and visit the Appaloosa Museum, devoted to the famous spotted horse—settlers referred to them as "a palouse horse" or "palousey"—of the Nez Perce Indians. The museum is just west of Moscow, Idaho, at the home of the national breed registry, the Appaloosa Horse Club, Inc.

Whether you're into peas or ponies, the Palouse, with its rolling hills and crystal blue skies, is a lovely area worth visiting. And it's good for you, too!

## FOR FURTHER INFORMATION

### General Information

Moscow Chamber of Commerce
411 S. Main St.
Moscow, ID 83843
(208) 882-1800 or (800) 380-1801

Pullman Chamber of Commerce
N. 415 Grand Ave.
Pullman, WA 99160
(509) 334-3565 or (800) 365-6948

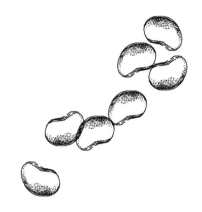

### Attractions and Events

Appaloosa Horse Museum
5070 Hwy. 8
Moscow, ID 83843
(208) 882-5578

National Lentil Festival
Contact the Pullman Chamber of Commerce

# ✿ Gilroy, California

GARLIC CAPITAL OF THE WORLD

No other bulb is so revered or feared as garlic: It can ward off vampires and blind dates, and make or break a sauce. It's also the star attraction in America's most unforgettable world capital: Gilroy, California, the Garlic Capital of the World.

Until the late 1970s, this central California community was not unlike dozens of other agricultural towns whose specialized crops gave them a growing economy. It wasn't until the locals decided to throw a garlic festival in 1979 and then took on the capital claim, that the town landed on the map for Americana buffs. At first, folks laughed at Gilroy—the bad breath capital, some jokers dubbed it. Then came the 1980s and the culinary awakening of the American palate. Garlic became a staple for cooks nationwide, roasted garlic became a hip appetizer in upscale restaurants, and Gilroy finally got some respect.

Today, the Gilroy Garlic Festival, held every July, is one of California's most popular events; it draws 130,000 visitors, who come to see the Garlic Queen crowned, to taste the hundreds of garlic-infused foods along Gourmet Alley (food booth central), and shop for garlic-themed tools and crafts, such as wreaths and garlands (Dracula beware!). But year-round, the town is garlic-scented, -flavored, and -decorated. Virtually every shop sells garlic memorabilia. And a magnificent Wall of Fame garlic mural painted on the south side of the old J.C. Penney building (now home to the Garlic Festival Store & Gallery) captures the community in all its garlic glory.

The stinking rose, as garlic is sometimes called, has indeed changed the economy of Gilroy, turning it from a sleepy agricultural community into a brand-name tourist attraction. Plans are even in the works for a garlic theme park. But though visitors come for the garlic, they also get a taste of something else. The town's historic district is worth visiting even without the flavorful incentive.

Gilroy was founded in 1815 by a Scotsman, John Cameron, who was on the run after jumping a British ship in Monterey Bay. He traveled inland to the Santa Clara Valley; there, using his mother's maiden name, Gilroy, he lived and worked at Rancho Ortega, one of the val-

Gilroy's Garlic Capital mural is a colorful tribute to the "stinking rose" that brought the town glory. *Photo by Caroll Hurd, courtesy Gilroy Visitors Bureau*

ley's largest spreads. After marrying the boss's daughter, he became a Mexican citizen and half-owner of the ranch. During his lifetime, a small town grew up around the ranch, and it, too, took on Cameron's mother's maiden name. Though Gilroy, the man, lived an ultimately unhappy life—his penchant for gambling left him broke and ranchless when he died in 1869—Gilroy, the town, thrived and grew.

In the 1860s, Gilroy Hot Springs, 12 miles northeast of town, became popular among health buffs. The Southern Pacific Railroad built a depot in Gilroy, where

Gilroy's Old City Hall is a local landmark and one of the state's few such architectural gems. *Photo by Caroll Hurd, courtesy Gilroy Visitors Bureau*

regular stagecoach service picked up visitors and delivered them to the hot springs. Gilroy became a major railroad junction—foreshadowing its modern placement at the junction of I-101 and Highway 152 (which links to I-5)—thus putting the community at the center of the main distribution route between San Francisco and Los Angeles.

Gilroy was altered in several ways in the early twentieth century. The first, and most noticeable, changes were in its physical appearance. Gilroy experienced several building booms that transformed it from a sleepy railroad town into a sparkling Main Street community. The first boom took place just after the turn of the century and led to the construction of the town's magnificent Old City Hall, Gilroy's most important historic building. Built in 1905, it's a jewel of a place, so eccentric with its turrets and gables that a definition of its style has been hard to come by. Its builder explained it was done in the "mission style," but experts have called it an example of the obscure, whimsical school of Flemish baroque. Whatever it is, the locals cherish it—and with good reason. Though similar city halls were built in the region at the time, all the others have fallen to the wrecker's ball.

The townspeople were devastated when their treasure was badly damaged by the 1989 Loma Prieta earthquake. A restoration effort, completed in 1994, saved the building. No longer used as the city hall, the "Grand Old Lady," as the building is affectionately known, now houses a restaurant and playhouse complex.

A local philanthropist, Lin Wheeler, funded another building boom during the 1920s, creating a magnificent collection of Art Deco structures such as Wheeler Auditorium, the Strand Theater, and Wheeler Hospital, which still stand as monuments to his architectural generosity. Another historic landmark, the Carnegie Library building, built in 1910, is now home to the Gilroy Historical Museum, which houses exhibits, a library, and archives covering local history and culture.

The second, and when it comes to garlic, most important alteration of Gilroy's landscape was not structural but rather human. An influx of immigrants from southern Italy between 1910 and 1930 swelled Gilroy's population and spurred its garlic farming industry. Italian farmers found the warm, welcoming soil of the Santa Clara Valley similar to that of their Mediterranean homeland and began growing the garlic they had cultivated back home. Gilroy's future was secured.

California farms produce 90 percent of the country's garlic, and the majority comes from this region. But Fresno accounts for the bulk of this production—it has 15,000 acres of farmland devoted to garlic, while Gilroy has only 500 to 700 acres. Still, Gilroy's garlic industry brings in $100 million to the local economy. And Gilroy Foods, Gilroy's largest employer, is the world's largest producer of dehydrated onion and garlic flakes.

Gilroy's largest garlic farm, the Christopher Ranch, is a 120-acre facility that produces 60 million pounds of garlic a year. The company also produces specialty prepared foods such as sauces and garlic braids. Don Christopher, the ranch's owner, has been

**CYBERSPACE CONTACTS**

## Christopher Ranch

http://www.christophergarlic.com/

America's largest garlic farm, the Christopher Ranch, has a savory site on the World Wide Web, featuring garlic facts, recipes, and a ranch history. There's also an online catalog selling goodies such as herb and garlic bouquets and a Garlic Lovers Gift Basket.

instrumental in making Gilroy the world capital it is today; he was one of the festival founders in 1979.

Promotion has been the key to creating a public image of Gilroy as the world's garlic capital. But Gilroy's garlic flavoring does not end with its popular festival; the town is filled with purveyors of pungent products, from the Garlic Grocery to the Garlic Shoppe and Garlic City Mercantile.

Perhaps Gilroy's most famous store is Garlic World, a huge free-standing building redolent with the ripe root. Owned by two leading growing families, the Christophers and the Tognettis, Garlic World sells everything from garlic wreaths and roasters to garlic presses and prepared pastas; it also does a blockbuster mail-order catalog business. Another unique shop is the Garlic Festival Store & Gallery, where visitors can buy garlic festival goodies as well as the wares of local artisans, who show and sell their useable art, such as pottery and woodworking, in the gallery. As noted, the side of the building, which was once a department store, is painted with the now-famous Garlic Capital mural.

Garlic may be Gilroy's ticket to fame, but it's not the only growth industry in town; indeed, one of the world's largest breeders of hybrid flower seeds, Goldsmith Seeds, is just west of downtown Gilroy. Visitors are invited to take self-guided tours of the facility, or just stroll the elaborately landscaped, flower-filled grounds. Gilroy is also moving to become a force in computer technologies. But no matter what other business comes to town, there's no mistaking that special smell of success that has brought it fame, fortune, and a fun family festival: Garlic is Gilroy's glory.

## For Further Information

### General Information

**Gilroy Chamber of Commerce**
7471 Monterey Hwy.
Gilroy, CA 95020
(408) 842-6437

**Gilroy Visitors' Bureau**
7780 Monterey Hwy.
Gilroy, CA 95020
(408) 842-6436

### Attractions and Events

**Garlic City Mercantile**
55 W. Sixth St.
Gilroy, CA 95020
(408) 842-6501

**Garlic Festival Store & Gallery**
7526 Monterey Hwy.
Gilroy, CA 95020
(408) 842-7081

Garlic Grocery
8300 Arroyo Cir., Suite 3330
Gilroy, CA 95020
(408) 842-3330

Garlic Shoppe
4310 Monterey Hwy.
Gilroy, CA 95020
(408) 848-3646

Garlic World
4800 Monterey Hwy.
Gilroy, CA 95020
(408) 847-2251

Gilroy Garlic Festival
Association
P.O. Box 2311
Gilroy, CA 95021
(408) 842-1625

Gilroy Historical Museum
195 Fifth St.
Gilroy, CA 95020
(408) 848-0470

Goldsmith Seeds
2280 Hecker Pass Hwy.
P.O. Box 1349
Gilroy, CA 95020
(408) 847-7333

## ❂ Pekin, Illinois

MARIGOLD CAPITAL OF THE WORLD

Former Senate Minority Leader Everett McKinley Dirksen (R-IL) was a powerful, conservative orator who left his stamp on the institution during his years in office (the 1950s and 1960s). There's even a Senate office building named in his honor. But Dirksen was more than a consummate politician: He had a not-so-secret passion for a particular flower, the marigold. He so admired this sunny blossom that he waged a long but unsuccessful campaign to have it named the official national flower.

Though Dirksen died in 1969, "The Honorable Mr. Marigold," as some affectionately dubbed him, has had a lasting influence on his hometown of Pekin, Illinois. It became the Marigold Capital of the World as a tribute to Dirksen's floral efforts, displayed most brilliantly during the Annual Marigold Festival, held the weekend after Labor Day. The festival, started in 1972 to honor Dirksen, was con-

Pekin's Mineral Springs Park Lagoon and its historic pavilion are the site of many a Marigold Festival event. *Courtesy Pekin Area Chamber of Commerce*

ceived to promote two causes close to Dirksen's heart: naming the marigold as national flower, and the reinstatement of school prayer.

The national flower campaign died on the vine after President Ford showed support for the rose in 1976, and school prayer faded as a festival focus as the fair evolved into a civic pride celebration and fund-raiser for local charities. But the marigold theme remains strong in this city where, come summertime, area gardens grow pleasantly plump with these beauties. During the Marigold Festival, a Garden Contest involves judging throughout the city, and many a festival-goer tags along to catch a glimpse of the finest flowers in Pekin.

Pekin is a city of parks as well as flowers (its district has the fourth largest park system in the state), and many of the festival events take place in Pekin's lovely Mineral Springs Park, with its magnificent turn-of-the-century pavilion overlooking the lagoon. Festival events also are held, naturally, in Everett McKinley Dirksen Park, just outside of town.

Many of the events are typical of a hometown festival, from the naming of a marigold queen and princesses to a variety of sports and games, including a Race for Congress, volleyball competitions, the Marigold Golf Tournament, and the Marigold Road Rally. And just about everyone joins the carnival and parade.

There's more to marigolds and to their festival than meets the eye. The marigold seemingly has as many varieties as the sun has rays, and a tour of Pekin's gardens and nurseries reveals plot after plot of marigold mutations, from the big, bold African marigolds (sometimes called American marigolds, they can grow up to three feet high) to the delicate-colored "spice series" of the French marigolds. Deep gold or pale yellow, pumpkin-colored or sunshine-hued, marigolds bloom in a spectrum that delights the eye.

And the Marigold Festival is about more than flowers and local pride: It continues to honor the memory of Everett Dirksen. A speech competition during the festival commemorates his famed oratorical skills; and one event, which helps kick off the festival, is "Time Out for Marigolds," a one-man reenactment of Dirksen's life and legacy performed at his namesake research center.

The Everett McKinley Dirksen Congressional Leadership Research Center, part of the Pekin Public Library, is open year-round, so even those who miss the festival can learn about the minority leader and his efforts to promote the marigold. The research center features an exhibit area on Dirksen's life and legacy, as well as a facility for scholars to study the congressional power structure.

Marigolds are meaningful to the people of Pekin for reasons that are more than soil deep: Every summer when the marigolds bloom, they reflect not only the community's gardening acumen, but also the city's remembrance of a hometown hero who helped shape U.S. policy—even if he never did get the marigold named national flower.

## FOR FURTHER INFORMATION

Pekin Chamber of Commerce/
Marigold Festival Committee
P.O. Box 636
Pekin, IL 61555
(309) 346-2106

Everett McKinley Dirksen Congressional
Leadership Research Center
Pekin Public Library
301 S. 4th St.
Pekin, IL 61554
(309) 347-7113

# ✿ Kennett Square, Pennsylvania

〜〜〜〜〜〜〜〜〜〜〜〜〜〜〜〜〜〜〜〜〜〜

WORLD'S MUSHROOM CAPITAL

Fungi fans rejoice! The town of Kennett Square, Pennsylvania, is a sure bet for 'shroom lovers of all makes and models. If you seek the morel equivalent of edible ecstasy, this, the World's Mushroom Capital, is your kind of town.

Kennett Square lives, breathes, and (of course) eats mushrooms. It's hard to find another town with a deeper devotion to its local cap crop (though Muscoda, Wisconsin, is known as the Morel Mushroom Capital). Kennett Square and the surrounding Chester County farms form the state's single largest mushroom growing area, and Pennsylvania accounts for nearly half of the nation's mushroom supply.

With Americans discovering exotic mushrooms, from Portabello to shiitake, and learning new ways to prepare them, from grilled to batter-dipped, it's a crop and industry that's, well, mushrooming.

So Kennett Square has a lot to celebrate come National Mushroom Month (September); and in mid-September, it pulls out all the stems for the Mushroom Festival, which draws 'shroomers from all over.

Festival-goers may run into local mushroom mascot Freddy Fungus, who might, were he at a bake sale, be mistaken for a lean popover or an elongated cupcake. It's just hard to capture that fungal flair when enlarged to adult-sized costume standards. But he's a fun guy nonetheless.

Of course, visitors can sample mushroom dishes from the standard (sautéed mushroom caps) to the sublime (delicate soups and ragouts). And most folks head home with enough mushrooms for a month of Sundays.

This capital community offers more, however, than a chance to buy mushrooms year-round. It also educates the public. Phillips Place, run by the Phillips Mushroom Farm (one of the state's biggest producers, it's known for its exotic varieties), is a sort of mushroom mini-mall. And it's home to the Phillips

Mushroom Museum, where visitors learn about the history, culture, and cultivation of mushrooms.

Where else would you be likely to find a mushroom diorama? Or discover that ancient Egyptians thought mushrooms could ensure immortality, and that Romans and Greeks reserved mushrooms as a delicacy for their royalty? It's a small museum, but you'll leave knowing more than you ever thought possible about the mushroom and its heritage.

Phillips Mushroom Place and the Mushroom Festival are just the beginning. If you've really got the 'shroom bug, farms and inns throughout the region host mushroom weekends, seminars, and hunts throughout the year. Call the Brandywine Valley Tourist Information Center at (800) 228-9933 for a list of seasonal mushroom events.

Perhaps we have the kind people of Kennett Square to thank for the growing popularity of unusual mushroom varieties, since it's their crops that are providing the raw materials to cooks now learning there's much ado about mushrooms. Still, as with all food cycles, it was inevitable that this savory, unusual vegetable would be reborn as a delicious diversion.

## FOR FURTHER INFORMATION

### General Information

**Chester County Tourist Bureau**
601 Westtown Rd., Suite 170
West Chester, PA 19382
(610) 344-6365 or (800) 228-9933

### Attractions and Events

**Mushroom Festival**
c/o: Chester County Tourist Bureau

**Phillips Mushroom Place/Mushroom Museum**
U.S. Route 1
Kennett Square, PA 19348
(610) 388-6082

# ❁ Bradley County, Arkansas

〜〜〜〜〜〜〜〜〜〜〜〜〜〜〜〜〜〜〜〜〜〜〜

PINK TOMATO CAPITAL OF THE WORLD

T hink pink and you probably imagine panthers or roses, valen-
tines or baby clothes. Tomatoes are no doubt pretty far down on
the list of pink things that come to mind. But not in Bradley County,
Arkansas, the Pink Tomato Capital of the World!

This southern Arkansas county grows the tasty Bradley County
Pink, and no matter whether you say to-mah-to and I say to-may-to,
it's a crop that local farmers are proud to say is their own. So proud,
in fact, that in mid-June, the county seat of Warren hosts one of the
state's oldest festivals, the Bradley Pink Tomato Festival.

Miss Pink Tomato gets crowned at a pageant that begins the
week-long series of events. But beauty alone can't make her a contender in the tomato-eating contest: There's some stiff competition
from serious tomato-stuffers, so the chow-down is always a crowd-
pleasing spectacle.

Even noncontestants can dine on heaping helpings at the popular All Tomato Luncheon, held at a local church; and those who prefer fried green tomatoes may be surprised to hear that these are
offered at the festival as well.

A crown alone can't assure victory in the tomato-eating contest. *Courtesy Bradley County
Chamber of Commerce*

Bradley County's pink tomatoes can draw high bidders at the annual auction. *Courtesy Bradley County Chamber of Commerce*

The festival got going in 1956, originally as a way to honor local tomato farmers. What began as an event to bestow the Farm Family of the Year Award has grown so large that it often makes the American Bus Association's Top 100 Events in North America, a prestigious annual listing of the best fests around the United States and Canada.

Beyond the festival, there's the Tomato Auction. It starts in early June and continues every day at the Warren Tomato Market, auctioning locally grown tomatoes until around mid-July when the tomatoes have all been sold. The action can get pretty lively, as buyers from all over bid for entire crops from the local farmers. And given the prized flavor of the Bradley Pinks (considered by some to be the masterpiece of 'maters), the bidding can reach surprisingly dramatic heights.

Bradley County's tomato crop, which accounts for half of the state's annual $7.5 million tomato yield, is grown on more than 150 tomato farms, small and large, scattered throughout the county. These farms, many still family-operated, are the heart and soul of Bradley County; they define the agricultural heritage of the region, just as the area's famous tall pines define its treeline.

## FOR FURTHER INFORMATION

Bradley County Chamber of Commerce
104 N. Myrtle
Warren, AR 71671
(501) 226-5225

# ⚙ Morton, Illinois

PUMPKIN CAPITAL OF THE WORLD

If Linus were serious about hunting down the Great Pumpkin Pie this Halloween, he'd skip his local bakery and head straight for Morton, Illinois. They don't call this community of 15,000 the Pumpkin Capital of the World without cause. If you've eaten a pumpkin pie made with canned filling anywhere in the United States this year, that sweet and tangy filling was probably processed in Morton. Eight miles east of Peoria, Morton is home to the Nestlé/Libby's Pumpkin Packing Plant, which processes more than 80 percent of the world's canned pumpkin. Though there are other pumpkin capitals—Circleville, Ohio, also calls itself the Pumpkin Capital of the World, and Half Moon Bay, California, calls itself the Pumpkin Capital of the West—Morton is definitely the *processed* pumpkin capital.

The pumpkins come from more than 50 farms within a 60-mile radius of Morton. They arrive by the truckload to the plant, where— especially during the highest consumption seasons of fall and

Even the kids get into the pumpkin spirit at Morton's bright orange festival. *Courtesy Morton Chamber of Commerce*

winter—the plant is busy, busy, busy, canning the filling for the 88 million pumpkin pies consumed on Thanksgiving Day alone!

But Morton's backyard gardeners aren't in it just for front stoop decor: The Morton Pumpkin Festival, held the second week of September, draws pumpkin lovers from near and far, including the farmers who supply the plant and the locals who grow the gourd for the pleasure of it.

Morton's annual Pumpkin Festival draws more than 100,000 visitors who come to eat, browse, and decorate their pumpkins and themselves. Collectors snatch up the annual Pumpkin Festival Pin, and you'll see a plethora of past and present pins fastened to lapels and baseball caps. You'll also see kids dressed up as little pumpkins, stem and all. And then there's the Pumpkin Princess Pageant, where the wide and winsome smiles rival those on the festival jack-o'-lanterns.

The food is the star, though. There's plenty of pumpkin pie, but every other pumpkinable edible is also available, from the all-you-can-eat pumpkin pancake breakfast held at a local grade school to creamy pumpkin ice cream, thick pumpkin chili, and tasty pumpkin fudge served at the festival grounds.

If you're curious about that huge factory, you can visit it during the fair. Nestlé also supplies food for the event, including the pumpkin filling and evaporated milk for pies (some 2,400 are consumed during the bash), and the coffee with which to wash them down. The company also sponsors several festival events.

The Midwest's other big pumpkin festival, the Circleville, Ohio, Pumpkin Show (a.k.a. the Greatest Free Show on Earth), takes place the third Wednesday of October, and it's an event you may have seen on the news, highlighted by those beanbag chair–sized pumpkins being weighed in by beaming farmers. Pumpkin-lovers in the know hit both festivals, since there's a month in between to recover from pumpkin pie overdose.

Morton's pumpkin festival is a darn sight more entertaining than what used to pass as the local fun fest: The Pumpkin Festival was created after years of less-than-inspiring civic events, such as the 1948 affair put together by the Morton Business Men's Association, with a theme of Morton— City of Beautiful Homes. Not much of a crowd-pleaser, that one. But then the pumpkin packing plant moved to Morton in 1960, and in 1967 the seed was planted for what would become the Pumpkin Festival.

Sure, when you think of pumpkins you think of Halloween decorations and Thanksgiving pies, but here in Morton, Illinois, the pumpkin has staked out a patch for all seasons.

## FOR FURTHER INFORMATION

### General Information

**Morton Chamber of Commerce**
416 W. Jefferson St.
Morton, IL 61550
(309) 263-2491

### Attractions and Events

**Morton Pumpkin Festival**
Contact the Chamber of Commerce

**Circleville (Ohio) Pumpkin Show**
216 N. Court St.
Circleville, OH 43113
(614) 474-7000

# ✪ Wellington, Kansas

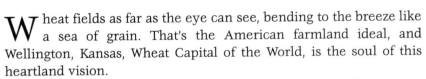

WHEAT CAPITAL OF THE WORLD

W heat fields as far as the eye can see, bending to the breeze like a sea of grain. That's the American farmland ideal, and Wellington, Kansas, Wheat Capital of the World, is the soul of this heartland vision.

Just 25 miles south of Wichita on I-35, Wellington's claim stems from being the seat of Sumner County, which tops the nation in hard red winter wheat production. It's a crop that owes its heritage to

Amish-Mennonite immigrants who came to the area more than a century ago from the Ukraine; each immigrant is said to have brought one hand-picked bushel of his or her homeland's finest Turkey red hard winter wheat. To this day, Sumner County farmers continue to reap what those early settlers sowed.

Though still leading the country in crop size, production of the hard red winter wheat peaked in 1952, when the county's 425,000 acres yielded a record 10.5 million bushels.

Wellington celebrates its grain of fame at the annual Kansas Wheat Festival. Held the second week of July, the event dates back to the 1900 Sumner County Jubilee and Wheat Carnival, which celebrated a then-record 7-million-bushel crop.

As you might guess, the Wheat Festival is part agrarian exposition, part local heritage celebration. The first big event is the Miss Wheat Capital Pageant, held as a prelude to the Miss Kansas Pageant; it takes place on the first night of the festival, and the queen then reigns over the remainder of the events.

Even those knee-high to a wheat stalk get their hopes up at the Baby Contest and Little Miss Wheat Queen Contest. And then there's the big bake-off (no flourless cakes, puhlease!). Tractor pulls for kids and grown-ups are also highlights, as are the horseshoe tournament, car shows, pancake feed, and numerous other events. And at the heart of it, the Festival Parade gives everyone a chance to cheer the family farmers.

Just wandering around the Kansas Wheat Festival makes you feel like you belong: the folks are friendly, the air is dense with the scent of baking. It's the kind of event that Norman Rockwell lived to portray.

Though there's no wheat museum in Wellington, the Chisolm Trail Museum, a three-floor local history collection, exhibits artifacts from the pioneer days, including items from the lives of those early wheat-planting immigrants. The museum also has displays on the 1900 wheat carnival, including the first Jubilee Queen's crown and fan.

For anyone who has ever salivated at the aroma of home-baked bread, Wellington is a place to stop and savor the joy America's wheat farmers have given us all.

## FOR FURTHER INFORMATION

**Wellington Area Chamber of Commerce**
207 S. Washington
Wellington, KS 67152
(316) 326-7466

CHAPTER 4

# GOOD EATS

ome cooking: It's as American as apple pie, meat loaf, and tuna casserole. The cuisine of our country is nothing if not diverse, from the down-home delights of Southern fare to the upper-crust edibles of Manhattan's culinary intelligentsia. The food we cook, serve, and eat says as much about who we are (or think we are) and where we come from (or pretend to come from) as the clothes we wear or the cars we drive. Almost like a genetic marker, the dishes that delight our native tongues stay with us for life as comfort foods and celebratory dishes, to linger on our palates as oral accompaniment to our sorrows and joys.

Food is so personal because it is so regional. Entire books have been devoted to the delightful differences in American cuisine from town to town and region to region, making volumes such as Jane and Michael Stern's delicious *Roadfood* guides to live by for exit ramp epicures. And just as towns and cities identify themselves with a particular crop, industry, or activity, many also consider a particular dish their own. Hence, you'll find world capitals all over the country devoted to the simple pleasures of good local cooking.

A modern-day Ben Franklin finds Philly's famous cheesesteak a liberating lunch treat. *Courtesy Philadelphia Convention & Visitors Bureau*

Towns that really cook with capital status do so for a number of reasons. Like other sloganeering communities, they're hoping to promote the best of their local culture and character — and in the process, bring in some tourist dollars. For some communities, such as **MATTOON, ILLINOIS** (the Bagel Capital of the World), and **BATTLE CREEK, MICHIGAN** (the Cereal Capital of the World), there's a hometown pride in an industrial heritage at work. These are company towns where food processors (Lender's Bagels in Mattoon and Kellogg's and other cereal companies in Battle Creek) have contributed mightily to the fabric and economic life of the community. Some towns and cities are known for a particular food because of local ethnic groups (the sausage capitals of the Midwest are perfect examples) or regional or local cooking traditions (barbecue capitals can be found all across the country). In the end, it doesn't matter much why a cooking capital claims its fame as long as you get there before the last crumb is gone.

Some places are so famous for their food that the community has been blended with that of a favorite local dish — take Boston baked beans, hence Boston's nickname of Beantown, or Philly

Cheesesteak. Philadelphia is indeed the Cheesesteak Capital of the World (though the city points out that this is an unofficial claim). If you stroll the streets of the City of Brotherly Love, the aroma of sizzling, thin-sliced beef, grilled onions, and melting cheese wafting out onto the sidewalks from dozens of shops and restaurants is enough to make you forget your business meeting or museum hopping and leave you munching happily away all afternoon.

Philadelphia is also the unofficial Pretzel Capital of the World, namely because tens of thousands of soft pretzels are baked and sold in the city every day. Pretzel purveyors on street corners and in storefronts sell these chewy, yeasty treats as fast as they can twist them. Philadelphia even has a Pretzel Museum (at 312 Market St.), operated by the PretzCo Soft Pretzel Bakery, where you can learn the history of pretzels and do the twist yourself.

Chicago, naturally, is the Deep Dish Pizza Capital of the World, and Boston is, as noted, the Baked Bean Capital of the World. But smaller cities can get just as much — and often more — mileage from a capital claim.

Take **MATTOON, ILLINOIS:** It's the Bagel Capital of the World — this despite the fact that when most folks think of these holey breads, New York City comes to mind as the place where "a bagel with a schmeer" is heard as often as "Hey, buddy, that's MY cab!" But Mattoon is home to the huge Lender's bagel factory; the company, which effectively introduced bagels to the heartland of America, produces more than 2 million bagels a year at its Mattoon bakery.

Frazzled parents soon learn that frozen bagels make great teething rings; and if you're traveling with little ones who can't eat solid foods yet, they'll go goo-goo over Fremont, Michigan, home of Gerber Products, which calls itself the Baby Food Capital of the World.

If you're still in the mood for breakfast, you might want to set your alarm early enough to pay a call on **BATTLE CREEK, MICHIGAN,** the Cereal Capital of the World. This is where cold cereal as we know it was born, developed first as a health food for the Battle Creek Sanitarium and then packaged by numerous companies. The city is still home to Kellogg's, the world's largest cereal producer; Purina-Ralston and Post also have their roots in Battle Creek. Every June, the town hosts the World's Largest Breakfast Table, where everyone is welcome to pull up a chair and grab a bowl.

For some folks, it ain't breakfast without grits, and if you're one of those people, head south to St. George, South Carolina, the Grits

Capital of the World. St. George hosts the hilariously weird World Grits Festival the third week in April, where the big event is the Rollin' in the Grits competition. Prizes are awarded to contestants who emerge from a vat of grits with the most grits still stuck to them (they weigh contestants before and after to figure out the sticky details).

Then again, pancakes are a pretty good way to start the day, too. To find flapjack heaven, click your heels twice and wish yourself to Liberal, Kansas, Pancake Capital of the World, which holds the International Pancake Day festivities at the end of February. The big event is the International Pancake Race, an annual competition that has been going on for more than 45 years, pitting the women of Liberal against the women of Olney, Bucks, England. Dressed in traditional outfits and aprons, the women must run a serpentine 415-yard course while carrying a skillet with a pancake in it.

Liberal is also home to the Wizard of Oz House, a tourist attraction designed to look like Dorothy's farmhouse, which delights munchkins of all ages. Villa Grove, Illinois, a tiny town just off Old Route 66, is another pancake capital, though it's also known for its maple syrup.

If you're in the mood for a cup of chili, **SPRINGFIELD, ILLINOIS,** just down Route 66 from Villa Grove, may be the place for you. Make that chilli, though, for this capital of the world spells its bean-rich dish with two *l*s, allegedly from the original Native American term. However you spell it, famous Springfield chilli parlors like the Den fill up quickly, so get in early to taste the best of the Midwest chilli bowl. If you prefer your chili with one *l*, head for Belle Chasse, Louisiana, the Chili Capital of the World — but be warned, it's gonna be spicy!

If you're in the mood for soup, the town of Utica, Illinois, has gained its reputation as the Burgoo Soup Capital, thanks to its famous (or perhaps infamous) dish, a vegetable and meat stew that can include just about any critter caught lurking around the kitchen door. But most cooks use beef and chicken, especially for the big Burgoo Soup Festival in October. And Bradford, Tennessee, is the self-proclaimed Doodle Soup Capital of the World — named for its hot chicken soup spiced with cayenne or red peppers and served 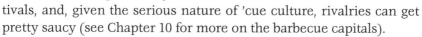 over chicken livers, gizzards, and eggs. Bradford dishes out its own Doodle Soup Festival in July.

Barbecue capitals dot the map like so many grease spots on a tablecloth: From Kansas City, Missouri, to Owensboro, Kentucky; Lexington, North Carolina, to Memphis, Tennessee, big cities and small towns alike lay claim to being the ultimate barbecue capital. They hold cook-offs and festivals, and, given the serious nature of 'cue culture, rivalries can get pretty saucy (see Chapter 10 for more on the barbecue capitals).

Speaking of sauce, the sauce revolution of the 1980s — when cooks began marinating and simmering as never before — gave birth to Orange County, North Carolina's growing cottage industry of sauce bottlers — which in turn has given Orange County its reputation as the emerging Sauce Capital of the South.

The case could be made for sausage as a perfect meal, and plenty of places are renowned for their local versions. Sheboygan, Wisconsin, and New Braunfels, Texas, both claim to be the best Wurst Capital of the World, while Iowa's Amana Colonies are known a little more formally as the Bratwurst Capital of the World. New Braunfels, by the way, is home to the renowned Wurstfest, held in early November, while Sheboygan hosts its own Bratwurst Days in August. And St. Charles, Illinois, is the Dry Sausage Capital of the World, in case you were wondering.

That spicy sausage andouille has La Place, Louisiana, as its world capital, and it's not the only cajun country dish to be capitalized. If you're looking for a savory serving of rice and meat, head to Gonzales, Louisiana, the Jambalaya Capital of the World; or if you'd rather have a spicy stew, then Bridge City, Louisiana, the Gumbo Capital of the World, is for you.

In the midst of all this extraordinary eating, don't forget the nutritional necessities — like poultry and dairy products, for instance. Shell seekers head for Gaylord, Minnesota, the Egg Capital of the World, which hosts the fragile but fun Gaylord Eggstravaganza Festival. Petaluma, California, has been called the Egg Basket of the World. At one time, it was even home to the world's first and only chicken pharmacy (presumably for those times when chicken soup didn't do the trick).

Petaluma, California, has long been known as the World's Egg Basket; once, it was even home to the world's only chicken pharmacy. *Historical photo property of Petaluma Area Chamber of Commerce*

Harvard, Illinois, the Milk Capital of the World, celebrates its dairy heritage at Harvard Milk Day, a wholesome event featuring milk exhibits, a Milk Run, and the crowning of a milk princess (who would presumably grow up to be a dairy queen). And Owatonna, Minnesota, has the melt-in-your-mouth title of Butter Capital of the World, while Hopkins County, Texas, deep in the heart of cattle country, is known as the Dairy Capital of Texas (they can't live by beef alone down there).

Naturally, Wisconsin, the Dairy State — a.k.a. the Cheese Capital of the Nation — has its share of dairy areas. Madison is sometimes called the Dairy Capital of the World; it milks the title for all its worth in early June during the Cows on the Concourse festival, where locals cozy up to dairy cows. Cheese capitals include Plymouth and Little Chute, which produced the world's largest wheel of cheese back in 1988 (40,000 pounds) and has been partying ever since. Every June it holds the Great Wisconsin Cheese Festival, where events include cheese-sculpting competitions and cheese factory tours.

Though the previous chapter has plenty of salad solutions for veggie lovers, don't overlook the tasty offerings of Cairo, Georgia, the Pickle Capital of the World, home of W.B. Roddenbery Co., Inc., a pickle-packing company that dates back to 1889 (Roddenbery also packages peanut and syrup products). Ocanada, Wisconsin, is another Pickle Capital, and Berrien Springs, Michigan, merrily celebrates its status as the Christmas Pickle Capital of the World. Come early December, they even have a parade featuring Rudolph the Red-Nosed Pickle.

You'll need something to wash all this down with, of course. For that morning perk-me-up, fly west to Seattle, the Coffee Capital of the World; it's the homebase of Starbucks, which helped launch the coffee bar craze that has transformed many of us into card-carrying American espresso fiends. Farther west, Kona, on Hawaii's Big Island, is another coffee capital. Its famous Kona beans brew up one of the world's best java jolts. Kona also hosts the Kona Coffee Festival in November, which features a big parade and street party; and the nearby Ritz-Carlton Mauna Lanai stages gourmet coffee cooking demonstrations and tastings.

Those in search of a stiffer drink should consider the offerings of **BARDSTOWN, KENTUCKY,** the Bourbon Capital of the World, so dubbed because at one time some 22 bourbon distilleries were situated in and around this historic town. Now, only a handful remain, and distilleries are banned from handing out samples of their product; so don't plan on tippling during the tour. The small town of Lynchburg, Tennessee (population 350), has gained a big reputation as a whiskey capital, largely because Jack Daniel's bottles its famous brew there. Visitors can tour the distillery and breathe in the aroma of aging spirits in the Barrelhouse, but, since the distillery is in the bone-dry Moore County, no sampling is done there either.

If tasting is what you want, your luck improves in California's Napa Valley, the Table Wine Capital of the World. Here, just about every winery offers tastings and

The Jack Daniel Distillery uncorked Lynchburg, Tennessee's claim as the Whiskey Capital of the World.
*Courtesy Jack Daniel Distillery*

tours; you can even take the Napa Valley Wine Train for the ultimate wine and rail experience. And Fresno has the palatable reputation as the Sweet Wine Capital of the World.

When it's time for dessert, you can savor the sweet treats of Mackinac Island, Michigan, the Fudge Capital of the World (though it's more famous as the Lilac Capital of the World, and for its world-class Grand Hotel). Chocoholics can indulge in their favorite flavor in **HERSHEY, PENNSYLVANIA,** which calls itself both Chocolate Town, U.S.A. and The Sweetest Place on Earth. The town was founded by Milton S. Hershey in 1903, and his chocolate company is still the center of attention in this community, where the streets have names like Cocoa Avenue and the scent of chocolate fills the air.

Another tasty area is the section of U.S. Highway 90 between Bay St. Louis and New Orleans, which Louisiana has dubbed the Praline Capital of the World because of the numerous places along that road that sell this delicious confection of brown sugar and pecans. And one more sweet place: Randolph, Nebraska, the Honey Capital of the Nation, where the ultimate buzz comes from the hundreds of hives local beekeepers tend.

If you were to travel coast to coast, stopping at every capital community and indulging in every food festival, the one town you would probably need to visit at the end is Durham, North Carolina, the Diet Capital of the World. It's home to several major diet clinics, including the world-renowned Duke Diet and Fitness Center. This "waist-land" extends beyond the clinic doors: Restaurants in town feature low-fat menus, and the thriving sporting goods stores stock extra-large workout ensembles and every imaginable piece of exercise equipment.

If a visit to Durham doesn't do the trick, there's one last place you can go to (possibly) lose your appetite: Clinton, Montana, the Testicle Festival Capital of the World, so-named because of its annual (cooked) testicle festival. The event, held in early October at Rock Creek Lodge, serves up more than 5.5 tons of Rocky Mountain oysters and other victuals. Also for sale are a variety of souvenirs — from

baseball caps and T-shirts to beer can wraps and even ladies' panties — imprinted with the event's slogan: "I Had a Ball at the Testicle Festival." For those who want to say they've been to the event but can't stomach the main course, the menu also includes chicken, cowboy beans, and Texas toast.

No matter where you travel in America, you're never far from a city or town with a capital cuisine, and part of the fun of visiting new places is trying the food; so time your trip around a local food fest and you'll be amazed at the endless variations on the same theme you'll find. And just visiting a Main Street lunch counter or diner offers a window into the culture and lifestyle of the locals, and gives you a taste of any town, whether you're just passing through or planning to stick around for the next meal.

## ❀ Mattoon, Illinois

BAGEL CAPITAL OF THE WORLD

For years it seemed that New Yorkers were the only ones who took their bagels seriously. The round, chewy breads were considered a Big Apple deli food, right up there with blintzes and New York style cheesecake. Across the land, if anyone else was eating something with a hole in the middle, it was probably a doughnut. Then came the 1980s food revolution, when everyone wanted to eat cosmopolitan, and the good-for-you, big-city bagel could be found in freezer sections and bread shelves of supermarkets across the country.

A large part of the national love affair with the bagel can be credited to Lender's Bagels. The family-run (but corporate-owned) bagel baker made believers out of millions of Americans with its low-fat but high-taste product. And Lender's has made the town of Mattoon, Illinois, site of the company's biggest bagel factory, the Bagel Capital of the World.

As often happens when a major corporation settles in a small town, Mattoon has taken on the bagel as its favorite food. The annual BagelFest, held the last weekend in July, draws tens of thousands of bagel lovers to such events as the World's Biggest Bagel Breakfast (Lender's donates the bagels). The event is launched with the traditional tossing of the first bagel, and then ensues an array of bagel-related festivities. Bagel beauties are crowned, bagel recipes are tasted and exchanged, local kids perform in shows, craftspeople exhibit their wares (anything shaped like a bagel sells big), and there's even a Bagel Buggy Derby.

Mattoon, with its population of nearly 18,500, sits in the heartland of south central Illinois. It was just another small city until Lender's began baking its way onto America's breakfast tables. Now Mattoon boutiques and gift shops offer bagel baseball caps and T-shirts, postcards, and magnets, and other souvenirs commemorating the toast of the town.

Can this bagel bonanza last? The BagelFest just keeps growing and growing—estimated attendance in 1995 was 40,000. And Lender's, which is owned by Kraft Foods, appears content in Mattoon. It seems the perfect place for a company still intimately connected with its namesake family of bagel bakers. Patriarch Harry Lender came to America from Poland in 1927, bringing his baking skills and trade with him. His family carries on the tradition; Harry's son Murray, who appears in Lender's commercials, helps keep the legacy alive. The Mattoon Lender's factory rolls out more than 2 million bagels a year and continues to be a wholesome force in the community.

## FOR FURTHER INFORMATION

**Mattoon Area Chamber of Commerce**
1701 Wabash
Mattoon, IL 61938
(217) 235-5661

Mattoon's BagelFest rolls out a colorful parade and all-you-can-eat bagel breakfast. *Courtesy Mattoon Chamber of Commerce*

# ✪ Bardstown, Kentucky

BOURBON CAPITAL OF THE WORLD

Bourbon, bourbon everywhere, but not a drop to drink. Ironically, in Kentucky, home to such distilling legends as Jim Beam and Maker's Mark, more than half the counties are dry, including Bourbon County. But in and around Bardstown, Kentucky, the Bourbon Capital of the World, you can visit some of these great liquor labels even if you can't sample their wares on site. Even in the wet counties, you have to go to a restaurant or package store to sample the local makes; Bardstown, fortunately, is in the decidedly damp Nelson County, so you needn't travel far to toss one back.

Bardstown and its environs were once home to 22 operating distilleries — distilling records from the region date back to 1776 — although a mere handful remain. Heaven Hill is the only one left in Bardstown itself, but the surrounding area boasts several others open to the public, notably, Jim Beam's (in Clermont) and Maker's Mark (in Loretto). A little farther afield are Ancient Age (in Frankfort) and Wild Turkey (in Lawrenceburg). All have variations on the theme of visitors' centers and tours.

Touring a bourbon factory is an astonishing experience; you don't smell the alcohol but rather the sweet, woodsy aroma of the fermentation process. You might think you were touring a bakery, but for the barrels.

During your tour, you'll probably see the stages of whiskey making, from the fermentation of grains — usually rye (though Maker's Mark uses red winter wheat for a distinctive flavor) and barley malt — to the varying stages of distillation. From its early, high-proof forms (the kind that moonshiners made in their stills), the white lightning can soar to as high as 130 proof before being watered down to around 110 proof, at which point the aging process begins. After aging, most makers dilute the whiskey to a lower proof for public consumption.

Exhibits vary among distillers. Jim Beam's American Outpost complex is designed as a real tourist destination — sort of a Disney World for drinkers. It includes a large visitors' center with displays on company history and the life and times of Jim Beam (he died at

Visitors to the Kentucky
Bourbon Festival can see how
the white oak barrels necessary
for the aging process are made.
*Courtesy Office of Special Events,
Bardstown-Nelson County Tourist &
Convention Commission*

home in Bardstown in 1947) and his ancestor who founded the company, Jacob Beam. Jim Beam's grandson, Booker Noe, is now the Master Distiller, and Noe knows everything there is to know about Kentucky bourbon.

The Outpost also has a complete set (said to be the world's only) of Jim Beam decanters — those figural bottles that collectors lovingly display behind their wet bars in their finished basements. Also at the Jim Beam complex is the Hartman Cooperage Museum, which details the history and construction of the oak barrels essential to the whiskey-making process.

Maker's Mark is a smaller establishment, but its lovely grounds make it worth the 20-mile drive from Bardstown to see this national historic property. Visitors enter the distillery grounds through the beautiful old red Toll Gate House. The Visitors' Center, originally built in 1889 as the resident distiller's house, has displays on the company and its products. The oldest continually operating distillery in the country (it dates back to the early 1800s), it has been bottling the Maker's Mark label since 1953.

Considered by some connoisseurs to be the ultimate bourbon, Maker's Mark makes its traditional sour mash the old-fashioned way, in barrels that are moved through a series of warehouses, aging in the upper levels of storehouses for several summers before being moved to lower, cooler warehouse quarters for the final processing. Visitors get to see much of this process, along with such distillery landmarks as the Quart House, probably the nation's earliest package liquor store, where locals used to bring their jugs and bottles for filling before Prohibition banned liquor altogether; after Prohibition was repealed, regulated packaging ended the jug-filling station tradition.

In Bardstown itself, Heaven Hill, the largest family-owned distillery in the country, shows a videotaped introduction to the company and its whiskey-making process. The distillery ages some 25 million gallons of bourbon at one time — that's 10 percent of the world's future bourbon! Visitors also can witness the entire bottling process, and, having seen the barrels emptied into the screened draining troughs in the Gauging Room (one of the last steps before bottling), Heaven Hill even allows guests to grab a souvenir. "To remind you of your journey," their brochure promises, "you can reach into the Gauging Room's draining trough and retrieve a barrel bung, fresh from the barrel and still soaked with great Kentucky Bourbon. It's an experience your senses will never forget."

If your senses need a little time to recover, Bardstown is also home to the Oscar Getz Museum of Whiskey History, where you can see artifacts such as a real mountain still, old aging barrels, an exhibit on Carry Nation (the axe-wielding matriarch of the Temperance movement) and other "liquorish" delights. The museum was created from the personal collections of Oscar Getz, a Bardstown businessman with a passion for whiskey paraphernalia that spanned a half-century. Getz died in 1983, and the museum opened the following year in Spalding Hall, the site of Kentucky's first Catholic men's college.

The Bardstown Historical Museum shares the same quarters as the Oscar Getz collection; so you can bone up on your local lore, such as the story of Stephen Foster, an area native, who, when writing his famous song "My Old Kentucky Home" was referring to a cousin's Bardstown plantation where he was a frequent guest. One of the commonwealth's most popular tourist attractions, the house, built in 1818, is the centerpiece of

## DID YOU KNOW...

### Colorful Barrels

If you assume that, like wine, whiskey gets its coloration from its ingredients, you're looking down the wrong barrel: it's the kind of wood used in whiskey barrels that gives the liquor its distinctive hue. Red-amber whiskey comes from new, charred white oak barrels, while paler yellow whiskeys were aged in used or uncharred barrels.

My Old Kentucky Home State Park in Bardstown. During the summer, the park stages a popular musical show, "The Stephen Foster Story," relating the life and times of the songwriter also renowned for such tunes as "Oh, Susannah" and "Camptown Races."

In case you were wondering how the bourbon capital celebrates its heritage, Bardstown does indeed have a Bourbon Festival, held the third weekend in September. The event includes distillery tours, demonstrations of oak barrel making, barrel painting, and a walking tour of downtown Bardstown featuring Kentucky bourbon memorabilia and landmarks. And, unlike the laws governing the distilleries themselves, there's no ban on sharing the local liquor at the festival, and one of the biggest events is the Great Kentucky Bourbon Tasting — but bring a designated driver if you plan on indulging.

## For Further Information

### General Information

**Bardstown-Nelson County Tourist and Convention Commission**
107 E. Stephen Foster Ave.
P.O. Box 867
Bardstown, KY 40004
(502) 348-4877 or (800) 638-4877

### Attractions and Events

**Kentucky Bourbon Festival**
Contact Bardstown-Nelson County Tourist and Convention Commission, Office of Special Events
(502) 348-0255

**My Old Kentucky Home State Park**
501 E. Stephen Foster Ave.
Bardstown, KY 40004
(502) 348-3502 or (800) 323-7803

Oscar Getz Museum of Whiskey History
and Bardstown Historical Museum
Spalding Hall
114 5th St. at Xavier Rd.
Bardstown, KY 40004
(502) 348-2999

The Stephen Foster Story
P.O. Box 546
Bardstown, KY 40004
(502) 348-5971 or (800) 626-1563

## Distilleries Open to the Public

Ancient Age
1001 Wilkinson Blvd.
Frankfort, KY 40601
(502) 223-7641

Heaven Hill Distillery
1064 Loretto Rd.
Bardstown, KY 40004
(502) 348-3921

Jim Beam's American Outpost
Hwy. 245
Clermont, KY 40110
(502) 543-9877

Maker's Mark Distillery
3350 Burks Spring Rd.
(Hwy. 52 East)
Loretto, KY 40037
(502) 865-2099

Wild Turkey
1525 Tyrone Rd. (off Hwy. 62)
Lawrenceburg, KY 40342
(502) 839-4544

# ⚙ Battle Creek, Michigan

CEREAL CAPITAL OF THE WORLD

When Battle Creek, Michigan, first gained international fame, it was as the Health City, home to Dr. John Harvey Kellogg's renowned Battle Creek Sanitarium. The turn-of-the-century spa helped spawn the health and fitness revolution; and Dr. Kellogg, in his zeal for promoting colonical-ly clean living, became famous for the special breakfast food he served his clientele.

So was born our cold cereal society of wheat flakes, raisin bran, and all manner of sugary, shapely tidbits. The company Kellogg founded is still headquartered in Battle Creek, and the city is also home to Ralston Foods and Post (a division of Kraft Foods) — a breakfast bunch that's given the city its reputation as the Cereal Capital of the World.

It's hard to believe that today's big-league breakfast food industry sprang from the slightly eccentric but nearly messianic Dr. Kellogg, whose Victorian regimen of sexual and carnivorous abstinence enthralled a generation. But though Dr. Kellogg developed the wheatflake as well as a cereal-based coffee substitute for his clients at "the San" (as his institution was nicknamed), he didn't think to package any of his nutritional foods for public sale.

That idea was C.W. Post's, a San fan from Texas who realized the commercial potential in the stuff guests were chowing down on every morning. Post founded the Postum Cereal Co. in Battle Creek in 1895, selling bran cereal (Grapenuts) and a coffee substitute (Postum). It was another decade before the Kellogg name graced store shelves, and then it was under the direction of Dr. Kellogg's younger brother, Will Keith (W.K.) Kellogg, who founded the Toasted Corn Flake Co.

Hundreds of entrepreneurs jumped on the bran wagon after C.W. Post made his cereal killing, and soon the town was flooded with would-be breakfast barons. By 1902, the town was home to more than 100 breakfast cereal and coffee substitute companies, but most such schemes turned to mush as the small market was overwhelmed with product. Novelist T. Coraghessan Boyle wrote a wickedly wacky novel (later turned into a film) about that era in the cereal city, titled *The Road to Wellville* (1993).

Today's Battle Creek is a modern city with all the amenities, but its cerealized story is still its biggest draw. To commemorate its breakfast-food fame, the city

hosts the annual Battle Creek Cereal Festival the second weekend in June. The event kicks off with the World's Longest Breakfast Table, which stretches through downtown in a seemingly endless line of red-and-white-checked cloth, laden with milk, bowls, and boxes of cereal. The free feast draws more than 60,000 eager eaters every year, with cereal and accompaniments donated by Kellogg, Post, and Ralston-Purina.

The giant breakfast table tradition dates to 1956, when, to celebrate its 50th anniversary, the Kellogg Co. closed off part of downtown and set up 222 picnic tables in anticipation of about 7,000 celebrants for its Golden Jubilee bash. The sponsors were shocked when more than twice that number showed up for breakfast.

The Cereal Festival grew up around the breakfast table tradition, but it wasn't until 1976 that a committee was formed to develop other events to mark the occasion. Now, it's a full-fledged festival, and, though the consumption of cereal is an important ingredient, not everyone is there to eat: Among the crowds you'll see an advertiser's dream team of cereal-box characters shaking hands and posing for pictures. As you might imagine, Tony the Tiger (of "Tastes G-r-r-r-eat" fame) is a favorite feline, while the Snap, Crackle, and Pop elves and other characters work the crowd like PR pros.

Battle Creek may have changed since the days when the elite came to diet and exercise their cares away, but the town still shows its flaky roots (and that's meant in the nicest possible way). Though the San is long gone, the property, now listed on the National Register of Historic Places, is still there. It serves as the Battle Creek Federal Center, housing various government and military offices. Traces of the past are visible, however, in the building lobbies and dining room.

Throughout the city, you can't help but see the Kellogg name. It graces everything from the Kellogg Arena (home to concerts, sporting events, and exhibitions) and Kellogg Forest (716 acres owned by Michigan State University, with public trails and recreation areas) to the Kellogg Bird Sanctuary (home to ducks, geese, swans, and other wild fowl) and the Kellogg Farm-Dairy Center (a state-of-the-art dairy that offers free tours to the public).

As the city's promotional video expounds, "Battle Creek — it's more than a place to stop for breakfast," there are many noncereal sights to see. During summer months, the skies are often filled with hot air balloons, taking part in the National Hot Air Balloon Championship and Air Show. The city also boasts the lovely Binder Park Zoo, the Leila Arboretum (a 72-acre English landscape garden, part of the Kellogg Forest), and other pleasant diversions. And to pay your respects to Battle Creek's greatest citizens, visit the lovely Oak Hill Cemetery, where you'll find the final resting place of the city's most famous resident, Sojourner Truth, the former slave who rallied the abolitionist battle cry and led crusades for women's rights and temperance. The cemetery also includes the graves of cereal kings C.W. Post and W.K. Kellogg as well as of the San man himself, Dr. John Harvey Kellogg.

But whatever you do while you're in Battle Creek, don't forget to eat your breakfast. After all, in this city above all others, it is the most important meal of the day.

## FOR FURTHER INFORMATION

### *General Information*

**Greater Battle Creek/Calhoun County**
**Visitor and Convention Bureau**
34 W. Jackson St., Suite 4-B
Battle Creek, MI 49017
(616) 962-2240 or (800) 387-2240

## *Attractions and Events*

**Battle Creek Cereal Festival**
Contact the Visitor
and Convention Bureau

**Battle Creek Federal Center**
74 N. Washington St.
Battle Creek, MI 49017
(616) 961-7015

**Binder Park Zoo**
7400 Division Dr.
Battle Creek, MI 49017
(616) 979-1351

**Kellogg Bird Sanctuary**
2 miles north on 40th St. to C Ave.
Battle Creek, MI 49017
(616) 671-2510

**Kellogg Farm-Dairy Center**
3 miles north of M-89 on 40th
Battle Creek, MI 49017
(616) 731-4597

**Kellogg Forest**
7600 N. 42nd St. near Augusta
Battle Creek, MI 49017
(616) 731-4597

**Leila Arboretum**
W. Michigan at 20th St.
Battle Creek, MI 49017
(616) 969-0270

**Oak Hill Cemetery**
255 South St.
Battle Creek, MI 49017
(616) 964-7320

# ✪ Springfield, Illinois

CHILLI CAPITAL OF THE WORLD

Springfield, Illinois, is perhaps best known for its Lincoln links: It was here that Honest Abe practiced law before moving to Washington, and here that he was entombed after his assassination. The city has a variety of other claims to fame: It's the state capital, the birthplace of the Steak n Shake restaurant chain, and a major stop along old Route 66. But there's one more thing about Springfield that might shock some southwesterners who thought they had left the chuckwagon parked safely back home at the ranch: Springfield is the Chilli Capital of the World. That's right, Chilli with two *l*s.

Some say the extra *l* is for Lincoln, or that it's to remind the Illini (Illinois folks) of the best state's chilli, but actually that extra letter crept in thanks to Joe Bockelmann, whose renowned Dew Chilli Parlor helped give Springfield its well-deserved capital reputation.

In 1909, when Bockelmann opened the Dew with its misspelled sign, he explained that it was the way it was supposed to be spelled (and some agree, contending it's the original Native American spelling). In this double-*l* state, why not? Governor Dan Walker even made a special proclamation to officially adopt Bockelmann's spelling of the word.

Springfield chilli is heavy on the beans, light on the meat, and rich on the cayenne and cumin. It's the kind of chili — er, chilli — that could keep a cowboy powered up on the range for days. Folks here like it that way, and if they enter those beanless chili cook-offs down in the enemy territory of say, Texas, well, they'll gripe and grumble and talk about how too much meat spoils the flavor.

Not that Springfielders dislike unique flavorings: Beer seems to be a popular ingredient in local chillis, though it's hard to get most folks to reveal their prized recipes. That's especially true during the Heartland Regional Chilli Cook-off, held the first weekend of June, when the heavy hitters from Springfield and several surrounding

Chilli cook-offs stir some local competition in Springfield. *Courtesy Springfield Convention and Visitors Bureau*

Springfield, Illinois, may be famous as Lincoln's hometown, but its chilli is its capital claim to fame. *Courtesy Springfield Convention and Visitors Bureau*

states stir things up in the city's biggest competition. Recipes are guard-ed like state secrets, and the winners, even in their rejoicing, may be happy to dish their award-winning chilli, but will rarely share their magic ingredients.

Still, from tasting around, you can figure out the Springfield chilli basics: Beans (chilli hot beans and/or kidney beans), finely chopped onions and celery, perhaps carrots and green peppers, tomato sauce, ground beef, chilli powder, cumin, and cayenne seem to be in most of the chillis. Meatless chillis go heavier on the beans and vegetables. Some locals will, Cincinnati style, add a little cinnamon to sweeten the mix. But the beans are the key; and, though some can be spicy, the hotness of chilli here is not paramount the way it is in Texas or Louisiana, so nervous palates can rest a little easier (hot chillis are well labeled at local parlors, so you always know what you're dipping into ahead of time).

You can get a good bowl of chilli all over Springfield, even at the classic roadside restaurant Steak n Shake, which, despite its name, is well known for its chilli. Then there are the real chilli parlors. The Dew was a local landmark until it was torn down, but there are plen-ty to choose from, including the Den Chilli Parlor, which has served up steaming chilli to hungry Illini since the mid-1940s. If you're looking for a fine bowl of chilli without the Texas hots, head for the Land of Lincoln, where two *l*s are better than one, especially when it's time to chilli out.

## For Further Information

### General Information

Springfield Convention and Visitors Bureau
109 N. Seventh St.
Springfield, IL 62701
(217) 789-2360 or (800) 545-7300

### Attractions

Den Chilli Parlor
1121 S. Grand Ave. E
Springfield, IL 62703
(217) 544-3000

Den Chilli Parlor
3419 Freedom Dr.
Springfield, IL 62701
(217) 698-4477

# ✪ Hershey, Pennsylvania

CHOCOLATE TOWN, U.S.A.

With a name like Hershey, it has to be chocolate, right? Nevertheless, some people are surprised to discover that Hershey is more than a state of salivation — it's a place in Pennsylvania. So what nickname does this sweet city go by? Chocolate Town, U.S.A., naturally. Hershey's other slogan, which accompanies attractions brochures — The Sweetest Place on Earth — is equally cavity-inducing.

Everything about Hershey whispers (some might say moans) chocolate. Driving into the downtown area, with its boulevards named Cocoa and Chocolate, you should keep your windows rolled down and breathe deeply. This has to be the only community in America that actually smells of chocolate. The very air is impregnated with the aroma of delicious decadence.

And there's more. The street lights downtown are a goofy tribute to that ultimate show of affection, the Hershey's Kiss. They're designed to resemble the famous pointy-tipped chocolate drop, and alternate silver, brown, silver, brown, representing a wrapped or unwrapped Kiss.

Yep, this town takes itself about as seriously as Disney World, and so a visit here is basically a trip to Candyland. Not surprising for a city built by Milton S. Hershey, founder of the Hershey Co., which is still head-quartered here. Also not surprising is the number of sweet-natured amusements Hershey offers its visitors.

During the warm months, Hersheypark is the big draw. An old-fashioned amusement park, it has a variety of roller coasters and other thrill rides, a wildlife park called ZooAmerica, and, of course, lots of ooey, gooey goodies to gorge on. The costumed creatures that roam the grounds are, appropriately, Kisses, Hershey and Kit-Kat Bars, and other overgrown candy characters. And they show amazing restraint in not decking the dozens (perhaps hundreds) of witty tourists who, on blisteringly hot summer days, insist on quipping, "You must be *melting!*"

Chocolatey street signs are a downtown treat in Hershey. *Courtesy Harrisburg-Hershey-Carlisle Tourism & Convention Bureau*

The Hotel Hershey, which overlooks the theme park, is a grand, mission-styled place with sweeping staircases, towering columns, dazzling reception rooms and 72 holes of golf on its lavishly appointed grounds (Hershey also calls itself the Golf Capital of Pennsylvania). And every February the hotel offers the ultimate getaway indulgence: A Chocolate Lover's Weekend. The splendid hotel can be a pricey place to stay, so start saving up those pennies for more than candy if you're planning a visit. But it's hardly the only hotel in town; other, less expensive accommodations dot the landscape as well.

The best bargain in town is the free Hershey's Chocolate World visitors center; open year-round, it is one of the nation's more entertaining trips down manufacturing lane. As the scent of chocolate overwhelms you, you step from a moving conveyor belt into a motorized chaise that transports you through the world of chocolate making. As you ride along, you see dioramas and demonstrations on the history, cultivation, and production of chocolate. And when you step off again, you're given a product sample as a parting gift. Not that you'll need it: The exit deposits you firmly in a huge gift shop and food court.

Hershey, Pennsylvania, is far more than a corporate town, though; indeed, it's more that the Hershey Foods Corp. is a town corporation. The M.S. Hershey Foundation, formed in 1935, is a charitable trust that provides funding and support for local education and cultural opportunities. But perhaps the company's greatest impact on the community has been the Milton Hershey School. Hershey and his wife Catherine had no children of their own; so, in 1909, they established a school for orphaned and disadvantaged boys.

Rather like Boys Town with a sweet tooth, the Hershey School (which began enrolling girls in 1976) continues to be an admired and academically competitive institution: 85 percent of the school's graduates go on to four-year colleges. To learn more about the school, visit Founders Hall, a grand building that's part administration, part memorial; here, you can see exhibits and a film on Milton Hershey and his school.

If this entices you to learn more about Milton, the man and his legacy, tour the Hershey Museum next door to the Hersheypark Arena. Here you'll find exhibits that tell his life story, one of perseverance in the face of collapsed dreams. Born in Derry Church, Pennsylvania, in 1857, and raised as a Mennonite, Hershey failed as a candy maker in New York, Philadelphia, Denver, and Chicago before earning sweet success (and millions) as a caramel manufacturer in nearby Lancaster. He sold the caramel company to start his own chocolate factory and, in 1903, established the town that bears his name. In 1907, he built the amusement park that has evolved into today's Hersheypark.

The museum has exhibits on the development of both the town and the corporation. It also displays Milton Hershey's collection of Native American artifacts and common goods from his Pennsylvania German heritage (yes, German — the misunderstood term "Pennsylvania Dutch" is actually derived from "Pennsylvania Deutsch," meaning the German-speaking immigrants who settled much of the commonwealth's farmlands).

If the overwhelming cocoa aroma of the community makes you long for the great outdoors, you can always take a break at Hershey Gardens, a 23-acre botanical park created by Milton Hershey in 1937. It's particularly renowned for its rose gardens, which, thankfully, smell like roses, not chocolate. Rarely have a company and its town melted so deliciously together, making both stronger and sweeter with time.

## FOR FURTHER INFORMATION

### General Information

**Hershey Information**
300 Park Blvd.
Hershey, PA 17033
(717) 533-3131 or (800) HERSHEY

### Attractions

**Founders Hall of the Milton Hershey School**
Hershey, PA 17033
(717) 534-3500

**Hershey's Chocolate
World Visitors Center**
Park Blvd.
Hershey, PA 17033
(717) 534-4900

**Hershey Gardens**
P.O. Box 416
Hershey, PA 17033
(717) 534-3493

**Hershey Museum**
170 W. Hersheypark Dr.
Hershey, PA 17033
(717) 534-3439

**Hersheypark**
100 W. Hersheypark Dr.
Hershey, PA 17033
(800) 242-4236 or (800) HERSHEY

**Hotel Hershey**
P.O. Box 400
Hotel Rd.
Hershey, PA 17033
(800) 533-3131

**ZooAmerica**
100 Hersheypark Dr.
Hershey, PA 17033
(717) 534-3860

# ❂ Salley, South Carolina

## WORLD CHITLIN CAPITAL

Some world capitals are created by the local industry or crop, which leads to the capital claim, and usually a festival or event later evolves around the title. But there are a few dogs whose tails wag them, and in the case of Salley, South Carolina, it dubbed itself World Chitlin Capital because of the growing popularity of its Chitlin Strut.

First, for those not in the know (and those who've managed to forget), chitlins are hog guts. Though those who speak the King's English would have them spelled and pronounced "chitterlings," the folks in Salley and other points Deep South know better. Those pig innards are chitlins, and they're worth struttin' about.

South Carolina has a couple of super struts — a strut being a fun word for festival, a chance to strut your stuff by showing off your best recipes and regalia. The Okra Strut in Irmo, South Carolina, is another biggie. But Salley's Chitlin Strut is a thing to behold.

During the weekend after Thanksgiving, this town, whose population teeters around 450, suddenly swells by the tens of thousands as strutters from around the South arrive to devour nearly five tons of chitlins. Along with all those interior edibles, the 40,000 festivalgoers also devour more than 150 bar-becued hogs and 1,500 chickens. But those are just side dishes, so if you don't like chitlins, *stay away!*

The Chitlin Strut was a dream of Jack Able, the former mayor of Salley, who died in 1993. In the fall of 1966, Able needed a fund-raising event to help fatten the town's coffers for local Christmas decorations. Able and his council representatives took a field

trip to Cayce, South Carolina, to pick the brain of Friendly Ben Dekle, a philosophizing country-and-western disc jockey at WCAY radio. They thought Dekle might have a few suggestions for an event that would raise money.

Well, Dekle did. Half-jokingly, so the story goes, Dekle told his visitors that he'd always wished for a Chitlin Strut, but, as the community literature puts it, "he was never able to find anyone with the 'guts' enough to do it." Able announced that Salley had the guts, and that same year, on the Saturday after Thanksgiving, the first Salley Chitlin Strut came to pass. Despite being stuffed with turkey, strutters managed to devour more than 600 pounds of chitlins that year, and Friendly Ben even served as master of ceremonies at the first Strut's Country Music Show, an event that has become a festival highlight.

Two decades later, the town and its Strut have grown gutsier with age. The Country Music Show is still a big event, but folks also come to watch the parade, cheer on their local lovelies at the Chitlin Strut Beauty Contest, and dance till midnight at the Strut in the Gymnasium. Aside from the obvious pig-related attraction, savvy soooo-eee sayers can enter the Hawg Calling Contest (if there are any live pigs left in the area by struttin' time).

The people of Salley are proud of the way they make their chitlins. They'll tell you that, unlike those big pig packers, they don't chemically strip their chitlins. They clean them the old-fashioned way: "twice slung and pulled through a forked limb," one excessively descriptive account in a festival program puts it. It goes on to note, "How do they smell? Just like the word sounds —

raunchy! According to some people, the smell will send flies, gnats, and mosquitoes away; others say the smell is so strong that even leaves on the trees turn the other way." But how do they taste? "Similar to pork skin . . . but definitely a taste of [their] own."

Though in the workaday world chitlins are usually used as sausage casing, as the Chitlin Strut Souvenir Program warmly notes, in this small town, chitlins are used "like glue to hold the people together, working for a united goal, to make life more interesting for the citizens. Some have said that chitlins are to Salley what Chanel No. 5 is to Fifth Ave." Ah, the sweet smell of success.

## FOR FURTHER INFORMATION

Town of Salley
Office of the Mayor
P.O. Box 484
Salley, SC 29137
(803) 258-3485

CHAPTER

# GONE FISHIN'

 ew sports in America are as revered, lingered over, and passed down through the generations as fishing. It's a mystical thing, a romantic machismo activity. But even if the Robert Redford soft-focus movie *A River Runs Through It* is your only fishing experience, no doubt you still enjoy a good salmon steak or lobster dinner now and then.

In many a lakeside town and coastal village, the catch of the day is more than a fish dish: It's a way of life and a livelihood. So any town that calls itself the Bass Capital of the World or the Sailfish Capital of the World is probably hoping to haul in a hefty tourist trade. But reeling in a capital claim and keeping it fresh are two different things. So some places offer more than just good fishing or dining: They have festivals and events to show off the regional cuisine and celebrate the tastiest denizens of the local deep.

You can tell what sorts of capital towns you'll find by where they're situated. Trace a finger on a map around the freshwater lake areas and you'll touch on such capital communities as Fairmont,

Minnesota; Toledo, Michigan; and Mille Lacs, Minnesota, all of which claim to be the Walleye Capital of the World; Walker, Minnesota, the Muskie Capital of the World; and Alexandria, Minnesota, the Bass Capital of the World.

The American South seems to have an abundance of capitals, perhaps because of the southern tradition of weekends spent lingering around the local fishing hole. You'll find Dixie fish capitals from Weldon, North Carolina (Rockfish Capital of the World), to Eufala, Alabama (another Bass Capital of the World). And there's the collection of catfish capitals that includes Belzoni, Mississippi, probably the best known of the breed. It's surrounded by some of the country's most productive catfish farms, and hosts the World Catfish Festival, with its quotient of goodies like catfish hushpuppies and catfish gumbo.

Other catfish capitals that hold parades, cook-offs, and other fishy fests include Des Allemands, Louisiana; Chetopa, Kansas; and Savannah, Tennessee—the last of which only recently reinstated its big event, the National Catfish Derby, a fishing contest that started in 1952 and brought great fame to Savannah before dying out in the 1960s. Locals polished up their capital claim in 1994 when they brought the fishing derby back, and it's now a full-fledged festival featuring the crowning of a Catfish Queen and a catfish skinning contest (in which presumably the queen is not involved).

Drive up the Mid-Atlantic coast and you'll come to towns such as Chincoteague, Virginia, the Oyster Capital of the World. Though it's more famous for wild horses than mouthwatering mollusks, you'd be hard-pressed to find a more succulent oyster stew; the small community even has its own oyster museum and Oyster Festival. Cross into Maryland and you'll come to Crisfield, a quaint Chesapeake Bay seafood capital known for its tasty crab cakes.

Another crab capital—this one celebrating the delicious Dungeness variety—is on the West Coast, in Newport, Oregon. And in Louisiana, they like their crabs alive enough to run for it. The St. Anthony Catholic Church Festival in Jean Lafitte, Louisiana, was proclaimed Crab Race Capital of the World by the state legislature.

Deep-sea lovers can go fish from numerous big game fish waterfront communities. Serious sportspeople head to Ocean City, Maryland, which, along with its hip-to-be-single beach scene, boasts a reputation as the White Marlin Capital of the World. Florida is particularly famous for its sportfishing. Islamorada calls itself the Sport Fishing Capital of the World, while in **STUART**, the Sailfish Capital of the World, avid adventurers charter boats to match wits with one of the wiliest fish in the ocean. But sailfishers out of Stuart have also learned they're expected to throw back their catch, since a history of indiscriminate fishing severely depleted the population of this sworded sea creature.

Some places are famous more for the good eats than the sporting life. Crisfield's a good example; people go there for the local crab cakes, not to go crabbing themselves—that's a job best left to the old pros who've long crabbed the Bay. **ROCKLAND, MAINE,** Lobster Capital of the World, in the heart of the state's lobstering region, holds the Maine Lobster Festival every August, featuring the World's Largest Lobster Cooker—pound for pound, one of the New England summer's tastiest traditions.

For those who prefer their fish on the fiery side, there's **BREAUX BRIDGE, LOUISIANA,** the Crawfish Capital of the World—though if the locals had their way, they might rename it the Mud Bug Capital to honor the nickname natives have given their favorite little bayou beastie.

Shrimp fans can head to one of several towns for the traditional blessing of the fleet and its harbor parade of decorated shrimp boats—usually the centerpiece of shrimp capital festivals. Fernandina, Florida, where the modern shrimping industry was born, celebrates its heritage and blesses its fleet at the Isle of Eight

The World's Largest Lobster Cooker stands out at the Maine Lobster Festival. *Photo by Paula Lunt, courtesy Rockland-Thomaston Area Chamber of Commerce*

The Golden Isles of Glynn County, Georgia are known for their seafood and shrimping.
*Courtesy Brunswick & the Golden Isles of Georgia Visitors Bureau*

Flags Shrimp Festival in late April; and on the first Saturday in May, McClellanville, South Carolina, hosts the Low Country Shrimp Festival, which also includes a fleet blessing.

One of the more intriguing shrimp capitals is Morgan City, Louisiana, the Shrimp and Petroleum Capital of the World. This unusual twin capital city celebrates its dual industries—oil and shrimp—at the annual Louisiana Shrimp and Petroleum Festival, held Labor Day weekend.

And though **GLYNN COUNTY, GEORGIA,** is dubbed the Seafood Capital of the World because of its seafood processors, the town of **BRUNSWICK**, within Glynn County, is also home to a large shrimping fleet, so it is considered a shrimp capital as well. It traditionally blesses its shrimp fleet on Mother's Day.

Sometimes prepared fish is the local star. **MADISON, MINNESOTA,** makes much of its claim as Lutefisk Capital, U.S.A. The townspeople devour more of the traditional Norwegian dish (dried codfish soaked in lye before preparation) than those of any other town in the state. They even have a town mascot, Lou T. Fisk, whose likeness appears as a painting on the watertower and as a monument in the town park. They also have some lutefisk competition, for Glenwood, Minnesota, calls itself the Lutefisk Capital of the World. Likewise, Mille Lacs (pronounced Mlax), Minnesota, is a walleye capital that also carries the claim of Fish House Capital of the World because of its thousands of ice fishing houses on or near the lake, where sportspeople settle in during the winter for some cool catches.

Because fish have to eat too, why not visit Lonoke, Arkansas, Minnow Capital of the World, where the Anderson Minnow Farms produces millions of minnows and goldfish for use as bait or fish food? Another Arkansas town, Paragould, has a reputation as the Goldfish Capital of the World, thanks to its glittering fish industry.

In this fish-eat-fish world, one capital has a

**DID YOU KNOW...**

**Lutefisk in Your Ear**
As if the briny codfish dish weren't famous enough, MTV viewers swallowed an unanticipated dose of fisk, courtesy of Lutefisk, the band. The group—whose members include a guitar player named Frosting and a drummer named Qazar—released its first album, "Deliver from Porcelain," in 1995. MTV has played their "Doctrine" video on the show "120 Minutes."

slightly scary reputation: Venice, Florida, near Sarasota, is the Sharks' Tooth Capital of the World, where beachcombers can hunt for the fossilized dental remains of ancient sharks that once trolled the Gulf Coast waters. Sharks teeth are so plentiful that the chamber of commerce hands out baggies of them like party favors to tourists. Though visitors are assured these are *prehistoric* sharks teeth, what swimmer, after unearthing one of these infamous incisors, wouldn't think twice before taking the plunge?

Pick a fish, any fish, and you'll often find a whole school of towns with a telltale slogan. Like crappie? Both Bernice, Oklahoma, and Weiss Lake, Alabama, call themselves Crappie Capital of the World. How about bass? Eufala, Alabama, is the Bass Capital of the World, while Clear Lake, California, has taken the more modest title of Bass Capital of the West. Ketchikan, Alaska, is still called the Salmon Capital of the World, though the welcoming gateway that once proclaimed that title is long gone; nowadays, the town sometimes goes by the better preserved title of Canned Salmon Capital of the World. Back in the lower 48, Waukegan, Illinois, on the shores of Lake Michigan, proudly calls itself the Freshwater Salmon Capital of the World.

Whether saltwater or freshwater, farm-raised or ocean caught, the fish that keep the tourism and industrial boats afloat in America's heartland towns and coastal communities are worthy of celebrating, honoring, and most of all, eating.

## ❂ Breaux Bridge, Louisiana

CRAWFISH CAPITAL OF THE WORLD

There are some foods you just naturally associate with Cajun country: po' boy sandwiches, etouffee, chicory coffee, gumbo. And crawdads—little, succulent shellfish, their tender meat ready to absorb those fire-hot sauces and spices.

If crawdads—or crawfish, as the rest of the country knows them—are your kind of seafood, then Breaux Bridge, Louisiana, the Crawfish Capital of the World, is your kind of town. Situated just east of Lafayette on Bayou Teche, this place is crawdad crazy and proud of it: if Crawdad Helper were being developed as a product, this would be the place to set up the test kitchen.

The town of about 6,600 is in the heart of the crawfish-abundant bayou country; Louisiana produces more of these little lobster-like critters than anywhere else in the country—a good thing, since the state is also their largest consumer. As far back as the 1920s, Breaux Bridge's restaurants and hotels (with names like the Hebert Hotel, the Rendez-Vous, Mim's, and Breaux's, among others)—were renowned for succulent dishes such as crawfish bisque and crawfish fricassee.

In 1959, the Louisiana legislature passed a resolution naming Breaux Bridge La Capitale Mondiale de L'Ecrevisse (Crawfish Capital of the World), in honor of the town's 100th anniversary. That same year, to celebrate both the town's capitalization and its centennial, Breaux Bridge held its first Crawfish Festival, an event that has become one of the state's biggest bashes.

The first weekend in May, some 200,000 crawfish fanatics descend on the town for good cooking and Zydeco partying. And boy, do these people get into the mood. Wandering through the festival grounds at Parc Hardy, you'll find more than a few folks dressed like crawdads, complete with wiggly feelers on their heads.

The festival has a couple of big attractions. One is the series of Crawfish Races, during which contestants pit their "mud bugs" (as crawdads are affectionately known) against each other in a competition of skitterish speed. The other main event is the Crawfish Eating Contest, wherein participants suck down multiple pounds of crawdads in the minimum amount of time.

Breaux Bridge's Crawfish Festival makes for some silly celebrants.
*Courtesy Louisiana Office of Tourism*

During the competition, contestants chow on five-pound servings of crawfish; when they finish one serving, another is delivered to their place. Some of these crawdad cravers will wolf down 10, 15, even 20 pounds or more at a sitting. The record-holder, Breaux Bridge's own Andrew Thevant, gobbled down 33.3 pounds in one hour.

The average serving size consumed by a typical crawdad eater is anywhere from 1 to 3 pounds, with about 10 to a pound; the only part of a crawdad you can really sink your teeth into is the tail. The sickly-yellow liver is considered a savory treat, not unlike the lobster's.

At the festival, celebrants can dine on servings of boiled crawdad for around five bucks for a pound and a half. And though contestants devour only boiled crawfish, festival-goers can indulge their taste buds with any number of crawfish delicacies. Try a crawfish pie, a crawfish etouffee, crawfish gumbo, or fried crawfish. Any way they can cook it, they serve it at the festival. Then folks dance it all off to the slithering thrum of the Zydeco music that pervades the fair.

Breaux Bridge may come as close to the perfect bayou country town as they make them, and during that first weekend in May, the rest of the state just sits back with a big grin and lets this crawfish capital crank up the Cajun cooking.

## FOR FURTHER INFORMATION

**Breaux Bridge Area Chamber of Commerce**
P.O. Box 88
Breaux Bridge, LA 70517
(318) 332-5222

**Breaux Bridge Crawfish Festival Association**
P.O. Box 25
Breaux Bridge, LA 70517
(318) 332-6655 or (800) 346-1958

# ⚙ Rockland, Maine

LOBSTER CAPITAL OF THE WORLD

If your mouth waters at the thought of melted butter caressing the crevices of a moist lobster tail, then come summer, head north to Rockland, Maine, the Lobster Capital of the World.

Rockland's Maine Lobster Festival, held the first weekend in August, is a near-perfect seafood fantasy, part silly local ritual, part lobster pot party. And lobsters are only the half of it. The all-you-can-eat Maine blueberry pancake breakfast that kicks off the event is worth attending even if shellfish makes you break out in hives.

The region's oldest annual festival, dating back to 1947, it celebrates midcoastal Maine's lobstering heritage. And it's the perfect place for the celebration: Rockland lies at the heart of the state's most productive lobstering waters—fresh-caught lobsters are shipped worldwide from this seaport community. Chances are, if you've eaten a Maine lobster, it came from somewhere around here.

The festival is presided over by King Neptune—a local guy in a cape and crown, wielding a triton. He's joined in his duties by the

Rockland's Maine Lobster Festival gets even the littlest crustaceans in the mood for some fun. *Photo by Paula Lunt, courtesy Rockland-Thomaston Area Chamber of Commerce*

Maine Sea Goddess, who's crowned the first night of the festival; she then gets her own coronation parade. Even the kids dress up as lobsters for the big parade. But aquatic royalty take a back seat to the lobsters: The real star of this show is the World's Largest Lobster Cooker, in which volunteers prepare thousands of lobsters for hungry hordes.

Though it costs just a few bucks to get into the festival (and it's a bargain, considering all the shows, entertainment, and events), you will have to pay separately for the fruit of the sea: Lobster is sold from the giant cooker at the local market price, which varies year by year, but usually costs $5 to $7 per pound (still considerably less than in most restaurants around the country).

If you need to work off a bit of that melted butter, you can enter—or just aggressively cheer on—the Great International Lobster Crate Race, one of the final events of the festival. Or just stroll down to the harbor; it will take your breath away, and leave you aching to stay a while longer.

Rockland is Maine as storybooks would have it: craggy coast, picturesque harbor, the call of gulls, and the barking of seals.

Rockland Harbor, which feeds into Penobscot Bay, has another capital claim—Schooner Capital of Maine—as it's home to the country's largest fleet of schooners.

During the warm months, schooners and windjammers such as the *American Eagle* and the Schooner *Victory Chimes* offer cruises of the harbor and bay. The second weekend in July, Rockland celebrates Schooner Days with a tall ships parade through Rockland Harbor to the cheers of throngs on shore.

Ferryboat rides to the Penobscot Bay islands also are popular maritime adventures for tourists. Visitors can take in the sights of Islesboro, Matinicus, Monhegan, North Haven, and Vinalhaven from ferries that depart from Rockland or other nearby ports. The islands—which range from the tiny Monhegan, less than a mile long, to Vinalhaven, which stretches for 14 miles—have inns and museums, galleries and lighthouses worth exploring.

If all this sea sighting makes you long to learn more about the area's maritime history, visit the Shore Village Museum at the Grand Army Hall in Rockland. Sometimes called Maine's Lighthouse Museum, it has the country's largest collection of lighthouse and Coast Guard-related artifacts. One of the highlights is a second-grade Fresnel Lens, a huge, honeycomb-shaped glass bulb built in 1855 for one of Maine's tallest lighthouse towers, Petit Manan. The museum also has a fascinating collection on New Englanders who fought in the Civil War, notably members of the Fourth Regiment of Maine.

But whether you're festival-going or island-hopping, museum-touring or schooner-cruising, you can be sure that, come mealtime, there's lobster on the menu—and that's perhaps the most luscious reason of all to spend a little time in this rockbound, crustacean-blessed edge of America.

## FOR FURTHER INFORMATION

### General Information

**Rockland-Thomaston Area Chamber of Commerce**
Harbor Park
P.O. Box 508
Rockland, ME 04841
(207) 596-0376

### Attractions and Events

**Boater Information**
Rockland Harbor Master
Rockland-Thomaston Area Chamber of Commerce
(207) 594-0312

**Maine Lobster Festival Committee**
P.O. Box 552
Rockland, ME 04841
(207) 596-0376 or (800) LOB-CLAW

**Schooner Days**
Contact Rockland-Thomaston Area Chamber of Commerce

**Shore Village Museum**
Grand Army Hall
104 Limerock St.
Rockland, ME 08481
(207) 594-0311

# ❂ Madison, Minnesota

## LUTEFISK CAPITAL, U.S.A.

T here's just something about those northern Americans, the ones descended from Nordic stock, whose blood seems to thrill at the colder months, who live to ice fish, who listen to Garrison Keillor and not only laugh but nod their heads knowingly, smiling secretly. And you know, they like lutefisk. They really do.

What, you may ask, is a lutefisk? It's a codfish that's soaked in a lye solution before cooking. Not the kind of stuff that most folks crave, but the people of Madison, Minnesota, not only enjoy lutefisk, they eat more of it per capita than those of any other town in Minnesota. Hence Madison's self-proclaimed title of Lutefisk Capital, U.S.A.

The town of Glenwood, Minnesota, calls itself the Lutefisk Capital of the World, so this lutefisk thing is no fluke among Minnesotans. Lutefisk is a beloved dish in Minnesota, served for generations since many in the state came across the ocean from Northern Europe.

But what does a lutefisk capital do to honor its favorite fish dish, other than eat it? Well, Madison's mascot is Lou T. Fisk, a jaunty cod-

Lou T. Fisk, Madison's fish mascot, has his own statue in the town park. *Courtesy Madison Area Chamber of Commerce*

fish with a great wardrobe. And he is everywhere you turn in this town of around 1,950.

Madison's J.F. Jacobson Park boasts a quite realistic statue of Mr. Fisk. Though larger than your average codfish, Lou's monument captures his codishness in all its spotted splendor, despite the tendency of locals to dress him up for special occasions in, say, a red beret. On U.S. Highway 75 as it passes through downtown, there's another Lou sculpture, this one carved out of a tree trunk. And the Madison watertower has a painting of Lou.

You can't escape this cute cod; he even shows up as a costumed character in local brochures and visitors' guides. In these, Lou wears overalls to help sell John Deere tractors, then changes to full fishing gear (traitor!) to promote the area's outdoor recreation. He dons lederhosen for Oktoberfest, and even shows up as a Minuteman (er, Minutefish) in a Chamber of Commerce write-up—presumably to show that he's an all-American lutefisk.

Madison celebrates its special affection for this cod dish at the Norsefest/Lutefisk Fest, held the second weekend in November. One of the biggest draws is the Lutefisk Eating Competition, and Jerry Osteraas has been the local champ since the late '80s. In 1989, his fame grew as he easily took the National Lutefisk Eating Contest championship (held in Poulsboro, Washington).

But it can get lonely at the top of the lutefisk-eating chain: In 1991, Madison had to cancel the contest because there were no challengers. In subsequent years, after much prodding, challengers have come forward, but Osteraas seems unbeatable. And as a local mascot, he's right up there with Lou T. Fisk. He and his family often dress in Norwegian garb and appear at regional parades and other events.

The festival is more than just an excuse to watch people shovel down cod. For instance, there's Lutefisk Madness! during which Madison stores slash prices and shoppers make a mad dash through the aisles to buy marked-down goodies. Then there's the big Lutefisk Supper, a banquet where festival-goers devour lutefisk, roast beef, and potatoes; it's followed by entertainment in the school gymnasium.

An outhouse race is another highlight that's recently been added to the roster of events. As described by the chamber of commerce, it "shows the strength of the big Norwegian guys who carry the outhouse through a maze, with one person sitting in it. What fun!"

To give the lutefisk its due, it's a high-protein dish that, considering it has been dried then soaked in lye, keeps very well for months—perfect for feeding the family during those cupboard-is-bare winter months back in the old country. And somehow—as often happens in a land where many a child grew up hearing grandparents' tales of the Old World—the lutefisk has become almost sacred in Minnesota as a food of the forebears.

Situated in southwestern Minnesota not far from the South Dakota border, Madison, which lies not far from Laq qui Parle (the Lake that Talks), was founded in 1885 by Norwegian, Swedish, and German settlers who came to America to farm. The town is a bit off the beaten track, something Madisonians don't seem to mind. As a brochure proudly proclaims, "Many communities in Minnesota are situated in high-traffic tourist areas. In contrast, Madison is parked right in the middle of the rich prairie lands." In other words, this is not your standard interstate exit kind of town.

But if you have a hankering for lutefisk, a trip to Madison is a must—if for no other reason than to pose for a photo with Lou T. Fisk.

## FOR FURTHER INFORMATION

**Madison Area Chamber of Commerce**
404 6th Ave.
Madison, MN 56256
(320) 598-7373, ext. 14

# ❂ Stuart, Florida

SAILFISH CAPITAL OF THE WORLD

For sportfishers, the sailfish is one of those great catches they dream about beforehand, exult in during, and brag about afterward. And Florida's Martin County, with its 100 miles of recreational waterways, is home to some of the best sailfishing in the world. One of the county's major recreation areas, Stuart, Florida, calls itself the Sailfish Capital of the World.

Situated on Florida's Treasure Coast, by the warm waters of the Gulf Stream and a variety of natural and man-made reefs, Stuart is a sportfisher's paradise. Though the sailfish are most abundant during the winter months (some are also caught in the summer), the waters are teeming year-round with other fish, including freshwater bass and sea trout, kingfish and bluefish.

Still, the sailfish is the area's big draw, and the Stuart Sailfish Club sponsors numerous tournaments to give fishermen and -women a sporting chance at competition. The largest of these is the annual Members Tournament, held the first weekend in January. Though a members-only event, outside contestants can join the club up to tournament time.

But Stuart's claim to fame has been a double-edged sword: The once plentiful fish, so prestigious a catch, were depleted by years of over-fishing. Nowadays, you're still welcome to reel in a sailfish, but not for the keeping. Good sports lucky enough to catch one of these graceful fish are now expected to tag them and send them back to sea for the future. Though there are times when a sportsman or -woman can keep the fish—notably if it's the first sailfish he or she has caught—most charter boats play by the accepted throwback rules unless there's good cause to do otherwise. Sportfishing, especially sailfishing, is one of Stuart's main industries, and fishing guides are wise about protecting their livelihood and that of future generations.

Sailfishing boats from the Stuart area often return with their signal flags flying to announce, "We caught him and we let him live." *Courtesy Gary Guertin, Pirates Cove Resort*

That's why you'll see many charters returning to port with a red flag raised proudly over the deck. It signifies "We caught him and we let him live." And in these waters, where the graceful sailfish still swims, it's a welcome signal that people are learning to wage a deathless battle for victory at sea.

Stuart has a variety of charter boat companies that specialize in sailfishing expeditions. Experienced captains and crews can teach novices the finer points of this special sport, which requires an unusually skilled and patient hand. Unlike most fish, sailfish often won't take the bait immediately; instead, they may try to stun it first with their swords, as they do with other prey. So fishermen and -women have to allow the bait to "play dead" for a few moments before striking and reeling in the catch, giving the sailfish time to think it has disoriented its prey before it takes the bait.

Perhaps it is this delicate game of cat and mouse that has traditionally made the challenge so enticing. A favorite fishing spot for presidents, the waters off Martin County have welcomed the rods of Teddy Roosevelt, Warren G. Harding, Chester Arthur, Grover Cleveland, and William Howard Taft.

## For Further Information

Stuart/Martin County Chamber of Commerce
1650 S. Kanner Hwy.
Stuart, FL 34994
(407) 287-1088

Stuart Sailfish Club
3178 SE Dixie Hwy.
Stuart, FL 34997
(407) 286-9373

# ⚙ Glynn County, Georgia

SEAFOOD CAPITAL OF THE WORLD

Nestled tightly to the edge of Georgia, just north of Florida, and tucked up against the Atlantic Ocean lie the coastal communities of Brunswick and the Golden Isles (Jekyll Island, St. Simons Island, Sea Island, and Little St. Simons Island). For most vacationers, they're either a much-anticipated golfing and sun-and-sand destination or the last stop before Florida (the mammoth Brunswick U.S.A. Interchange on I-95 is a motel, restaurant, and mall complex that's practically a city in itself).

But Glynn County, Georgia, which encompasses this lovely jumble of islands and waterfront towns, is also an industrious place, where the labor of shrimpers and factory hands is hardly a day at the beach. Between the hard-working shrimp fleet that sails from Brunswick and the five seafood packaging plants in the area, Glynn County has earned its bragging rights as the Seafood Capital of the World.

The communities of Glynn County are caught in a delicate balancing act between tourism as industry and industry as tourism. Recreational facilities—notably the growing collection of golf courses on the islands—have given the area a comfortable income from vacationing out-of-towners. But the county's hard-working heritage is still strong. A major point of pride is that Brunswick shipyards turned out many of World War II's Liberty Ships. So locals are happy to have their area recognized for more than golf and surf; and the Brunswick shrimping fleet is gaining a reputation as a tourist attraction in and of itself.

The shrimp caught in these coastal waters are a major component in the local seafood packagers' product lines, so it seems apt that Brunswick also calls itself Shrimp Capital of the World. More often, tourists on vacation stop by the wharves of Brunswick to watch the fleet at work.

As the fame of the local shrimp fleet grows, tourists have learned to show up at the Brunswick docks on Bay Street in the late afternoon, to watch the shrimp crews unload their daily catch and clean up the boats for another day.

One day in particular—Mother's Day—finds hundreds of tourists and locals crowding the waterfront to watch the traditional Blessing of the Shrimp Fleet, a ritual enacted not only in Brunswick but in other shrimp fishing areas around the South. This colorful parade of shrimp boats showing off their winter coats of paint and polish serves as the unofficial launch of the shrimping season, which runs from early June until about the end of February.

From the fleet ships, the shrimp goes to the packaging plants (the area has one of the country's largest concentrations of seafood proces-

Brunswick, Georgia's shrimping fleet is one of the nation's largest and puts on a colorful display during the fleet blessing in May. *Courtesy Brunswick & the Golden Isles of Georgia Visitors Bureau*

sors), and from there it's sold around the United States and the world. So next time you order a shrimp salad, think fondly of Glynn County and Brunswick, Georgia—and not just because you'd rather be golfing.

## FOR FURTHER INFORMATION

**Brunswick & The Golden Isles of Georgia Visitors Bureau**
4 Glynn Ave.
Brunswick, GA 31520
(912) 265-0620 or (800) 933-COAST

# CHAPTER 6

# ARTS AND CRAFTS AND CULTURE

he crafts and culture of our nation reflect our values and virtues, where we come from, and where we are going. In the sheen of a beautifully turned pot or the spicy tang of an ethnic meal, we can find our roots, both creative and cultural.

Towns across America take such pride in their local artisans that they proclaim themselves capitals in the name of their craft. Other communities, built by immigrants, celebrate their heritage with the sloganeering equivalent of dual citizenship, calling themselves the Swedish Capital of America or the Czech Capital of Oklahoma.

Of the American communities defined by the hand-hewn collectibles turned out by local artisans, one of the most renowned is **BEREA, KENTUCKY,** the Folk Arts and Crafts Capital of Kentucky. Home to the famed Berea College, where students work their way through school instead of paying tuition, Berea is known for the basketry, pottery, woodworking, and textiles made in the workshops of the college's Student Craft Industries, as well as for its numerous downtown artisans whose open-door studios offer visitors a chance to watch the creators at work.

Student crafters at Berea College in Berea, Kentucky, create useful and beautiful items to help work their way through school.
*Courtesy Berea College*

Asheville, North Carolina, is the Appalachian Folk Heritage Capital. It's home to numerous studios and boutiques, as well as to the Appalachian Folk Center. Opened in 1980, the center houses the Southern Highland Handicrafts Guild, whose crafters make quilts, leather goods, pottery, clothing, jewelry, and other decorative and useful goods. Asheville also hosts a number of Appalachian cultural events, including the Mountain Dance and Folk Festival, held the first week in August, and the Tell It in the Mountains storytelling festival in early September.

Another Southern town known for its crafts is Seagrove, North Carolina, the Pottery Capital of the World. As far back as the eighteenth century, European potters settled in this central North Carolina area, drawn by the red clay of local riverbanks, which pro-

Asheville, North Carolina, the Appalachian Folk Heritage Capital, is home to the stunning Folk Art Center. *Courtesy Price/McNabb and North Carolina Tourism Development Authority*

duced fine and functional pottery. Today, more than 60 potters still spin their wheels in and around Seagrove; their work is particularly popular as gifts, and many a southern bride registers her preferences with the local potters.

**HAVRE DE GRACE, MARYLAND,** is also famous for its crafts— though this Chesapeake Bay community's specialty is rather fowl. The Decoy Capital of the World, it's home to some of the world's finest waterfowl carvers, as well as to the Decoy Museum, which exhibits the best of their work. Havre de Grace's niche was carved by Madison Mitchell, considered one of the great decoy masters; his works and those of locals who followed are honored at the museum and during the annual decoy festival.

Monument, Colorado, has whittled a place for itself as the Carving Capital of America. It's home to the National Carver's Museum (on Woodcarvers Road), which showcases the best of this cutting-edge craft.

And speaking of woodcrafts, all those readers who fell in love with *The Bridges of Madison County* know only too well the magic of a romantic covered bridge. Though Iowa's Madison County may be a star of book and screen, it's Indiana's Parke County that bears the

Decoy Capital Havre de Grace, Maryland, has long been renowned for its master carvers. *Photo by George Hipkins, courtesy Havre de Grace Decoy Museum*

title of Covered Bridge Capital of the World. Home to 32 covered bridges, Parke County celebrates its timeless spans with an annual Covered Bridge Festival in October.

Another Indiana county is also renowned for its architectural wonders. Fulton County is the Round Barn Capital of the World. Such barns are a rarity, but just north of Rochester you can visit the Round Barn Museum to see one that was originally built in 1924. It was later damaged in a tornado and, after restoration, donated to the Fulton County Historical Society. Inside the museum, you'll discover a trove of local historical artifacts and exhibits, including displays on hometown hero Elmo Lincoln (the first movie Tarzan) and on the Cole Bros. Circus, which wintered in Fulton County between 1935 and 1940. And circle the second weekend in June on your calendar for Rochester's Round Barn Festival.

Another community where the architecture reflects the local craft is **WINONA, MINNESOTA,** the Stained Glass Capital of the United States. Home to five major stained glass factories, several of which you can tour, the Missouri River city sports an impressive collection of stained glass windows in its churches and business buildings.

The buildings of Hominy, Oklahoma, also are bedecked with local artwork. Known as the City of Murals, Hominy boasts more than 60 murals painted by Charles D. (Cha') Tullis, a Northern Blackfoot Indian and local jeweler and designer. The Mural Project began in 1990; though several paintings were destroyed in a 1994 fire, most still can be seen on building exteriors, depicting various Native American and local historical themes.

Those who prefer to decorate themselves may want to visit Gallup, New Mexico, the Indian Jewelry Capital of the World. Local

Native American artisans create silver and turquoise ornaments that are world-famous for their style and beauty. Their work is sold locally at more than 60 trading posts, galleries, and boutiques in and around Gallup.

Anadarko, Oklahoma, is another Native American capital. It calls itself the Indian Capital of the Nation and boasts a stellar collection of museums, cultural centers, and other attractions, including the National Hall of Fame for Famous American Indians and the Southern Plains Indian Museum. Anadarko is also home to Indian City, U.S.A., a re-creation of a Native American village, built as a living memorial to the area's native peoples. It stands on the site where a band of mercenaries massacred the Tonkawa Indians during the Civil War.

Anadarko is not alone in linking itself to its local ethnic heritage, but most other such capitals are related to imported cultures rather than native ones. One of the most famous is **SOLVANG, CALIFORNIA,** the Danish Capital of America. Founded in 1911 by Danish immigrants, the town held onto its culture in part by founding a folk school, which passed down traditions to the crucial first generation of American-born Solvangers. Solvang has turned its European charm into a major tourist draw. Aswirl with windmills and alive with Old World architecture, cuisine, and crafts, the town's carefully preserved and cultivated Danish heritage attracts a steady flow of visitors eager to experience its authentic charm.

The Midwest, in particular, has a plethora of communities whose roots are proudly revealed in their capital claims. Together, they read like a grand tour of Europe. Solvang has some competition in Dannebrog, the Danish Capital of Nebraska. And you'll find Swedish roots in Lindsborg, Kansas—Little Sweden, U.S.A. —and Stromsburg—Swedish Capital of Nebraska. And Czechoslovakian culture thrives in Wilbur, the Czech Capital of Nebraska, and Yukon, the Czech Capital of

## CYBERSPACE CONTACTS

# Immigrant Research Center

**http://www.umn.edu/ihrc/**

Looking for your roots? One of the world's best resources is the Immigrant History Research Center (IHRC), founded in 1965 at the University of Minnesota. Its Web site lets you search the IHRC library's collections and databases on-line for information on immigrants to America.

Oklahoma. And one of the nation's best St. Patrick's Day parties is in **O'NEILL, NEBRASKA,** the Irish Capital of Nebraska.

Why are there so many cultural and ethnic enclaves in the heartland? The prairies were often homesteaded by groups of immigrant families that traveled from the homeland to America, then headed west to the vast, uncultivated land available for settling in the nineteenth century. For all the talk of cowboys and Indians in the Wild West, it was more often than not these new immigrants from Germany and Sweden, Ireland and Poland, Czechoslovakia and Russia, among other nations, who transformed the West from open spaces to communities and farmlands.

During the late nineteenth and early twentieth centuries when America absorbed millions of newcomers, many of these immigrants also settled in the big cities of the East and the Midwest. They created urban ethnic cores—Chinatowns and Little Italys—where the language and culture of the homeland were passed down to future generations. The cultural capital communities share the same bloodlines as their city cousins—the only difference is that they had more room to spread out.

Then there are the towns with a tinge of place envy. Rather than recalling their own heritage, they invoke places whose very names hold a certain mystique. Take the allure of Athens. There's Athens, Georgia, most famous for its 1980s rock bands, but plenty of other places have Athenian aspirations: Waco calls itself the Athens of Texas, while Lexington, Kentucky (also called the Horse Capital of the World), is known as the Athens of the West. Fayetteville is the Athens of Arkansas, and Leonia calls itself the Athens of New Jersey. And Boston raises itself above all others by calling itself the Athens of America.

Some communities cast an envious eye on others within this nation. Two cases in point: Lincoln, Nebraska, the Hartford of the West, and Rapid City, South Dakota, the Denver of South Dakota.

The heritage and history of immigrant culture and the art and craft of creation often spotlight the unique talents and traditions of a town or city, giving it good cause to celebrate its special qualities.

# ✪ Solvang, California

DANISH CAPITAL OF AMERICA

When you think of California, you probably think of surfers and movie stars, rocky coasts and sandy beaches. Windmills and folk dancers don't usually come to mind. But that's just what you will find in the jewel-like town of Solvang, Danish Capital of America.

As if torn from a Hans Christian Andersen story, Solvang is a puff pastry of a town, with Danish architecture (brown wood with white trim, resembling Tudor style), sweet shops, and windmills galore. And it has fashioned this old-fashioned, Old World charm into a major tourist attraction. Thousands of visitors flock to Solvang, 35 miles north of Santa Barbara on Highway 154, to enjoy its European ambiance.

Yet Solvang is a surprisingly modern community; it was founded in 1911 by Danish immigrants, who re-created a typical Danish village on Spanish land-grant acreage. The California sunshine inspired the town's name, which means sunny fields in Danish.

Wherever you turn in Solvang, you feel as if you're in another country. Many of the locals who work in the town's shops and

Solvang, California's Old World architecture reveals its roots as the Danish Capital of America.
*Courtesy Solvang Conference & Visitors Bureau*

restaurants wear traditional Danish folk costumes. Danish souvenirs abound. And the tasty treats to be found in the numerous bakeries explain why sweet pastries are dubbed "danish."

Those pastries star in the annual Taste of Solvang festival, held in mid-March to celebrate the local goodies. From the Dessert Showcase (a local ballroom filled with yummies) to the World's Largest Danish (served in Solvang Park), the tempting tastes of Danish specialties leave festivalgoers well stuffed.

The other big Danish festivity of the year takes place the third week of September, when Solvang hosts Danish Days. Dating back to 1936, the event celebrates food, music, dance, and entertainment from Denmark.

Solvang's museum scene also reflects its Danish heritage. The Elverhøj Museum is a local and Danish history collection. Guides (again, in Danish folk costumes) lead you through the collection, which is housed in a ski chalet–style building that was once home to one of Solvang's most prominent and artistic families, the Brandt-Erichsens. Their 1950 home, designed in the style of an eighteenth-century Danish farmhouse, was renovated in 1987 to house the museum. There you'll see collections of exhibits on the Danish-American experience and on the founding of Solvang. The museum's name is derived from a popular Danish folk play, Elverhøj—meaning "elves on a hill"—about a king's visit to the world of lovely wood sprites.

Solvang also has a museum devoted to the life and times of Denmark's storytelling master, Hans Christian Andersen (1805–1875). Operated by the Ugly Duckling Foundation (named for one of Andersen's most famous stories) and devoted to preserving and disseminating his work, the Hans Christian Andersen Museum contains illustrations and settings inspired by his stories, as well as first editions of his works and other artifacts from his time. One surprising exhibit highlights his charming work as an artist; most people don't realize he was also an inspired illustrator. Another touching

Solvang's windmills are land-
mark remembrances of the
Old Country left behind.
*Courtesy Solvang Conference &
Visitors Bureau*

display focuses on the famous singer Jenny Lind, the "Swedish Nightingale," for whom Andersen experienced a long but unrequited love. He never married.

Though Danish culture predominates in Solvang, evidence survives of the town's earlier European inhabitants, the Spanish. Old Mission Santa Inés, founded in 1804, is touted as the Hidden Gem of the California Spanish Missions; the property is now an historic site where visitors can learn the story of the mission and its village. The 19th of the 22 missions built in California by Spanish Franciscan priests, Santa Inés was the first European settlement in the Santa Ynez Valley. Like other missions, it was established to colonize the area and convert the natives to Catholicism. Though much of the mission was destroyed in an 1812 earthquake, some portions, including the chapel, were rebuilt. It's one of only a handful of Spanish Mission chapels in continuous use since 1817.

America has its share of replicated European villages—indeed, theme park companies such as Disney take great pride in building little bits of the Old World into their New World attractions. But long before Uncle Walt dreamt of constructing Cinderella's castle in an orange grove, a group of Danes added a touch of their homeland to the California landscape. To this day, Solvang is truly and enchantingly the Danish Capital of America.

## FOR FURTHER INFORMATION

### General Information

**Solvang Chamber of Commerce**
P.O. Box 465
Solvang, CA 93463
(805) 688-0701

**Solvang Conference &**
**Visitor's Bureau**
1511-A Mission Dr.
Solvang, CA 93463
(800) GO-SOLVANG

### Attractions and Events

**Danish Days Foundation**
P.O. Box 1474
Solvang, CA 93464
(805) 686-9386

**Old Mission Santa Inés**
1760 Mission Dr.
Solvang, CA 93463
(805) 688-4815

**Elverhøj Museum**
1624 Elverhoj Way
P.O. Box 769
Solvang, CA 93464
(805) 686-1211

**Taste of Solvang**
Contact Conference
& Visitor's Bureau

**Hans Christian Andersen Museum**
1680 Mission Dr.
Solvang, CA 93463
(805) 688-2052

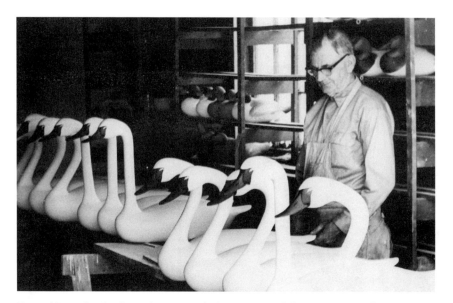

The crafting styles that have given Havre de Grace its capital claim are preserved in images such as this 1973 *photograph from the Decoy Museum. Photo by George Hipkins, courtesy Havre de Grace Decoy Museum*

# ✿ Havre de Grace, Maryland

DECOY CAPITAL OF THE WORLD

F akery, when done to perfection, is an art that can surpass the original in form and function. This is certainly the case with bird decoys, the best of which are sometimes more prized than the birds they are ostensibly used to hunt. And the best decoys are said to come from Havre de Grace, Maryland, the Decoy Capital of the World.

This small town, perched at the convergence of the Susquehanna River and the Chesapeake Bay, gained its decoy destiny through the carefully carved creations of its resident decoy artists, among them Madison Mitchell, considered an American master of the art form.

The Havre de Grace Decoy Museum, housed in a stucco building that was once a service structure for the old Bayou Villa Hotel next door (now luxury apartments), includes complete collections of decoys crafted by Madison Mitchell, Paul Gibson, Charlie Joiner, Charlie Bryant, and other artisans, along with exhibits of decoy-mak-

The Concord Point Lighthouse marks the spot where British invaders landed to sack and burn the town in 1813.
*Courtesy Havre de Grace Decoy Museum*

ing tools. The museum also hosts the annual Decoy, Wildlife Art & Sportsman Festival, held the first weekend in May, and the annual Duck Fair in September, where the best of old and new decoy art is celebrated.

Hunters and collectors come to Havre de Grace year-round to see the famous fakes and to buy new ones in the town's shops. Local artisans enjoy a national reputation, and often travel to shows and events around the country to sell their work.

An historic town, Havre de Grace dates back to the eighteenth century. Already a major community in the late 1700s, it was a serious contender to become the nation's capital; Congress decided to build a new federal city instead. Havre de Grace's downtown district still boasts many historic homes and buildings, including the handsome Rodgers House, a brick townhouse said to be the community's oldest surviving structure; built in 1787, it was visited by George Washington several times. Another architectural gem is the quirky

Harrison Hopkins House, built in 1868, which features eccentric, multilevel roof planes.

The majority of structures in the town post-date the War of 1812, for in 1813, more than half of Havre de Grace was destroyed by the British, who sailed up the Chesapeake and landed at Concord Point, where, under the command of Admiral Cockburn, they sacked and burned the town on May 3. Defended by two small batteries—one manned almost singlehandedly by the brave John O'Neill, still considered a local hero—Havre de Grace stood little chance against such formidable forces. The site where Cockburn's soldiers landed is memorialized by a stone marker in front of the town's historic white lighthouse at Concord Point, where the Bay meets the Susquehanna River.

Another Bay community, St. Michaels, Maryland, is said to have avoided a similar fate by blacking out the town and hanging lanterns high in the trees to confuse the enemy; when the British sailed in under cover of darkness, they fired on the lights, sheering off treetops but leaving the town intact.

The British may have burned it, but Havre de Grace regained its composure and rebuilt the community—as did Washington, D.C., after Cockburn's forces sacked and burned it in August 1814. Today, Havre de Grace is truly a lovely historic community with a solid hometown heritage—not some decoy.

## FOR FURTHER INFORMATION

### General Information

**Havre de Grace Chamber of Commerce**
P.O. Box 339
Havre de Grace, MD 21078
(410) 939-3303 or (800) 851-7756

### Attractions and Events

**Havre de Grace Decoy Museum**
100 Giles St.
Havre de Grace, MD 21078
(410) 939-3739

**Havre de Grace Decoy, Wildlife Art & Sportsman Festival and Annual Duck Fair**
Contact the Decoy Museum

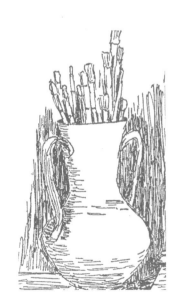

## ⊛ Berea, Kentucky

### FOLK ARTS AND CRAFTS CAPITAL OF KENTUCKY

S ome communities are forever changed by the institutions within them; this is particularly true of college towns. And, if the college happens to be as unique as Berea College in Berea, Kentucky, the institution affects not only its hometown but also the world at large. Berea College is an unusual tuition-free liberal arts institution where students work off their studies in a training-intensive work/study program.

Both Berea and its namesake college are renowned for their craftspeople, who turn out lovingly handmade items, from candles and ceramics to furniture and stained glass. To honor this tradition, the Kentucky legislature proclaimed the town the Folk Arts and Crafts Capital of Kentucky.

Berea College's student crafters make everything from brooms to baskets and placemats to pottery. *Courtesy Berea College*

Berea's crafters work in studios that are open to the public, so a visitor to Berea's Old Town can view workshop after workshop, seeing firsthand how the local artisans create their wares.

Though individual artisans and their work have gained Berea national acclaim, the community is also home to larger producers of crafts. One of the major companies in town is Churchill Weavers, which produces blankets, scarves, and other high-quality woven goods. Founded in 1922 by Carroll Churchill, an industrial engineer, and his wife Eleanor, a teacher, the company is still run by a couple handpicked by Mrs. Churchill. And like other weavers in town, Churchill invites visitors to watch its crafters at work. Free self-guided factory tours include a stop in the loomhouse, where weavers work at the handmade looms that date back to the company's founding. You can also shop at Churchill's factory outlet store.

Nestled in the foothills of the Cumberland Mountains, Berea is a community of around 9,125. It was founded in 1854 by the Reverend John Gregg Fee, an abolitionist fresh from divinity school in Cincinnati, who came to the slave state of Kentucky hoping to make a difference. He settled in the hill country of Lane County, where few if any slaves were held and where the people were more progressive in their views on the subject.

Another abolitionist, a flamboyant Kentuckian named Cassius Clay, sold Fee the land on which the community was built. Clay's elaborate Italianate mansion, White Hall, is now a historic house museum; it's situated 20 miles north of Berea, just off I-75.

In 1855, Fee was instrumental in founding Berea College as the South's first interracial college, encouraging students to learn and work together in a unique experiment that has become an institution. Its College Labor Program provides free tuition to all students—a Berea education costs around $13,000 per student—who are largely from the economically disadvantaged southern Appalachian region.

The school, which still operates under many of Fee's guidelines (including his wish that it remain a Christian institution), maintains an enrollment of 1,500 students drawn from applicants who can prove financial need. They are involved in a variety of work/study fields, from crafts to innkeeping. The popular 59-room Boone Tavern Hotel, opened in 1909 by the college, is still run by Berea students. The hotel's restaurant is also one of the community's finest dining rooms, and here, too, the students do the cooking and wait tables.

The College's Student Craft Industries employ about 15 percent of the students, who learn skills and produce sellable goods in such arts as broom making, pottery, weaving, woodcraft, and wrought ironwork. The program evolved from the Homespun Fairs held on campus in the late nineteenth century, where the parents of students came to sell handmade items to help pay for their children's education. Soon, the students were making their own tuition costs back by crafting goods themselves.

The Log House Sales Room at Berea College sells the crafts, textiles, and other creations of the students. *Courtesy Berea College*

Today, visitors can buy items made by Berea students at the Log House Sales Room on College Square. College Square, on the edge of campus, is also home to many crafters' studios.

Like those of local artisans, the college studios are open to the public so visitors can see the students at work. Many graduates stay in the community, joining the dozens of other craftspeople whose workshops give Berea its unique artist-at-work atmosphere. The college also operates the Appalachian Museum, which covers the history and culture of Appalachia as well as the school's own background and legacy.

The community hosts several major crafts festivals a year, drawing tens of thousands of collectors, designers, and art lovers who travel into the hills to see and buy the best that this talented community of artists has to offer.

## FOR FURTHER INFORMATION

### General Information

**Berea Tourist and Convention Commission**
201 N. Broadway
P.O. Box 556
Berea, KY 40403
(606) 986-2540

**Berea College**
CPO 2316
Berea, KY 40403
(606) 986-9341 or (800) 457-9846

## Attractions and Events

**Churchill Weavers**
100 Churchill Dr.
Lorraine Court
Berea, KY 40403
(606) 986-3127

**Crafts Festivals**
Contact the Berea Tourist and Convention Commission

# ✿ O'Neill, Nebraska

IRISH CAPITAL OF NEBRASKA

Here in Hay Country, as this section of northern Nebraska is known, you expect to find places such as Emmet, known as the Biggest Little Haytown in the World. But a heartland home for leprechaun-lovers? That's right. O'Neill, Nebraska, is the Irish Capital of Nebraska.

Nebraska, and the Midwest in general, are replete with communities that have created a capital claim out of their ethnic heritage. From Yukon, Oklahoma (the Czech Capital of Oklahoma), to Loupe, Nebraska (the Polish Capital of Nebraska), you can tell a lot about a place by the people who settled it, especially if their homeland traditions are still practiced today. And in O'Neill, this is certainly the case. Founded by an Irishman who made a concerted effort to bring his heritage to bear on the place, you could almost call it a planned ethnic enclave.

The idea for the city started as a kernel of hope in the mind of General John O'Neill, a Civil War veteran, while he was living in Burlington, Vermont, in 1871. He saw the desperation of the Irish immigrants who were so badly treated when they arrived in New England (Boston was a major immigration destination for the Irish).

The historic Kinkaid Building, now a museum and historical society headquarters, as it looked in 1884. *Courtesy Holt County Historical Society*

O'Neill conceived of a better place for his people in the Midwest, where they could farm or mine the land without the prejudices of the overcrowded eastern cities.

His idea became a dream, one that he wrote home to Ireland about. "I have always believed that the next best thing to giving the Irish people their freedom at home is to encourage such of them as to come to this country either from choice or from necessity to take up land and build homes in America."

In 1872 and 1873, O'Neill combed the Midwest in search of a place to lead his intended flock. He traveled through Illinois, Missouri, Wisconsin, and Minnesota. And then, in the prairie state of Nebraska, he found the perfect place. O'Neill made a deal with a pair of land agents to develop a townsite.

In 1874, he headed back east to Pennsylvania, where he traveled among the Irish miners, selling them on the idea of relocating to his new town in Nebraska, which was to be settled by and for Irish immigrants. "Why are you content to work on the public projects," O'Neill would lecture his rapt audiences, "when you might in a few years own farms of your own and become wealthy and influential people?" The first converts to O'Neill's dream began arriving on May 12, 1874.

Those early settlers had a difficult time; a lack of housing forced the first group of O'Neill pioneers to share a sod house they built together—they dubbed it the Grand Central Hotel—to provide shelter for their new community of 13 men, 2 women, and 5 children. And a severe drought the first year made farming a difficult proposition at best.

But O'Neill persevered; he traveled east again, recruiting more colonists. And slowly, the little community grew. O'Neill became so successful at talking up his settlement that he helped found two other towns nearby—Atkinson and Greeley—as Irish farming communities. And O'Neill's work inspired another Irishman, Moses P. Kinkaid, to further open up the area to settlers. Kinkaid, a U.S. senator, introduced the 1904 Kinkaid Land Act, which increased the amount of land given to homesteaders in the early twentieth cenutry. The historic Kinkaid Bank Building in O'Neill, where Kinkaid had his law offices, is now operated by the Holt County Historical Society.

Another Irishman of note who spent some quality time in O'Neill and went on to change the country was Father Flanagan, founder of Omaha's famed Boys Town youth complex. After being ordained in 1912 at the University of Innsbruck in the Alps, the Irish-born Flanagan was assigned his first post as an assistant pastor in O'Neill. Five years later, he founded his Father Flanagan's Boys Home in Omaha, which later became Boys Town.

Today's O'Neill still has its roots planted firmly in the Emerald Isle. The community of around 4,000 celebrates a blockbuster St. Patrick's Day with all the greenery and trimmings. Some 20,000 people come to O'Neill for the big day, with festivities that include the crowning of the Irish king and queen, dining on traditional Irish food, performances by Irish dancers, and a bright green parade. During the party, the townspeople traipse over to the intersection of Highways 20 and 281 to paint the World's Largest Shamrock—giving cause for the community's other nickname, Shamrock City.

It was on St. Patrick's Day, 1969, that Governor Norbert Tiemann officially proclaimed O'Neill the Irish Capital of Nebraska. Three years later, to the day, another Nebraska governor, J. James Exon, dedicated an historical marker with the same capital claim; and on St. Patrick's Day, 1977, the Nebraska legislature passed a resolution again making O'Neill the state's official Irish Capital. O'Neill has held firm to its emerald roots through its first century and will no doubt stay as green and inviting into the next.

## FOR FURTHER INFORMATION

**O'Neill Area Chamber of Commerce**
315 E. Douglas St.
O'Neill, NE 68763
(402) 336-2355

**Holt County Historical Society**
Kinkaid Bldg.
401 E. Douglas St.
O'Neill, NE 68763
(402) 336-2344

# ⚙ Winona, Minnesota

STAINED GLASS CAPITAL
OF THE UNITED STATES

There's a certain magic in the way stained glass projects shards of colored light, whether through church windows or lamp shades. Both an art and a craft, the creation of stained and other art glasses requires patience, skill, and thick skin; and the artisans of Winona, Minnesota, Stained Glass Capital of the United States, have all these in abundance.

Winona is home to six major art glass factories: Hauser Art Glass Co., Conway Universal Studios, Cathedral Crafts, Decker Stained Glass Studios, Jon-Lee Art Glass, and Reinart's Stained Glass Studio. Though the largest of these, Hauser—which, with its sister company, the Willet Studios of Philadelphia, forms the country's largest stained glass maker—recently filed for bankruptcy protection, Winona is still home to a thriving art glass industry.

The stained glass studios of this city of 26,000 on the banks of the Mississippi River have produced windows for prominent structures around the world. Reinart's, in business since the 1940s, has made windows for the Vatican Chapel in Jerusalem, and Hauser, founded in 1946 by James E. Hauser, has produced windows for structures as varied as the National Cathedral in Washington, D.C., Forest Lawn Cemetery in Los Angeles, and the Children's Research Hospital in Krakow, Poland.

Winona's art glass industry dates back to the late nineteenth century, and today, many of its studios still create windows using the time-tested methods of a century ago. Visitors can see the old-fashioned art of stained glassmaking on tours offered by two local factories: Conway Universal Studios of Stained Glass and Cathedral Crafts, Inc. Conway opened its doors in 1940, and makes stained glass using the traditional methods of kiln firing and leading. Cathedral Crafts also uses old-fashioned glass-cutting and glazing techniques. During its tour, you'll also see artists demonstrating stained glass window design and stained glass painting.

But you don't have to take a factory tour to see the evidence of Winona's glass-making heritage. Throughout the city, magnificent stained glass windows adorn many office buildings, banks, and churches. Some of the finest examples are visible in the J.R. Watkins Co. Administration Building (150 Liberty Street). When the building was constructed in 1912, after designs by renowned Chicago architect George W. Maher, it was thought

On the banks and bluffs of the Mississippi River, Winona is home to some of the nation's top stained glass crafters. *Photo by Kay Shaw, courtesy Winona Convention & Visitors Bureau*

 to be the world's finest private office building. One reason was the extraordinary window over the main entrance, which depicts Winona's famous Sugar Loaf Mountain in a naturalistic design reminiscent of the flowing work of Louis Comfort Tiffany. This window was created by Louis J. Millet, a frequent collaborator with both Maher and another famed Chicago architect, Louis Sullivan.

Another Maher-designed building, the Winona National Bank (204 Main St.), completed in 1916, boasts lovely windows from the famed Tiffany Studios themselves. The building was designed in the Egyptian Revival style, a sort of Art Deco exotica, and the detailing and windows match this mood. The Tiffany glass is a rich compendium of abstract lotus plants and bamboo-like trellises, so delicate they look as though they were just picked from a crystal garden.

Some of the earliest stained glasswork still visible is at the Winona County Courthouse (3rd Street, west of Johnson Street), a towering edifice built in 1889, which features windows created by the local studios of C.G. Maybury & Son. Done in the late Victorian style, the windows feature decorative floral and fan patterns in hues still surprisingly deep and vibrant more than a century later.

Another highlight in this city of windows are the marvelous geometric panels at the Merchants National Bank (102 E. 3rd St.). Completed in 1912, the windows reflect Frank Lloyd Wright's colorfully square Prairie School style—the artist, George Elmslie, is considered second only to Wright in this design school.

The Winona County Historical Society also has some wonderful windows, by a local artist, Ed Glubka of Conway Studios, depicting Winona County history; and the city's many churches have a wealth of the colorful windows. The Visitors Bureau is happy to hand out guides that point the way to these sites. And while you're seeing the sights, pick up a copy of the Historic Downtown Walking Tour, which points out landmarks in Winona's vintage Victorian downtown area, many of which are listed on the National Register of Historic Places.

Winona is known for more than beautiful glass, though, as Al Thurley, director of the Winona Convention & Visitors Bureau, points out. The community has a long list of unique claims; for instance, Winona is also home to Watkins, a major spice company, which once had a sales force of so-called Watkins men who traveled by horse and wagon, selling spices to farm wives. "The area around the Administration Building and factory, which occupy one block in Winona, really smells great when they're making one of those spices," Thurley says. The company also has a Heritage Museum and an outlet store where curious cooks can learn a little corporate history and spice up their shopping.

And in the historical trivia department, Winona has a humdinger: It's home to the only Revolutionary War soldier buried in Minnesota. "His name was Stephen Taylor," Thurley explains. "I'm still not sure how he ended up here. I haven't been able to figure that one out yet." Nevertheless, Taylor is buried in a local cemetery.

Winona was, and remains, a river city. In 1805, when explorer Zebulon Pike first came upon the river bluff landscape that would one day be Winona, he declared it a "...sublime and beautiful prospect." Nearly a half-century later, the community was founded on this lovely spot, in 1851, by a steamboat captain.

Winona grew rich in the 1880s as a lumber and industrial center. As its wealth increased, some of the finest architects of their time were hired to design buildings, and the stained glass industry first came to Winona as a result of creating windows for these magnificent new edifices. The artisans who came to work on Winona's buildings sometimes stayed to settle in the community. A renaissance in stained glass repair and creation in the 1940s, sparked by the neglect many churches suffered during World War II, gave new life to the industry; today's batch of studios dates from that postwar era.

Another important element in Winona's heritage is its riverboats; today, a new generation of these graceful vessels ply the waters, with pleasure cruise boats such as the *Julia Belle Swain* steamboat, the *Mississippi Queen* steamboat, the *Delta Queen* steamboat, and the *American Queen* steamboat docking frequently in Winona.

The city celebrates its steamboat heritage at the annual Steamboat Days festival, held in early July. And riverboat history is preserved at the *Julius C. Wilkie* Steamboat Museum, docked at Levee Park. The ship itself, the *Julius C. Wilkie*, is a replica of an earlier museum vessel that burned in 1981. This new boat, completed in 1982, includes some of the elements salvaged from its predecessor, including the twin smokestacks and paddle wheel. The ship itself is a museum, displaying a variety of exhibits, including boat models, artifacts, and a beautiful stained glass window of a riverboat in full steam.

Though Winona's past may be up the river, its future, at least in self-promotion, lies on another conduit—the information highway. The city has a Web site with community information, so cyber-tourists can visit Winona without leaving home. But stained glass still looks better in natural light.

## FOR FURTHER INFORMATION

### General Information

Winona Convention & Visitors Bureau
67 Main St.
P.O. Box 870
Winona, MN 55987
(507) 452-2272 or (800) 657-4972

### Attractions and Events

Cathedral Crafts, Inc.
730 54th Ave.
Winona, MN 55987
(507) 454-4079

Conway Universal Studios
of Stained Glass
503 Center St.
Winona, MN 55987
(507) 452-9209

Julius C. Wilkie Steamboat
Museum
Main St. at the Levee
Winona, MN 55987
(507) 454-1254

Steamboat Days
Winona Area Jaycees
P.O. Box 308
Winona, MN 55987

# SPORTS AND PASTIMES

he way we spend our leisure time says as much about us as the way we make our living. For some, relaxation means a weekend of canoeing; for others, it's epitomized by a day of outlet shopping. What's restful for one makes another restless; and one person's excitement is another's boredom. But from pleasurable pastimes to stimulating sports, America's love affair with leisure is as strong as ever. And there's a friendly clutch of capital communities eager to share their own special recreational opportunities.

In resort and wilderness areas dependent on family vacationers and sports enthusiasts, a catchy slogan or claim to fame can boost a town above the heads of other places competing for those same tourist dollars. The right recreational incentive can lure enthusiasts from great distances to do their thing—be it windsurfing or backpacking, water skiing, or snowmobiling—in the world capital for

Historic Cedar Point Amusement Park in Sandusky, Ohio, in a photo from the 1930s. *Courtesy Rutherford B. Hayes Presidential Center, Fremont, Ohio, Charles E. Frohman Collection*

their sport. Plus, being, say, the Thrill Ride Capital of the World (as is Cedar Point Amusement Park in Sandusky, Ohio) projects a sense of fun and enjoyment that paints a beaming portrait of the locals and their hometown.

America has so many sporting capitals that it takes stamina just to read the list. No matter what your sport, you'll find at least one place that claims to be the champion. From Eugene, Oregon—the Track Capital of the World (Nike "just did it" there first)—to Killington, Vermont, the Learning to Ski Capital of the World (home to the world-famous Killington Ski School)—sports capitals across the nation welcome participants of all levels from amateurs to pros.

Golf is perhaps the most capitalized sport in America, with more world capitals than a course has holes. You can putt your way across the country, from Myrtle Beach, North Carolina (the Seaside Golf Capital of America), to Pebble Beach, California (Golf Capital of the World). Pinehurst, North Carolina, Orland Park, Illinois, and even the entire state of Ohio also play through with the title of Golf Capital of the World.

All-season sports lovers can head to West Yellowstone, Montana, which has both warm and cold activities on tap. It's known as the Trout Fishing and Snowmobiling Capital of the World, because in the summer it's a great place for fishing and in the winter, the snowmo-bile trails into Yellowstone Park are outstanding. Or how about America's favorite pastime, played with an icy spin in Lake Tomahawk, Wisconsin, the Snowshoe Baseball Capital of the World?

No matter what the season, Florida's year-round warmth has cre-ated waves of watery world capitals. Ft. Lauderdale is the Boating Capital of the World, a nicely vague claim that covers the gamut of craft that frequent the busy port resort. Bigger boaters steer a course for Miami, the Cruise Capital of the World: the Port of Miami has more scheduled cruise ship departures than any other port in the world.

For spectators and participants alike, Winter Haven, Florida, is the Water Ski Capital of the World. It's home to Cypress Gardens, the celebrated attraction renowned for its acrobatic water skiers. Winter Haven also boasts the Water Ski Hall of Fame, which features a col-lection of costumes, skis, memorabilia, and paintings honoring the best of these well-balanced athletes. For a slower, drier pace, shuffle over to Lake Worth, Florida, the Shuffleboard Capital of the World; the National Shuffleboard Hall of Fame is on the other coast, how-ever, in St. Petersburg.

Yachters, meanwhile, have their pick of capitals, both in New England: Newport, Rhode Island, is the Yachting Capital of the World, while Marblehead, Massachusetts, is the Yachting Capital of America. They each lay claim to a capital title thanks to the America's Cup race—it was raced off the coast of Marblehead first, then later sailed south to Newport.

For fans of inland water sports, **ELY, MINNESOTA,** is the Canoe Capital of the World, thanks to its proximity to the Boundary Waters Canoe Area Wil-derness, home of some 14,000 square miles of waterways and lakes. Ely area outfitters provide canoers with all the essen-tials for their wet and wild adventures.

Even wilder is Salmon, Idaho, the Whitewater Capital of the World. The community was once a winter camp for such famous trappers and adventurers as Kit Carson and Jim Bridger. Situated at the forks of the Lemhi and the Salmon Rivers, it now serves as the launch point for rafting trips into the River of No Return Wilderness Area, the largest single wilderness area in the contiguous United States. The frightening moniker came from the ultimate adventure travel team, Lewis and Clark; but the Salmon's outfitters have good track records in bringing even their most white knuckled of rafters back in one piece.

For those who want to ride the wind above the waves, the Outer Banks of North Carolina are known as the Windsurfing Capital of the World. The area gained initial fame for another kind of windsurfing. It is the site of the first manned flight of the Wright Brothers, who launched their plane into the wind from the sandy dunes of Kitty Hawk in 1903. They chose the site in part on the advice of the local postmaster, William J. Tate, who, in 1899, wrote the Wrights to suggest the Outer Banks "would be a fine place [to test the contraption]; our winds are always steady generally from 10 to 20 miles velocity per hour . . . If you decide to try your [flying] machine here, I assure you . . . you will find a hospitable people when you come among us."

Today, the high flying is done atop the waves; even beginning windsurfers can pick up the sport like a breeze by taking classes from one of the many local shops that offer classes. Out West, windsurfers catch the currents that race up the Columbia River Gorge near the town of Hood River, Oregon, an area that likewise lays claim to the Windsurfing Capital title. The colorful parade of wind-

Kites on the beach are a blustery sight year-round at Lincoln City, Oregon, the Kite Capital of the World. *Courtesy Lincoln City Visitor and Convention Bureau*

surfing sails bobbing up and down the river give credence to the boast.

Oregon is such a breezy state that it could well call itself the wind sports capital of America. Lincoln City, Oregon, has the high-flying title of Kite Capital of the World, and was voted North America's best kite-flying location by *Kitelines Magazine.* Why is this such a windy city? According to Terri Cowling of the Lincoln City Visitor & Convention Bureau, "Lincoln City sits right on the 45th parallel, positioning it at the ideal point in the mixing process of the warm equatorial air and the cold polar air."

The title comes with a few strings attached, too: Lincoln City hosts annual Spring and Fall Kite Festivals and the Stunt Kite Championships, which attract thousands of kite enthusiasts from around the world. And what do they fly when they get there? Chances are, it's a kite from Catch the Wind, which manufactures kites at a local factory but sells them nationally. Catch the Wind invented the popular "spin sock" kite design now twirling at a beach near you; they also created the giant 90-foot spin sock and kite displays that have become landmarks of Lincoln City's breezy beach.

And while wrist-work can be the key to keeping that kite aloft, another wrist activity is the claim for Petaluma, California, which is gaining a reputation as the Wrist-Wrestling Capital of the World. It's home to the World's Wrist-Wrestling Championships in October, hosting more than 200 competitors from around the world. And after they've worked up an appetite, wrestlers can rest their wrists in one of Petaluma's 142 restaurants—a number that has gained the community the title of Restaurant Capital.

For those who really just like to watch, **BANDON, OREGON,** has been called the Storm Watching Capital of the World. The town is situated at the confluence of the Coquille River and the Pacific Ocean; and when the weather whips up the waves, it's a dramatic place to witness Mother Nature's blustery wrath. There's even a storm watcher's club, which is really more about promoting the town than about watching the weather, but its members are the first to grab their binoculars when the barometer begins to fall.

Another windy pastime, one that the Wright Brothers would surely have applauded, is soaring, and **ELMIRA, NEW YORK,** is the Soaring Capital of America. Visitors come to the National Soaring

Elmira is the final resting place for one of America's greatest writers, Mark Twain. *Courtesy Chemung County Chamber of Commerce*

Museum to explore the history of free-floating flight, and to take off themselves from the adjacent airport, which offers soaring rides. Those who prefer to stay grounded can stroll New York State's largest collection of Victorian architecture in a single district, or visit Mark Twain's Study and the Mark Twain Exhibit at Elmira College. Twain had a home in Elmira and wrote many of his famous works there. He's also buried in Elmira.

Literary pursuits are among the more cerebral ways we spend our leisure time, and those who do a lot of reading are inevitably tough competitors in trivia competitions. They're just the type to win it all at Appleton, Wisconsin, the unofficial Trivia Capital of the World, where the Midwest Trivia Contest is held annually.

Another game that has been capitalized as both a claim to local fame and a popular athletic activity is rope jumping. Bloomer, Wisconsin, the Rope Jumping Capital of the World, hosts the Annual Speed Rope Jumping Championship every January. The founder of rope jumping as a sport, Wally Mohrman, was a local physical education teacher.

Another fun pursuit that keeps kids of all ages howling with joy (or fear) is roller-coaster riding. No amusement park keeps riders happy better than **SANDUSKY, OHIO'S CEDAR POINT,** the Thrill Ride Capital of the World. It's home to 12 roller coasters, the world's largest collection, and is frequently voted tops in thrill rides by roller-coaster enthusiasts worldwide.

For those who prefer going 'round and 'round instead of up and down, Jacksonville, Illinois, is the place to go. It's the Ferris Wheel

Capital of the World, and it's home base for the Eli Bridge Co., which has been manufacturing Ferris wheels since 1900. The company's founder, W. E. Sullivan, saw the world's first Ferris wheel (created by George Ferris) at Chicago's Columbian Exposition in 1893. Wheels immediately began turning in Sullivan's mind: "I went to the Wheel and inquired of the ticket seller if they allowed visitors to examine the mechanism," Sullivan later wrote. "As well as I recollect, his answer was that if I bought a ticket, I could go in and examine it all I wanted."

Examine it he did; the mechanically minded Sullivan rushed home and told his wife he had found the machine he wanted to build. It took him years, but, after leasing a bridge factory in Jacksonville, Sullivan set to work on spinning his dream into reality; in 1900, his Big Eli Wheel (45 feet high, with 12 buggy seats for passengers) was completed, becoming the first of many Ferris wheels the company was to produce for America's midways. Today, the company's wheels still spin in amusement parks the world over.

Fun seekers have their pick of myriad capitals across the country. With so many amusement parks to choose from—Disney and Universal Studios are but the largest—Orlando, Florida, promotes itself as the Attractions Capital of the World.

For sheer laughs, happy faces abound in Bernardstown, Massachusetts, the Clown Capital of the World. Baraboo, Wisconsin, a.k.a. Circus City, was once a major circus winter quarter town, and still has a number of the original circus buildings, including the elephant barns. That midway spirit is perfectly captured at its Baraboo's Circus World attraction, featuring big top performers, side-shows, and the world's largest collection of circus wagons. Likewise, Peru, Indiana, calls itself the Circus Capital of the World because of its big top heritage.

Some folks like to get into the act themselves. Take the denizens of McAllen, Texas, which pro-

---

**DID YOU KNOW...**

**Big Top Treats**
Baraboo, Wisconsin's Circus World may be a midway marvel, but several other circus cities also boast three-ring attractions. Bridgeport, Connecticut, P.T. Barnum's hometown, has the delightful Barnum Museum, and Sarasota, Florida, once the winter camp of the Greatest Show on Earth, draws crowds for the John & Mable Ringling Museum of Art's Circus Collection of posters and other memorabilia.

motes itself as the Square Dance Capital of the World. Every year, the Rio Grande Valley community's population swells with the influx of "Winter Texans" (snowbirds from the Midwest), who flock there for the warmth, the relaxation—and the square dancing. You can dance the night away seven days a week in McAllen, which has enough dance clubs and social halls to make even a Virginian reel.

Then again, if those Winter Texans stayed home up north, they'd still find plenty of joint-jerking rhythm in Chicago, the Polka Capital of the World.

And as for music, well, Nashville, Tennessee, twangs supreme as the Country Music Capital of the World, thanks to that ever Grand Ole Opry; but fast-growing Branson, Missouri, is the Live Music Capital of the World, and with more country music performers building theaters in the bulging Ozark community, it might some-day spirit Nashville's title away altogether.

Mountain View, Arkansas, meanwhile, is the Folk Music Capital of the World. Fans travel many a mile to watch live performances at the Ozark Folk Center Theater and at other venues in and around Mountain View. One local legend, Jimmy Driftwood, plays his grandfather's guitar and is often joined onstage by other area per-formers at the Jimmy Driftwood Barn, a project of the University of Central Arkansas.

For sheer show-stopping razzmatazz, **LAS VEGAS, NEVADA,** is the Entertainment Capital of the World; though more famous for its gaming, the community has never officially called itself the world's gambling capital. Unofficially, it's sometimes been called the Wedding Capital of the World, thanks to its quick-hitch facilities;

Vegas even has drive-through wedding chapels, though somehow the ministers refrain from asking, "You want fries with that?" But for its official capital claim, Vegas made a slot for itself as the world's Entertainment Capital because almost every major singer or comic of the past half-century has strutted the stages of the Great Light Way. Even Ronald Reagan headlined there at the Last Frontier in 1954.

By then, Reagan was famous for his work in the Film Capital of the World, Hollywood, California, which was long before he was cast as the lead for an eight-year run in the ultimate world capital, Washington, D.C. Though

Hollywood is the film capital, Rochester, New York, is the Photography Capital of the World, where visitors can snap to it at the International Museum of Photography, housed in the 50-room mansion built in 1905 by George Eastman.

Though such spectator events are great fun for the audience, some folks prefer the interactive pleasures of shopping. Bloomington, Minnesota, calls itself the Shopping Capital of the World, thanks to the presence of the Mall of America, the biggest mall in the U.S. And recreational shoppers and hard-nosed bargain hunters alike charge to **READING AND BERKS COUNTY, PENNSYLVANIA,** the Outlet Capital of the World. The community is so proud of its outlet shops it even trademarked the title, so that other communities gaining inroads on the outlet scene couldn't attach the same label. Reading was once a major textiles manufacturing city and, today, through urban renewal, it has saved many of its factories and warehouses by converting them into beautifully renovated shopping centers.

Now, if you were a settler in the Old West, you shopped at the General Store. That may not sound like heaven to today's shoppers, but anyone who saw Billy Crystal in *City Slickers* knows that, for some people, playing cowboy is the ultimate relaxation. They're the kind of travelers who head for Wickenburg, Arizona, the Dude Ranch Capital of the World. Wickenburg is home to a herd of guest ranches, including the Kay El Bar Ranch, the Flying E Ranch, the Rancho de los Caballeros, the Wickenburg Inn & Guest Ranch, and the Rancho Casitas.

The Wild West also rides again in Dodge City, Kansas, the Cowboy Capital of the World, which has preserved and restored its famous gun-slinging image with staged battles and Wild West saloons. And visitors can still see the infamous Boot Hill Cemetery, created after a cowboy died in a gunfight and was literally buried with his boots on, on the spot. Many of the town's legends are recounted at the Boot Hill Museum.

Coast to coast and capital to capital, relaxing retreats and sports resorts await the pleasure of America's vacationers and weekend adventurers, who want nothing more than to sit and stay a spell.

## ❂ Ely, Minnesota

CANOE CAPITAL OF THE WORLD

Ely, Minnesota, is so serene and pristine that even the crowds who've recently discovered it can't put much of a dent in its peacefulness. And, anyway, most travelers who come to Ely aren't there to shop or mingle in the small downtown. They've come for the Great Outdoors, notably, the canoeing. For Ely has gained a reputation as the Canoe Capital of the World.

Canoes are a way of life in Ely. The community lies in the heart of the Boundary Waters Canoe Area Wilderness (BWCAW), a vast wilderness that includes 14,000 square miles of lakes and rivers. The BWCAW reaches up to Canada and down into Minnesota, offering some of the most unspoiled and primitive canoeing waters in North America. Ely is surrounded by the Superior National Forest—which has 2,021 lakes over 10 acres in size, along with 1,975 miles of streams; in 1909, it received one of the early national forest designations from Teddy Roosevelt.

Outdoors lovers from all over come to Ely for the canoeing and other wilderness recreation.
*Courtesy Ely Chamber of Commerce*

Ely outfitters offer canoers everything they need to explore this watery wonderland. Equipment rental and provisions are available, along with trip-planning assistance for those who want to do it themselves; outfitters also offer services such as guides, fly-in trips, and tent camps to make life easier for less adventurous explorers. A number of companies, including Ely Canoe Livery and Voyageur North Outfitters, offer partial outfitting, with various kinds of tents, canoes, and other equipment for a la carte adventurers who just need a few pieces of paraphernalia to fill in the gaps. Many of these outfitters also operate bunkhouses and/or cabins for canoers and campers.

And even those who have seen *Deliverance* once too often can rest assured about the safety of trips out of Ely: U.S. Forest Service Rangers patrol the local waters daily to provide assistance and security for canoers and other wilderness wanderers.

Though Ely has found its fortune lately in its recreational opportunities, it was founded by pioneering miners in the late 1880s who were searching for gold but found rich veins of iron ore instead. Though not as lucrative as gold, iron proved a necessary metal for the nation's manufacturing boom.

The first Ely area iron mine to send up its ore was the Chandler Mine, which shipped its first cargo in 1888; during the next 80 years, the Ely mines produced about 18,756,000 tons of ore. The Pioneer Mine, the last of Ely's 11 iron mines, closed in 1967—the iron was still there, but it had become too expensive to extract. Some mining still continues in this area, which is referred to as the Iron Range; but now it's for taconite, a low-grade ore with an iron content of about 20 percent. You can still visit the old headframe of the Pioneer Mine; it's near a park adjacent to Miner's Lake. And to experience the underground life up close, take a tour of the Soudan Underground Mine, 20 miles west of Ely.

Though iron brought Ely fame and canoes gave it a recreational reputation, the town has also gained renown among wildlife lovers for another reason—and this one's a real howl. The International Wolf Center, opened in 1993, is a wolf study and preservation complex. A resident wolf pack gives visitors an up-close look at this mysterious and beautiful animal. The Center also sponsors Howling Field Trips, which take visitors into the field to study wolf communications.

Whether you come for the canoes or the canines, Ely is a little bit of heaven in a lot of wild country. God's Country, some have called it; he'd be proud to take the credit, no doubt.

## FOR FURTHER INFORMATION

### General Information

**Ely Chamber of Commerce**
**Log Cabin/Information Center**
1600 E. Sheridan St.
Ely, MN 55731
(218) 365-6123 or (800) 777-7281

**Boundary Waters Canoe Area**
**Wilderness Permit Station**
International Wolf Center Building
Hwy. 169
Ely, MN 55731
(218) 365-7681
(Closed October–May)

### Attractions and Events

**International Wolf Center**
Hwy. 169
Ely, MN 55731
(218) 365-4695 or (800) ELY-WOLF

**Soudan Underground Mine Tours**
Soudan Underground Mine Park
1379 Stuntz Bay Rd.
Tower, MN 55790
(218) 253-2245

### Outfitters
Dozens of outfitters serve the Ely area; here's a sampling:

**Boundary Waters Canoe Outfitters**
Box 447
Ely, MN 55731
(800) 544-7736

**Ely Canoe Livery**
410 E. Sheridan St.
Ely, MN 55731
(218) 365-6287 or (800) 382-2041

**Voyageur North Outfitters**
1829 E. Sheridan St.
Dept. E
Ely, MN 55731
(218) 365-3251 or (800) 848-5530

# ❂ Las Vegas, Nevada

## ENTERTAINMENT CAPITAL OF THE WORLD

When you think of gambling, you think of Las Vegas; there's no getting around it. No state lottery games or riverboat and Native American casinos will ever change that, although they are all taking a hefty bite out of the city's profits. But that still leaves a lion's share of change for the casinos.

But what would Las Vegas be without the late great Liberace, or more recently Wayne Newton and Siegfried and Roy? Its star-spangled stageshows, barely bedecked showgirls, and sizzling nightlife are almost as famous as its Lady Luck legacy. Although Vegas basks in the neon-lit lime-light of its gambling fame, few visitors realize that its official capital claim isn't about slots or dice, but rather, about song and dance: Las Vegas is the Entertainment Capital of the World.

---

**CYBERSPACE CONTACTS**

## The Rat Pack Home Page

**http://www.primenet.com/~drbmbay**

Check out the crooniest tunes, facts, and photos from the greatest Vegas lounge lizards, the "Rat Pack"—Frank Sinatra, Dean Martin, Sammy Davis, Jr., Peter Lawford, and Joey Bishop—at the Rat Pack Home Page, which features loads of sound clips and other beautiful goodies, baby.

It has several other (unofficial) capital claims as well. One that rings a bell is the city's renown as the Wedding Capital of the World. Every year some 50,000 cupid-struck couples get quick-hitched in the city's ubiquitous wedding chapels. And, since Vegas is also famous for its glitzy sleight-of-handers who can pull rabbits from hats as quickly as the slot machines can suck coins from pockets, the city also has an enchanting reputation as the Magic Capital of the World (Colon, Michigan, shares the same claim).

Vegas history is as much legend and lore as reality. Anyone who's seen the film *Bugsy* might think the casino industry was founded by a gangster as a desert oasis for gamblers. In actuality, Benjamin "Bugsy" Siegel's Flamingo, which opened in 1946, was not the first casino in Vegas; gambling had been legal in the state since 1931, when Governor Fred Balzar signed the Wide-open Gaming Bill that was to transform the state.

That same year, the first superstar wedding took place in Vegas, when "It" girl Clara Bow tied the knot with movie star Rex Bell. It was a secret wedding conducted in a judge's chambers; since then, stars from Elvis (who wed Priscilla in 1967) to George Hamilton (who wed Alana in 1972) have married in far more public ceremonies.

In 1932, the Apache opened at Second and Fremont Streets, becoming the city's first 100-room hotel; within a decade of the gaming legalization, the Strip was taking shape with hotels such as the El Rancho Vegas, which opened in 1941. Other major players in the early days were the El Cortez Hotel, which opened the same year as the El Rancho, and the Last Frontier Hotel, which opened in 1942.

But Bugsy's Flamingo was a bird of a different color. His lavish casino hotel set the tone for the city's future, as its upscale atmosphere brought the glitz and sizzle of Los Angeles east to the desert.

The town gained its entertainment capital claim to fame from the big-time performers who earned big bucks playing to SRO crowds in the hotel theaters. After the hotels were in place, they began attracting serious players, both on and off the stage. Though small-time acts kept gamblers and vacationers amused at first, by 1944, Vegas was ready for high-wattage star power. And it got it in Sophie Tucker, "The Last of the Red Hot Mamas," who sizzled at the Last Frontier that year, becoming the first stellar performer to step up to the mike in Vegas. With Tucker came a new kind of cachet, and other name acts quickly followed, from Jimmy Durante (who made his Vegas debut as the Flamingo's first headliner) in 1946, to Frank Sinatra, who first crooned to swooning crowds at the Desert Inn in 1951.

The list of performers from those early days reads like a who's who of stars: Lena Horne, Bill "Bojangles" Robinson, Joe Lewis, Ella Fitzgerald, Ray Bolger, Danny Thomas, Marlene Dietrich, Ronald Reagan, Maurice Chevalier, Elvis Presley, and Judy Garland are just a few of the names who played Vegas in the 1940s and 1950s. And in the ensuing years, the list has continued to dazzle with an intensity to rival the city's neon.

Donn Knepp's *Las Vegas: The Entertainment Capital* (Menlo Park, CA: Lane Publishing, 1987) details the rise of the city's entertainment status with hundreds of historic photos and fascinating tidbits. As Knepp, formerly with the Las Vegas News Bureau (the city's media promotion agency) notes, "Since 1944 when Sophie Tucker was the first world-famous star to appear at a Las Vegas resort, virtually every name entertainer has found a Las Vegas engagement indispensable to career advancement and enhancement."

Vegas is indeed a star maker: Take the case of Liberace, Mr. Entertainment himself. The late Lee Liberace made his Las Vegas debut at the Last Frontier in 1944, at the age of 25, and initially he established himself as a serious performer. But when he began adding elaborate costumes and a comedy schtick to his routine, he sealed his fortune. His flamboyant wardrobe and self-deprecating humor made him a Vegas legend and earned him legions of faithful fans. He gave his last performance in 1986, but his legacy lives on at one of the city's most popular tourist attractions, the Liberace Museum, where visitors can see some of his astounding costumes—some weighing hundreds of pounds in beads and sequins—along with his famous collections of candelabra, pianos, cars, and rings.

Today, Vegas is as entertaining as ever. Along with the headline entertainers and sporting events (boxing remains a big ring draw), the city is evolving into a family destination by building up its base of nongambling attractions. Taking a cue from Walt and Mickey's empire, which has turned Orlando into the family entertainment world's capital, Vegas' famed Strip is being transformed into a whimsical wonderland of themed hotels that boast Disney-esque diversions.

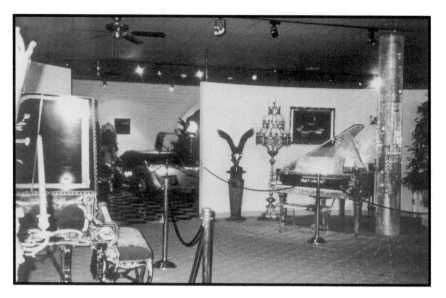

The Liberace Museum exhibits the glitzy pianos and costumes owned by the flamboyant Vegas performer. *Laura Bergheim*

From the Yo-ho-ho verve of the Treasure Island Hotel—fronted with a pirate village, it stages nightly battles between life-sized ships—to the Egyptian-styled Luxor Hotel—where guests can explore a replica of King Tut's tomb and float along an indoor Nile—entertainment-rich destinations are the hottest properties in Vegas. Even older hotels are updating their themes to attract a wider audience. Caesar's Palace built the Forum Shops, an enclosed shopping mall based on a Roman street theme, with fountain statues that come to animatronic life to perform for enthralled shoppers.

Not that the casinos are losing ground. Every hotel still has a huge casino, where the coin-clinking cacophony of slot machines serenades the ears night and day. But gambling alone can't keep the crowds coming in this lottery-mad world, hence these palaces of pleasure for all ages.

A city of about a million people, Vegas sprawls in all directions. Many who live here never venture to the hotel casinos; if they gamble at all (and most get that out of their systems early on), they satiate their taste at the slot machines in corner convenience markets and restaurants. The slots are everywhere, from laundromats and drug stores to souvenir shops and supermarkets. And, as it is for the locals of any tourist town, the major sites—here the hotels and shows—are seen mainly as distractions for visitors.

The Las Vegas climate, too, is appealing especially to retirees. The average annual temperature is 66 degrees Fahrenheit, with an average daily humidity of 29 percent—including rainy days. Another set of numbers attracts entrepreneurs and investors: Over 28 million visitors a year descend on Vegas for fun and games. Though most who come to play don't decide to stay, enough newcomers have settled here in the past decade to make it one of the country's fastest growing metropolitan areas.

If the glitz gets to be too much, you can still get a real feel for Vegas' past. Just get off the Strip and head to the older casinos, the ones where the main attraction is still, and always will be, gambling. Although many of these were torn down to make way for newer models, on the fringes the early places still operate.

Another good way to learn about Las Vegas and its entertaining history is to drive about 40 minutes southeast to the Clark County Heritage Museum in Henderson, which houses a treasure of a tiny exhibit on Las Vegas history. From an early penny slot machine (you can still put a coin in, but you can't win anything) to a collection of swizzle sticks and other casino collectibles, the history of this unique city unfolds in a disarmingly low-tech environment. The entertain-

The Clark County Heritage Museum's Las Vegas exhibit traces the glittering city's rise as a gambling and entertainment giant. *Laura Bergheim*

ers who made Vegas great are honored at the museum as well; one wall displays photos and memorabilia from earlier heydays of head-liners.

Somehow, by leaving Las Vegas you find it again in this simple museum. All that glitters is not gulch, and below this sequined surface lingers a lively history and heritage that offers greater insight into this thoroughly entertaining Entertainment Capital of the World.

## FOR FURTHER INFORMATION

### General Information

**Las Vegas Convention and Visitors Authority**
3150 Paradise Rd.
Las Vegas, NV 89109
(702) 892-0711

### Attractions and Events

**Clark County Heritage Museum**
1830 S. Boulder Hwy.
Henderson, NV 89015
(702) 455-7955

**Liberace Museum & Foundation**
1775 E. Tropicana Ave.
Las Vegas, NV 89119
(702) 798-5595

# ✷ Reading and Berks County, Pennsylvania

OUTLET CAPITAL OF THE WORLD

Some people see shopping as a metaphor for life: Some days, everything you want is on sale, practically a steal, while other days, no matter how hard you try, you can't find the one thing you're searching for. In the 1990s, shopping has evolved into a recreational pursuit akin to hunting, but without the blood.

Still, the American urge to shop is tempered by another facet of the national character: that of the budget-conscious consumer. Hence, the birth of the outlet store, where you can shop till you drop but still save money. If you're a bargain hunter, there's no place quite like Reading and Berks County, Pennsylvania, the Outlet Capital of the World.

The claim rests on more than the area's 300 outlet stores; the area has been a paradise for penny-pinchers as far back as the disco era, when the community spawned some of the first outlet stores. It took two decades before the discount trend took off nationwide, but today strings of outlet strip malls have sprung up along interstates and in resort towns across America.

Realizing that other outlet capitals could be lurking just around the corner, the Reading and Berks County Visitors Bureau trademarked the phrase "Outlet Capital of the World," staking out a legal as well as proprietary claim to the term.

The heart of the Pennsylvania Dutch country, where a simple life devoid of unnecessary trappings is an honored tradition, seems the last place that the consummate consumer would be likely to frequent. Then again, there's no sales tax on clothing in Pennsylvania, so perhaps it had to happen—if not here, then elsewhere in the state.

Despite growing competition from other outlet centers, Reading remains the top outlet shopping destination in America, with more than 10 million visitors a year swarming through the outlets to

The 1890s buildings that now house Reading's VF Outlet Village were once part of the nation's largest hosiery factory complex. *Courtesy Reading and Berks County Visitors Bureau* save thousands of dollars on brand-name and off-brand merchandise. Of course, they're actually spending money while they're "saving" it, so the local economy is thriving.

Reading's outlets also stand out architecturally. Whereas most outlet malls are characterless concrete constructions, many of Reading's shops are housed in buildings that previously served other purposes. This is urban renewal at its most lucrative. By turning sites such as the old railroad office, millhouses, and factories into shopping environments, the town has been able to restore and preserve its historic structures while creating a solid economic drawing card. The warm old brick buildings with their classic charm offer a retail therapy antidote to the bargain basement ambience of most outlet malls. And a happy shopper is a generous shopper.

Three of the largest outlet centers in the Reading area are the VF Outlet Village, the Reading Outlet Center, and the Reading Station Outlet. Each fills a space redolent of history. The complex that houses the VF Outlet Village—which includes subdivided outlet centers such as VF Factory Outlet and Designer's Place—was built in the 1890s as one of the world's largest hosiery centers. Its seven buildings included mills, manufacturing, and packaging facilities; and the neighborhoods that grew up around this industrial center were an early example of

The Reading Outlet Center fills structures once used for apparel manufacturing. *Courtesy Reading and Berks County Visitors Bureau*

"planned communities," built as housing for factory workers.

Likewise, the loft-like buildings that house the Reading Outlet Center were also once factories and warehouses for Reading's once-booming apparel industry. And the historic site of the Reading Railroad headquarters is home to the Reading Station Outlet.

Reading's stores run the gamut from the genuine factory outlet, where a particular manufacturer sells off overstock and discontinued or damaged goods, to cheap chain discount stores. Savvy outlet shoppers here and elsewhere learn to study the marketplace and know the true value of items before whipping out the credit card; but those looking for bargains will find them by the bin-full in Reading outlets.

Most of the area outlets are housed in large complexes—the VF Outlet Village, for instance, houses more than 75 stores. Though some concentrate on a certain product line appeal—the Reading Station Outlet specializes in upscale designer wear, with stores selling Brooks Brothers, Armani, Valentino, Ungaro, and other fashion leaders (ads for the mall promise "Factory Direct 20–75% Off Retail Every Day")—most of the outlet complexes offer a mix of apparel, accessories, and housewares.

Visitors to Reading have no problem finding the outlet stores. They seem to be down every street, at every corner, ever present, ever growing. Once in town, the biggest decision isn't where to shop, but where to shop first. Flip through local tourism magazines or the brochures in hotel lobbies and you're greeted by giddy off-the-rack rhetoric: "Rediscover Classic Savings!" "Big Deals" "1/2 Off Your Favorite Brands Every Day!"

Reading's outlets have successfully filled the void left by the apparel industry, which deserted the town as less expensive labor forces were developed in the South and overseas. Its evolution from industrial village to off-price mecca has set an example for many American communities to diversify the local economy by investing in tourism and trade attractions. A few other towns have also succeeded in this endeavor, notably, Freeport, Maine, where L.L. Bean's catalog store became an anchor for other outlets, virtually creating the cluster concept for discount stores.

But Reading has excelled in making a name for itself as more than just a popular bargain-hunters destination. Its homestyle, welcoming nature and whole-hearted embrace of the recreational shopping boom has made it a getaway for romantic weekenders and family travelers as well as for hard-core shoppers. Reading may have trademarked its capital claim, but it really needn't have: Its reputation is safe both as an outlet capital and a pleasant place to visit. Now that's a real bargain.

## FOR FURTHER INFORMATION

### General Information

**Reading and Berks County Visitors Bureau**
VF Factory Outlet Complex
Park Rd. and Hill Ave.
P.O. Box 6677
Reading, PA 19610
(610) 375-4085 or (800) 443-6610

### Major Outlet Malls

**Home Furnishings Outlet**
Exit 22, Pa. Turnpike
Morgantown, PA 19543
(610) 286-2000

**The Outlets on Hiesters Lane**
755 Hiesters Lane
Reading, PA 19605
(610) 921-9394

**Reading Outlet Center**
801 N. 9th St.
Reading, PA 19604
(610) 373-5495

**Reading Station Outlet Center**
951 N. Sixth St.
Reading, PA 19601
(610) 478-7000

**VF Outlet Village**
801 Hill Ave.
Reading, PA 19610
(800) 772-8336

# ⚙ Elmira, New York

〰〰〰〰〰〰〰〰〰〰〰〰〰〰〰〰〰

SOARING CAPITAL OF AMERICA AND MARK
TWAIN COUNTRY

Ever since Icarus flew too close to the sun with his waxen wings, melting back down to Earth from the grace of the skies, humankind has been seeking to break the bonds of gravity and ground. The Wright Brothers made it possible for us to hop a jet across the country or around the world, but there are somewhat simpler pleasures to be found in the floating, gossamer realms of non-powered flight.

These delights are paramount in the Finger Lakes community of Elmira, New York, the Soaring Capital of America. A mecca for the gliding set, Harris Hill Park just outside Elmira is home to the National Soaring Museum, which houses the world's largest collection of contemporary and neoclassical sailplanes. Adjacent to the museum is the Harris Hill Glider Field, where sailplanes take to the air year-round (weather permitting; and in this part of New York, the weather sometimes refuses permission).

Sailplanes are aptly named: As a ship rides the waves, so a sailplane rides the air current. In recent years, the popularity of lighter-than-aircraft and hang gliding has gained the sport legions of new fans, and attendance at the museum and at the sailplane events it sponsors have soared to new heights.

The National Soaring Museum is filled with artifacts and displays that tell the history of soaring from the dawn of human flight (many early planes, including the Wright Brothers', were gliders) to today's ultra-modern sailplanes. Many visitors are astonished to learn that the Space Shuttle is in fact the world's largest sailplane. Once those booster rockets are gone, it just floats around the planet until it reenters the atmosphere and glides back down to Earth.

The 28,000-square-foot museum has a little something for everyone. History buffs gawk at the display of wing cloth from the first

1903 Wright Flyer; action fans can settle into a cockpit simulator to experience what it's like to soar; and science lovers can explore exhibits on meteorology and aerodynamics. The museum has more than a dozen full-sized gliders on display, and houses the U.S. Soaring Hall of Fame, which honors great innovators, pilots, and soaring enthusiasts.

Even if you've never soared before, you can take a demonstration sailplane flight at the adjacent glider field with one of the pilots of the Harris Hill Soaring Corp. Lifting off into the welcoming clasp of the wind, you find yourself soaring out over the lakes and farmlands of the Chemung Valley. Unlike powered flight, the grace and natural flow of gliding lends itself to an almost contemplative peace as you watch the landscape below rise and fall with the breeze that carries you above the land. Just one flight and you might become hooked on a lifetime hobby.

Elmira's soaring reputation is only part of its draw for tourists. One of America's most down-to-earth authors did some of his best work in Elmira. Hence the area's other nickname, Mark Twain Country.

Though Samuel Clemens (Twain's real name) was a child of the Mississippi River region about which he frequently wrote, some of his most productive periods were spent in the Finger Lakes area. His local connection began when he met his future wife, Olivia Langdon, the daughter of a prominent Elmiran. The couple's Elmira residence, Quarry Farm, became their summer place for more than 20 years. It was here, in the intriguingly geometric building known as the octagonal study, that Twain worked on many of his classics, including *Huckleberry Finn, A Connecticut Yankee in King Arthur's Court,* and *Life on the Mississippi.* Twain fans can pay their respects at his grave site in Elmira's Woodlawn Cemetery.

Twain's famous study was relocated to the campus of Elmira College, where it's open to the public; the rest of Quarry Farm is now

## DID YOU KNOW...

### First in Flight
Though the Wright Brothers gained greater fame for their uplifting adventures at Kitty Hawk, N.C., in 1903, it was a German, Otto Lilienthal, who first successfully flew a heavier-than-air craft. In 1891, after more than thirty years of experimentation, he launched his bat-winged glider from a Berlin hillside, soaring more than 100 feet before touching down again. He died in a crash five years later.

Mark Twain's octagonal study is a legendary literary attraction in Elmira. *Courtesy Chemung County Chamber of Commerce*

home to the Center for Mark Twain Studies, an academic retreat that hosts symposia and lectures. Visitors also can see the Mark Twain Exhibit at the college's Hamilton Hall, which displays artifacts and photos from Twain's years at Quarry Farm.

Elmira's historic structures are more than Twain deep, however; the Near Westside neighborhood, listed on the National Register of Historic Places, has the State's largest concentration of Victorian homes. The neighborhood association has a walking tour pamphlet that points out the important structures and their histories, and sponsors guided tours on summer weekends.

From planes to Twain, this charming Victorian community of around 34,000 has earned a special place in the flight records and literary annals of history. Whether upwind or down river, it's a unique community with a heart that soars.

## For Further Information

### General Information

Chemung County Chamber of Commerce
215 E. Church St.
Elmira, NY 14901
(607) 734-5137 or (800) MARK TWAIN

Near West Neighborhood Association, Inc.
353 Davis St.
Elmira, NY 14901
(607) 733-4924

## Soaring Attractions and Events

**Harris Hill Soaring Corp. (Sailplane rides)**
Harris Hill Park  R.D. 3
Elmira, NY 14903
(607) 739-7899 (office)
(607) 734-0641 (field)

**National Soaring Museum**
Harris Hill Park
R.D. 3
Elmira, NY 14903
(607) 734-3128

## Mark Twain Attractions and Events

**Mark Twain's Study and Mark Twain Exhibit
Center for Mark Twain Studies at Quarry Farm**
Box 900
Elmira College
Elmira, NY 14901
(607) 732-0933

**Woodlawn Cemetery (Mark Twain's grave)**
1200 Walnut St.
Elmira, NY 14905
(607) 732-0151

# ✿ Bandon, Oregon

〜〜〜〜〜〜〜〜〜〜〜〜〜〜〜〜〜〜〜〜〜〜〜

## STORM WATCHING CAPITAL OF THE WORLD

For most people, a stormy night means cuddling up by the fire, hiding under the covers, or seeking solace in a cup of cocoa or something stronger. But that's not the case for the brave folks of Bandon, Oregon—or at least not for the members of the Bandon Storm Watchers club. Here, in what some have called the Storm Watching Capital of the World, a whipping wind, roiling sea, and torrential downpour is a ticket to adventure. Club members grab their binoculars and head for a local retirement center, which provides a room for the watchers to oooh and aaah through the winds and rain.

This coastal town's stormy reputation is well-earned. It's situated where the Coquille River meets the Pacific Ocean, which means a strong blast slamming into the area sets the tidal pools swirling, the boats in the harbor rocking, and the sand on the shore blowing in a dervish of devilish delight.

"Bandon's just a good place to watch a storm," explains Storm Watchers president Linda Ross. "We get very spectacular wave action. And with the amount of logging we have, there's a lot of wood floating around in a storm." And when there's no storm in sight? "On a calm weekend, when the tide is out, you can go out to the tidepools

A stormy day in Bandon is well worth watching. *Photo by Kay Meyrovich*

Bandon's other capital claim, cranberries, are harvested and celebrated as a major cash crop.
*Courtesy Bandon Chamber of Commerce*

and find agates," Ross says. Clamming is another popular fair-weather pastime here.

But Ross notes that the real goal of the Storm Watchers—which has about 350 members—is to promote the community as a tourist destination. "It's kind of a quiet town. We don't even have a movie theater, but there are other things to do here," Ross explains. The Storm Watchers sponsor events such as the big Memorial Day Weekend Seafood and Wine Festival, and a lecture series featuring speakers on topics such as surf-fishing, beachcombing, and local wildlife.

There's more to see in Bandon-by-the-Sea (the town's full name, which few use) than storms or speakers: It's also prime whale-watching territory. Mid-February to mid-May, watchers—even standing on the shore—can see gray whales migrating north from Baja California to the Bering Sea (often with calves in tow). The whales make their return trip south in winter; then, the best viewing is in December.

Bandon has another capital claim. As the Cranberry Capital of the State of Oregon, nearly 1,000 acres of the coastal strip from Sixes River to Hause are bogged down with the crop, making it a primary West Coast cranberry-growing region. Locals celebrate their berries at the Annual Cranberry Festival, held in late September. A cranberry queen is crowned, cranberry goodies are eaten, and participants generally relish their crop.

Whirlwind tourists find much to watch and munch in this seaside town; so bring binoculars and an appetite, and you'll soon be well-weathered and well-fed.

## FOR FURTHER INFORMATION

### General Information

**Bandon Chamber of Commerce**
P.O. Box 1515
Bandon, OR 97411
(541) 347-9616

**Bandon Storm Watchers**
P.O. Box 1693
Bandon, OR 97411

**Oregon Cranberry Farmers' Alliance**
P.O. Box 1737
Bandon, OR 97411

### Attractions and Events

**Cranberry Festival Association**
P.O. Box 348
Bandon, OR 97411
(541) 347-2277

**Seafood and Wine Festival**
Contact Bandon Storm Watchers

## ○ Sandusky, Ohio's Cedar Point

THRILL RIDE CAPITAL OF THE WORLD

R oller coasters are one of those hot-button amusement issues for people: You either love them or you hate them. Die-hard coaster buffs travel the country in search of the highest, fastest, and swirliest rides, leaving their nausea-prone pals politely waiting on a nearby bench.

Walt Disney World may have the Magic Kingdom, but the Thrill Ride Capital of the World is the Cedar Point Amusement Park in Sandusky, Ohio.

Cedar Point might be just another amusement park but for its devotion to developing some of the country's most breathtaking, nerve-wracking rides. If you need Dramamine to survive a drive to Grandmother's house, stay away from Sandusky. But if the face-flattening joys of centrifugal force send you into paroxysms of pleasure, then the thrill rides at Cedar Point are worth the trip.

The park originally coastered to fame because of its old-fashioned contraptions such as the Blue Streak, a classic wooden roller coaster. But in the past decade it has opened a number of major rides that have given the park a high-tech edge in the increasingly competitive thrill ride arena. In 1989, the park unveiled its Magnum XL-200, which, when it opened, was the world's fastest and tallest roller coaster.

But as engineers upped the ante at other parks across the country, Cedar Point had to find a way to respond. In 1994, it opened the diabolically dubbed Raptor, an $11.5 million inverted coaster that towers

---

CYBERSPACE CONTACTS

## Cedar Point Amusement Park

**http://www.cedarpoint.com**

For more on the thrilling rides of Cedar Point, visit the park's official Web site, which features a page describing the twist-and-shout machines that gained Cedar Point such fame. White-knuckled job seekers can also learn about the park's employment opportunities on-line.

137 feet into the sky and sends its passengers screeching down a 45-degree, 119-foot drop.

In 1996, it introduced Mantis, a $12 million coaster being promoted as the world's tallest, fastest, and steepest stand-up coaster. The park's literature describes the monstrous Mantis as "Towering 145 feet in height with a 137-foot drop angled at 45 degrees, riders . . . come within feet of the water's surface before challenging Mantis' swooping elements at 60 mph—all while standing up."

Despite the natural state of self-promotion to which amusement parks are prone, Cedar Point's thrill ride capital claim is more than just whistling in a wind tunnel. In a number of ways, it has genuine bragging rights to the title. It has the most roller-coaster rides, and also boasts the world's largest collection of stomach-churning contraptions. Mantis is Cedar Point's 12th roller coaster—making it the park's fifth new glide ride in six years—strengthening its footing as the record-holder.

Cedar Point isn't alone in proclaiming its status as the highest roller in the amusement park pack. In 1995, readers of *Inside Track*, an international magazine devoted to amusement parks and thrill rides, voted it Best Park for the fifth consecutive year.

Cedar Point's oldest building, the Grand Pavilion, erected in 1818, housed a huge theater, bowling alleys, photography studio, and beauty salon. *Courtesy Sandusky Library, Follett House Collection, Sandusky, Ohio*

Standing 70 feet tall, the Leap Frog Railway opened in 1918 at Cedar Point Amusement Park in Sandusky, Ohio, now known as the Thrill Ride Capital of the World. *Courtesy Cedar Point Historical Archives*

Cedar Point got its start in 1870 as a collection of bathhouse facilities on Lake Erie Beach. In the early 1880s, the park introduced rides, the first of which was an offshore water trapeze that would fling bathers into the lake. A sea swing and water toboggan soon followed. Drier heads soon prevailed with the opening of the Grand Pavilion in 1888; it featured an auditorium, dining room, bowling alleys, a beauty salon, and photography studio. Today, it's the oldest building at Cedar Point.

Cedar Point's first roller coaster, the Switchback Railway, debuted in 1892. As the park's history notes, "Guests were wowed by the 25-foot-tall height and 10-mph top speed." The park's oldest currently operating roller coaster is the Blue Streak, which dates to 1964. And its gentlest is the Jr. Gemini, built in 1979 as a "training coaster" for younger riders; it stands a mere 19 feet tall.

You know what you're getting yourself into when you climb aboard rides such as the aptly named Mean Streak (1991), one of the world's tallest and fastest wooden coasters, or the Disaster Transport

(1990), the park's only enclosed coaster, which zooms through a harrowing outer space setting, dodging asteroids and space pirates.

If you're wondering how parks like Cedar Point come up with all those evocative names for their rides, consider the case of the Mantis. It started out with the name of Banshee, "after the untamed ghostly entity of Irish folklore," according to a Cedar Point press release. But the term had such morbid associations that the park decided perhaps it was too scary even for this new hair-raiser: "After unveiling the massive project in September (1995), we had concerns that some of our guests may have found the doom and misfortune connotations associated with the coaster's original name inappropriate," explained Don Miears, the park's executive vice president and general manager. So Banshee became Mantis, but the death-defying thrills remained the same.

Despite its fame as a coaster's paradise, Cedar Point does have many of the traditional pleasures of an old-fashioned park. Notable among these is the Midway Carousel, the park's oldest operating ride. Built in 1912, it moved to Cedar Point in 1946 and continues to give visitors a gentle spin. In 1982, the carousel was named to the National Register of Historic Places.

But it's the coasters that many of the park's most devoted enthusiasts come to experience, and Cedar Point continues to propel its patrons with both classic and high-tech rides that will keep them speeding well into the next century. One bit of advice before taking on the sinister heights and corkscrew delights of Cedar Point: If you're planning a coaster-to-coaster trip with nonthrill-riding companions, tell 'em to bring a book to read, 'cause you may not be back to that park bench for a while.

## FOR FURTHER INFORMATION

**Cedar Point Amusement Park/Resort**
P.O. Box 5006
Sandusky, Ohio 44871-8006
(419) 627-2350

CHAPTER  8

# NO STONE UNTURNED

he foundation of this nation is rock solid — just ask those who live where geology is destiny, in, say, **ELBERTON, GEORGIA,** the Granite Capital of the World, or La Crosse, Kansas, the Post Rock Capital of the World. When the rock or stone beneath a town gives its economy a base upon which to stand, that's cause for celebration. And self-promotion. Just as some crops grow best in certain regions, the land offers up its rocky riches to a select few areas. For some, it can be a gold mine (literally); for others, it's a quarry. And in communities whose reputations are built on stone or rock, mineral or metal, their capital claims are cast to last.

The South has an abundance of such places. Some, such as Elberton and its granite quarries, produce rocks so familiar to us—in gravestones and other memorials—that we never even think about where they come from. New England also is famous for its granite: New Hampshire is known as the Granite State, and Barre, Vermont, used to be called the Granite Capital because of its prosperous granite quarries in the nineteenth century. Though its claim has been

It's hard work quarrying granite, but Elberton, Georgia, yields a world capital's supply.
*Courtesy Elberton Granite Association, Inc.*

eroded by time and the loss of local quarries, visitors can still view the community's impressive collection of granite buildings and memorials, and tour the Rock of Ages granite quarries just outside of Barre in Graniteville.

Other southern sites claim fame for substances few of us have ever heard about. **WASHINGTON COUNTY, GEORGIA,** for example, is the Kaolin Capital of the World. Kaolin, for the uninitiated (which is most of us), is an aluminum silicate clay obtained from the mineral kaolinate. Though its name may be unfamiliar, its use is commonplace, for it adds sheen to everything from magazine paper to house paints.

The South also has its share of earthy mysteries, especially **MOUNT IDA, ARKANSAS,** the Quartz Crystal Capital of the World. New Agers helped spawn a "crystal rush" in the 1980s that made crystal miners there rich. Even though the price has bottomed out, this area, in the Ouachita Mountains, is said to have the world's richest vein of quartz crystal.

Like the South, the Midwest has its share of stony success stories. La Crosse, Kansas, is the Post Rock Capital of the World, thanks to the abundance of this unique stone that's found in this part of Kansas. When the settlers moved west, they needed to build fences; with trees scarce in the plains, they had few solid materials to use for fence posts. But clever pioneers discovered that the local rock was a good substitute for wood. It could be shaped to the right size, and bored with relative ease for the insertion of fence boards or wire.

La Crosse even has a Post Rock Museum, which tells the story of the stone; it's right next door to the Kansas Barbed Wire Association Museum, which houses more than 700 kinds of barbed wire and related implements and artifacts. No wonder La Crosse also calls itself the Barbed Wire Capital of the World.

Then there's **BEDFORD, INDIANA,** the Limestone Capital of the World. Bedford and surrounding Lawrence County are home to some of the world's most productive limestone quarries. Lawrence County limestone has been used in the construction of landmarks such as the Washington National Cathedral, the Empire State Building, and Chicago's Merchandise Mart. Locally, many Bedford buildings are made from limestone; in fact, it has so many rocky worship houses it also bears the title of City of Stone Churches. The community is also famous for its talented stonecutters, and has a touching memorial to an artisan who died young: It depicts his workbench just as he left it, in the middle of a project.

One of Bedford, Indiana's limestone houses of worship. Bedford has so many it's also known as the City of Stone Churches. *Courtesy Lawrence County Tourism Commission*

Silver Capital Wallace, Idaho's miners have been striking it rich for more than a century.
*Courtesy Wallace District Mining Museum*

Out west, settlers got richer quicker by mining rare metals and minerals. **WALLACE, IDAHO,** the Silver Capital of the World, was originally the site of a minor gold strike. But the silver veins proved far more rewarding, and eventually the miners got rich themselves. Wallace is still home to four of the world's most productive silver mines.

One boom town that eventually went bust, at least in mining, was **GRANTS, NEW MEXICO,** once the Uranium Capital of the World. Uranium was discovered there in 1950, and within a decade, the population had soared from 2,200 to 10,000, with mining companies pouring resources and people into the community. The uranium mines disappeared in the 1980s, but the town's glowing history is still on record in the New Mexico Museum of Mining, the country's only museum devoted to uranium mining. Grand Junction, Colorado, is another community that called itself the world's uranium capital; and like Grants, its mining heritage faded along with the Cold War era of uranium demand.

The West has supplied fuel for more than just nuclear weapons. It's also home to such energetic places as Rifle, Colorado, the Oil Shale Capital of the World, and Hugoton, Oklahoma, the Gas Capital of the World. And Battle Mountain, Nevada, is the Barite Capital of the World, thanks to the wealth of the sulfate mineral found in the area.

Back east, the fires are kept burning at such capitals as Beckley, West Virginia, the Smokeless Coal Capital of the World, and Scranton, Pennsylvania, the Anthracite Capital of the World.

## DID YOU KNOW...

### Putting New Mexico Uranium on the Map

Maps and data on New Mexico's uranium resources can be obtained from the National Uranium Resource Evaluation (NURE) reconnaissance survey program, a 1974–1984 project. According to the New Mexico Bureau of Mines and Mineral Resources, "Elements of the NURE program include: geochemical surveys and maps, geologic maps, geophysical surveys, quadrangle assessments for uranium resources, miscellaneous geologic investigations, and drilling projects."

The town of Altoona, Pennsylvania, has a decidedly different reason to celebrate its holes in the ground: With tongue planted firmly in cheek, it calls itself the Pothole Capital of the World, thanks to its abundance of really big potholes.

In addition to the crystals from **MOUNT IDA, ARKANSAS,** the country has a few more sparkling spots. Franklin Township, New Jersey, is the Fluorescent Mineral Capital of the World; and another Franklin, this one in North Carolina, calls itself the Gem Capital of the World—thanks to the bejeweled landscape, where visitors from around the world go to hunt for rubies and sapphires.

But only diamonds will do for some, and they really dig Murfreesboro, Tennessee, the Diamond Capital of the World. It's home to Diamond State Park, where visitors can literally mine for diamonds.

Some of America's greatest wealth lies beneath its surface, but it takes the dedicated and proud people of their namesake capital communities to mine these riches and bring them forth so that others might build skyscrapers or carve memorials, burn fuel or cut gems. Whether quarried or mined, the discovery and recovery of these underground resources is a both a duty and a blessing for those who live above them.

# ⚙ Elberton, Georgia

∾∾∾∾∾∾∾∾∾∾∾∾∾∾∾∾∾∾∾∾∾∾∾∾∾

GRANITE CAPITAL OF THE WORLD

Elberton's granite quarries yield some of the finest memorial stone in the world. *Courtesy Elberton Granite Association, Inc.*

Driving into Elberton, Georgia, you can't help but notice there are an awful lot of stonecutters and monument companies around. Elberton, the Granite Capital of the World, leads the nation in dimension stone production (mainly granite), according to 1992 statistics from the U.S. Bureau of Mines. And it does more than quarry the stone, as proclaimed in the community's other slogan (more of a mouthful than Granite Capital of the World): "Elberton Produces More Granite Monuments Than Any Other City in the World."

The Elberton area has 35 quarries and more than 100 manufacturing plants, so there's no lack of competition for the stone and its finishing. And though the quarries are the ultimate proof of Elberton's solid foundation, the community cements its claim with the Elberton Granite Museum and Exhibit.

The three-level museum, operated by the Elberton Granite Association, features exhibits on the history of granite quarrying and processing, including tools from the chiselling age as well as those from the machine era. It also shows how granite is cut, sandblasted, and polished.

One of the most fascinating exhibits is a miniature replica of Elberton's other great granite attraction, the Georgia Guidestones. These mysterious beacons of modern wisdom were erected 7 miles north of Elberton, in a field next to Highway 77. Like an American Stonehenge, they stand in alignment to the sun at certain points in the sky, and are engraved with 10 statements that seem to be guidelines for preserving, or—heaven forbid—rebuilding civilization. But these are not ancient runestones left by some long-lost civilization. The grouping of stones, weighing a total of 119 tons, was erected in 1979. They were financed by a mysterious man who identified himself only as "Mr. Christian."

The message on the Georgia Guidestones appears in 12 languages, both living—English, Russian, Spanish, Swahili, Chinese, Hindi, Hebrew, Arabic—and dead—Sanskrit, Babylonian cuneiform, Egyptian hieroglyphic, and classical Greek. No matter the language, the message is the same:

Maintain humanity under 500,000,000 in perpetual balance with nature.

Guide reproduction wisely — improving fitness and diversity.

Unite humanity with a living new language.

Rule Passion — Faith — Tradition — and all things with tempered wisdom.

Protect people and nations with fair laws and just courts.

Let all nations rule internally, resolving external disputes in a world court.

Avoid petty laws and useless officials.

Balance personal rights with social duties.

Prize truth — beauty — love — seeking harmony with the infinite.

Be not a cancer on the earth — Leave room for nature — Leave room for nature.

The mysterious Georgia Guidestones, just outside Elberton, bear a message of hope for humanity in 12 languages. *Laura Bergheim*

Elberton is a magical place to visit, just to see the Guidestones alone. They have a power and presence that make you believe in miracles, or at least in mankind. Add into the mix Elberton's monumental granite industry and you have a community with rock-solid roots in a lasting industry.

## FOR FURTHER INFORMATION

**Elberton Granite Museum and Exhibit**
1 Granite Plaza
P.O. Box 640
Elberton, GA 30635
(706) 283-2551

## ❀ Washington County, Georgia

KAOLIN CAPITAL OF THE WORLD

In this high-tech world of polymers and plastics, manufactured materials and space-age substances, it's nice to know that Mother Nature still has a few tricks up her sleeve. Take kaolin, for instance. Ever heard of it? Probably not. It's a white, aluminum silicate clay, predominantly composed of the mineral kaolinate. But chances are, you have come in contact with it. From magazine pages to house paints, plastics to pharmaceuticals, it's used as a filler or coating pigment agent in numerous everyday products. And 60 percent of the world's kaolin is mined in and around Washington County, Georgia, the Kaolin Capital of the World.

Georgia's most important mineral resource, kaolin is mined in three major locations—Sandersville, Wrens, and the Dry Branch-Gordon-McIntyre area—along a stretch known as the Tuscaloosa Fall Line that runs diagonally across the state from Macon to Augusta. This line tells much about the geologic history of the state. A transitional zone between the Piedmont Plateau and the coastal plain, it was the continental shoreline during the Cretaceous Period, about 70 million years ago. Thus, the land to the east of the fall line—most of central Georgia—was once covered by the prehistoric waters of the Atlantic Ocean. In fact, fossilized sharks' teeth, sand dollars, and other ancient sea creature remains are often found in kaolin deposits.

During the Cretaceous Period, heavy mineral deposits were left on the shoreline rocks from water flowing out of mountain streams and rivers toward the ocean. The erosion of these crystalline rock sediments eventually formed the kaolinate deposits that now provide a livelihood for area kaolin miners and manufacturers.

Kaolin mining first began in China; then the British began digging for the stuff when the bright white clay became an important ingredient in fine porcelain. In North America, the Cherokee Indians are believed to have also mined kaolin for their pottery. Though driven from their homelands along the Trail of Tears, the Cherokees' use of Georgia's fine white clay led, at the turn of the century, to a nationwide demand for kaolin, and the region's kaolin mining took off. Today, kaolin is one of the state's major exports—indeed, it's the single largest Georgia export shipped from the port of Savannah.

One of the largest kaolin mining companies, Thiele Kaolin Co., is situated in Sandersville. Its pit-mining operations use heavy equipment to extract the raw kaolin from beneath the layer of "overburden"—topsoil, sand, and clay—up to 100 feet deep that covers the crystal layers. Using draglines, scrapers, and bulldozers, the overburden is cleared away, the crude kaolinate crystals are retrieved and sent to processing, where they are pulverized and purified, using either an airfloat or waterwash method, both of which remove trace impurities. After chemical leaching and magnetic separation, which improve brightness and color, the kaolin is processed for shipping. Depending on industrial needs, it's shipped in powdered or slurry forms.

It's all pretty high-tech for a bunch of crystals formed in prehistoric times, but the people of Washington County—which includes the communities of Warther, Sandersville, Davisboro, Deepstep, Tennville, Oconee, Riddleville, and Harrison—have found this snow white clay to be a rare gift from nature. Around here, its nickname is "white gold." Local businesses, even those having nothing to do with kaolin mining, such as a Sandersville florist, include kaolin in their names.

Sandersville, Georgia, Washington County's seat, is home base for a major kaolin mining company, and also hosts the annual Kaolin Festival. *Courtesy Cal Duke & Associates*

The citizenry even celebrates its magical mineral with a Kaolin Festival, held in mid-October in Sandersville. The festival spotlights local craftspeople and their pottery, naturally, but also features beauty and talent contests, a parade, a golf tournament, and even a Cemetery Ramble through the local graveyard.

The next time you flip through a glossy magazine, paint your living room, or arrange flowers in a porcelain vase, you may not be thinking of Georgia or its kaolin; but chances are, a tiny piece of Washington County has just taken a sedimental journey into your world.

## FOR FURTHER INFORMATION

Washington County Chamber
of Commerce
119 Jones St.
P.O. Box 582
Sandersville, GA 31082
(912) 552-3288

# ○ Bedford, Indiana

LIMESTONE CAPITAL OF THE WORLD

Limestone is the stuff of skyscrapers and statues. Softer and warmer than marble, lighter and more malleable than granite, it's one of the most commonly used building stones in America, and it comes in abundance from the quarries of the Hoosier heartland. Bedford, Indiana, the Limestone Capital of the World, is home to some of the nation's most productive limestone quarries.

It was here, in central-southern Indiana's Lawrence County, that the stone for the Empire State Building was quarried—in the aptly named Empire Quarry. And having been used in a structure that could handle the likes of King Kong, limestone quickly gained acceptance as the stone of choice for other mammoth building projects. Many famous Big Apple structures both secular (Saks Fifth Avenue, Rockefeller Center, and Radio City Music Hall) and sublime (the St. John the Divine Cathedral) were built from Bedford-area limestone.

Likewise, Chicago's skyline boasts limestone landmarks such as the Tribune Tower and the Merchandise Mart; and the Nation's Capital has a number of Lawrence County limestone structures, including the Pentagon and the National Cathedral. Whether it's scraping the sky or reaching toward heaven, Indiana limestone has developed a faithful following among architects and builders.

The local limestone industry's roots are traced to one man, Dr. Winthrop Foote, a Yale-educated physician who came to the Indiana Territory as an untested pioneer after his brother, Ziba, drowned there while surveying. Foote lost his greenhorn status quickly, and decided to stay to treat the settlers, who were sorely in need of medical assistance—especially since most had homesteaded in Palestine, the Lawrence County seat, situated along the malarial

This touching memorial honors a young stonecutter, Lewis Baker, who died in his prime; it captures the image of his workbench as it was the day he died. *Courtesy Lawrence County Tourism Commission*

White River. But Foote was more than a frontier doctor; he was a visionary. He was instrumental in moving the county seat to higher ground—Bedford—and opened the county's first limestone quarry, the Blue Hole. When he died in 1856, he was buried in a magnificent tomb (still visible, just off Bedford's Main Street) alongside the remains of his long-lost brother, Ziba, for whom he had the memorial erected.

Bedford's limestone is renowned, but the town is also famous for the fine workmanship it lavishes on the stone after it has been culled from the earth. Master stonecutters have given Bedford numerous and poetic monuments, including the Foote Tomb; and their artistry continues to this day.

Many Lawrence County graveyards include Bedford stonecutters' works, but one of the finest collections is in Bedford's Green Hill Cemetery, where a unique kind of memorial seems to grow from the ground. Many graves are marked with intricately carved "tree stumps," appearing to have been chopped off in their prime. Standing as tall as 12 feet high, these late nineteenth-century and early twentieth-century monuments feature realistically sculpted bark, creeping vines, and flowers, and even a few stubby branches jutting out from their trunks. The inscription facades are smooth, as if the bark had been peeled away. As metaphors for life and death, the stump stones are wise, gentle memorials.

The cemetery is also home to a monument that captures the spirit of Bedford's famous artisans. It's a memorial to a young stonecutter, Lewis Baker, who died suddenly while at work. Erected in

1917, the memorial re-creates his workbench, with his whisk broom and tools laid across it just as they were the day he died.

Another remarkable stone monument is a life-sized statue of local Tom Barton, memorializing him as he lived—as a golfer, his clubs and bag in one hand and wide-brimmed hat in the other.

The nearby community of Mitchell has another fascinating limestone memorial, a haunting monument to astronaut Virgil "Gus" Grissom, who died in a January 1967 fire during a ground test of the Apollo I module he was to have piloted. A hometown hero, Grissom is remembered with a beautifully carved rocket ship, poised as if to perpetually propel him toward the stars.

To get the whole story on Lawrence County's limestone, visit the Land of Limestone, an Indiana Heritage Exhibition at the Bedford Campus of Oakland City University. The exhibit, housed in a 1926 landmark limestone building, traces the local stone's natural, industrial, and architectural history.

Lawrence County limestone is the sturdy stuff of some of America's most famous buildings;

Mitchell, Indiana, features this landmark memorial to Apollo I astronaut and hometown hero Virgil "Gus" Grissom. *Courtesy Lawrence County Tourism Commission*

and at its heart is Bedford, a classical hometown community, where the local industry has also become the local art. From the quarries of limestone to the carvers who transform it into monumental works, it's a place where the people and their land are intimately linked, as chisel to stone.

## FOR FURTHER INFORMATION

**Bedford Area Chamber of Commerce**
1116 W. 16th St.
Bedford, IN 47421
(812) 275-4493

**Land of Limestone Exhibition**
c/o Lawrence County Tourism Commission
P.O. Box 1193
1116 16th St.
Bedford, IN 47421
(812) 275-7637 or (800) 798-0769

# ❁ Mount Ida, Arkansas

QUARTZ CRYSTAL CAPITAL OF THE WORLD

Ever watch one of those New Age cable programs and wonder where they get all those crystals? The citizens of Mount Ida, Arkansas, can tell you. That mystical rock comes in abundance from the earth beneath their feet. Mount Ida prides itself on being the Quartz Crystal Capital of the World.

Mount Ida's crystal-clear claim is buried in the heart of the Ouachita Mountains, where quartz crystal miners uncover the cool gemstone that has become a hot seller since psychics and channelers began touting the rock's supposed powers. The demand for the quartz became so great in the late 1980s, the height of the New Age craze, that the media dubbed the surge in interest the "crystal rush." The boom glutted the market with the stone, however, so the rocks-to-riches saga faded as crystal prices dropped. But the region still benefits greatly from the continuing demand for its crystal.

The championship Quartz Crystal Dig features a crystal gem show, where shoppers stop to browse and buy quartz. *Photo by Debbie Baldwin, courtesy Mount Ida Chamber of Commerce*

About 99 percent of the crystal mined in the United States comes from this area, and its market value is said to top $100 million. Other crystal mines around the world can be found in Brazil, Madagascar, and Mexico, but the pure quartz crystal that lies beneath Montgomery County, home to Mount Ida, is said to be the world's largest such deposit.

Though professional mining companies dig for crystal using heavy machinery, you don't have to be a pro to hunt for quartz in the mountains. Numerous outfits offer rockhounds the chance to dig for crystal themselves; drive around Mount Ida and it seems every corner has a rock shop with a dig-it-yourself mine attached.

A number of the public mines, including Robins Mining Co., Ocus Stanley and Son, Fiddler's Ridge Rock Shop, Starfire Mines, and Crystal Pyramid, help put on the Annual World's Championship Quartz Crystal Dig in mid-October.

Started in 1986, the competition pits diggers against each other in a race to find the largest chunk or cluster of quartz crystal; the winners receive cash awards. Everyone goes home with at least a bit of quartz, since it's so abundant in the mining areas. But be prepared to get your fingernails dirty—hand tools are the only equipment allowed. Those who prefer their crystal a little more refined come for the gem and crystal show that accompanies the big dig.

Though collectors of all stripes show up for the event, the clear believers are the New Agers, who attribute to crystal the power to calm and focus the mind, to heal the body, and to inspire creative energies. Some people even believe crystals can help their cars get better gas mileage and their home appliances work more efficiently. This may or may not be true, but certainly the thousand or so residents of Mount Ida have experienced the economic power they hold.

## FOR FURTHER INFORMATION

**Mount Ida Chamber of Commerce**
P.O. Box 6
Mount Ida, AR 71957
(501) 867-2723

### Crystal Mines

**Crystal Pyramid**
HC 63
Box 136A
Mount Ida, AR 71957
(501) 867-2568

**Fiddler's Ridge Rock Shop and Crystal Mines**
HC 63
Box 211J
Mount Ida, AR 71957
(501) 867-2127

**Ocus Stanley & Son**
Pine St.
P.O. Box 163
Mount Ida, AR 71957
(501) 867-3556

**Robins Mining Co.**
Box 236
Mount Ida, AR 71957
(501) 867-2530

**Starfire Mines**
HC 63
Box 306
Mount Ida, AR 71957
(501) 867-2341

# ⚙ Wallace, Idaho

SILVER CAPITAL OF THE WORLD

Gold may be the metal of wedding bands and fili-grees, but it's silver that sets our tables, plates our tea sets, and rings our bells. And though many a Western town's gold rush background brought it glory and gunfights, no town shines with quite the spirit of Wallace, Idaho, the Silver Capital of the World.

Wallace's shimmering veins are tapped by four of the world's largest silver mines—the Sunshine, Coeur, Galena, and Lucky Friday—which, by 1985, had produced a combined total of a billion ounces of silver. Wallace's mining activity achieved significant levels of production shortly after the turn of the century, though largely as the by-product of lead mining. But major silver strikes in the 1930s and 1950s proved the region was more than a flash in the pan.

Gold fever initially sparked interest in the region's riches after word spread of an 1882 strike about 20 miles north of present-day Wallace. Thousands of prospectors soon descended on the area. In 1884, outcrops of silver-lead ores were located to the south, and a cedar swamp at the mouth of the canyon soon became a settlement. The entire area became known as the Coeur D'alene Mining Region.

By the late nineteenth century, the growing wealth of mining companies attracted bandits. And though train robberies were a popular way of snatching the loot en route, sometimes the bad guys went straight to the source. In 1891, the town was both shocked and amused by the underground robberies of two miners in the Standard-Mammouth Mine, in which a pair of masked men discovered that the miners were hardly a mother lode of money. The bandits got away with only $478 (still a lot of money in those days).

The mines often had internal problems of another kind. In 1892, a bitter labor dispute between the mine owners and the miners led to the dynamiting of the Frisco Mill. Six people were killed, and federal troops placed Wallace under martial law for four months. The

This 1896 view of Sixth Street looking north from Bank Street reveals a mining town on the verge of its biggest boom years. *Courtesy Wallace District Mining Museum*

following year, the fallout from the labor dispute and a sudden drop in silver prices forced many of the mines to shut down. Though the market and the mines soon recovered, in 1899, an even more violent labor war broke out, landing 1,200 miners in a makeshift jail dubbed the "Bullpen." The town was again placed under martial law—this time for two years.

To understand the magnitude of the boom during those mining rush days, consider that today Wallace has a population of about 1,010—nearly 200 fewer than the number of miners jailed in the Bullpen a century ago.

The history of silver mining in Wallace has been neither pretty nor polished; but after the strife of the late nineteenth century, with silver prices again on the rise, technologies easing the hardships of mining, and labor laws protecting the miners' rights, the Wallace silver mines finally began living up to their potential. The new century saw a rebirth and rededication to mining that helped keep the town afloat even through the Depression.

Today, silver mining is still a major part of Wallace's economy, but so too is tourism. The Sierra Silver Mine Tour, one of the state's most popular summer attractions, takes hard-hatted visitors on an underground tour through a "depleted" silver mine. Tourists learn how miners "follow the ore vein" as a road map, and see exhibits and equipment that tell the history of mining from the early days of mules and hand-drills to today's machine-based extraction methods. The tour guide even encourages you to do a little mining of your own. You can keep a piece of history if you pick up a few rocks along the way, but even if you don't get your own piece of the rock, you will still feel like part of the team—and the tour ticket is a replica of a mine stock certificate.

Another mining-related attraction is the Wallace District Mining Museum, opened in 1956, which houses an extensive collection of mining tools and artifacts. Exhibits include examples of mine lighting—from the old stearic candles to today's battery-operated mine lights—and drilling equipment—from wrist-shattering hand-drills to modern machines. Though mining is the focus here, the museum also has other local artifacts, including early phonographs and office machinery.

For those who prefer their silver in a more refined form—say, as jewelry—local stores such as the Idaho Silver Shop and Silver Capital Arts cater to shoppers.

If you still want to go for the gold, drive an hour north to Murray. This tiny town, little more than a memory, flashes its gold rush roots in numerous ways. As you drive through the Murray Valley, you'll see giant piles of rocks that were dredged up by the Yukon Gold Mining Co., where lucky lookers sometimes can find gold nuggets buried in the rubble. Murray is also home to the Sprag Pole Museum, which has artifacts and photos of the old gold-mining days. Driving west from Murray toward Prichard (named for Andy Prichard, who started the gold rush), you'll find the remains of Eagle City, a former tent camp where some 1,500 gold miners camped during the winter of 1883, at the height of the rush.

But there's more gold in them thar hills than meets the eye: Recreation dollars pour into the Silver Mountain and the Lookout Pass area during the winter months when skiers, snowmobilers, dog mushers, and other winter sports enthusiasts arrive by the hordes. In the summer, those same hills are alive with campers and hikers. And year-round, tourists line up for a ride on the World's Longest Gondola, which offers a scenic mountain view.

Wallace's turn-of-the century Main Street can set off a bout of déjà vu with its almost generically American hometown

The Sixth Street view, as seen in the 1970s, shows why the town's careful preservation of its downtown structures earned it a place on the National Register of Historic Places. *Courtesy Wallace District Mining Museum*

appeal; the downtown historic district is listed on the National Register of Historic Places. You might also recognize the town if you were one of the few people who saw the epically unsuccessful Hollywood western *Heaven's Gate,* which was filmed in Wallace.

Wallace celebrated its silver centennial in 1984 (the town was officially founded in 1884). In the century since its birth, much has changed. It has grown from a mountain mining camp into a serious industrial community, evolving into a town that balances mining with recreation, where the skier-filled slopes of its white-capped mountains are adding new economic luster to the old silver strands that still lie beneath them.

## FOR FURTHER INFORMATION

### General Information

**Wallace Chamber of Commerce**
P.O. Box 1167
Wallace, ID 83873
(208) 753-7151

## Attractions and Events

**The Idaho Silver Shop**
417 6th St.
Wallace, ID 83873
(208) 556-1171

**Sierra Silver Mine Tour (seasonal)**
P.O. Box 712
Wallace, ID 83873
(208) 752-5151

**Oasis Bordello Museum**
605 Cedar St.
Wallace, ID 83873
(208) 753-0801

**Wallace District Mining Museum**
509 Bank St.
Wallace, ID 83873
(208) 556-1592

# ○ Grants, New Mexico

(FORMER) URANIUM CAPITAL OF THE WORLD

The atomic age has traced a generation-splitting path of progress that ricocheted from wonder and worry to fervor and fear before settling into ambivalent acceptance of its peril and promises. And in its initial flush came the 1950s uranium boom out West, an era earmarked with all the exuberance and instant millionaire success stories of a twentieth-century gold rush.

Those days are gone, but the towns that prospered from them still remain, though diminished by the loss of the mines. Grants, New Mexico, is prominent among them. Once proudly touting itself as the Uranium Capital of the World, it now has no operating uranium mines. But the memory lingers like a radiant glow, and the industry has left a legacy in the form of a popular tourist attraction.

The history of Grants' economic development has been almost tidal in its rhythms, with one industry washing ashore as another receded, only to ebb and be replaced by another. Grants, like so many western towns, began as a frontier town. It was named for the three Grant brothers—Angus, Lewis, and John—who were contracted to build a railroad through the area in 1882. Grants' early settlers were sheep and cattle ranchers, drawn by the lush pastures and fresh water supplies. By the turn of the century, a second local industry—logging in the Zuni Mountains—was growing. It overtook ranching as the area's primary economic base after a 1918 drought led to overgrazing.

Crops made a brief comeback in the 1940s, after the completion of the Bluewater Dam in the Bluewater Valley created good irrigation for vegetable growers. Carrots became the crop of choice—Grants was even briefly known as the Carrot Capital of the World—but this growth spurt was short-lived, as post–World War II supermarkets began buying vegetables in bulk from larger farm areas.

Around this same time, U.S. Route 66, which ran through Grants, helped boost the local tourism industry. As one of the only main towns between Gallup, New Mexico, and Phoenix, Arizona, it became a stopping point for road-trippers. Motels and diners opened and thrived from the traffic along this legendary highway, though Gallup, famous for its hotels, still swallowed up most of the overnight business. The interstate system eventually replaced Route 66, with Interstate 40 swooping past Grants, leaving the Mother Road to decay into a crumbling conduit by the 1980s.

After carrots and cars came uranium. As the 1950s dawned, the federal government was buying up uranium for its weapons projects; and a new breed of western prospector began getting rich quick. In 1950, Paddy Martinez, a local Navajo-Mexican, discovered a piece of rock the color of the Sun and took it into Grants to be assayed. It was uranium, and suddenly Grants was a boomtown. In 1958 alone, five uranium mills—Anaconda, Kerr-McGee, Phillips, Homestake New Mexico Partners, and Homestake Sapin—were built in the area.

With the uranium mines came a prosperity the little town had never known before. Roads were finally paved; libraries built; schools improved; and new stores, banks, and other businesses flooded the community. People came with the package too; the 1950 census listed Grants' population at 2,200. By 1955, the town had grown to 7,000; by 1960, it had a population of 10,000.

The 1970s were a period of recession for the area; growth slowed and cutbacks were implemented at the mines. Still, the population held firm; in 1980, it had peaked at 11,450. But, then, what had been

The New Mexico Mining Museum replicates a uranium mine right down to the track draft where the carts were loaded with ore for the journey to the surface. *Photo by Lee Marmon, New Mexico Mining Museum*

a slump became a landslide for the uranium business. By 1983, the last of the mines and mills had closed. Businesses failed. People lost their jobs and left town. The 1990 census listed the population at 8,626.

Yet, as it has in the past, Grants is bouncing back, though its latest industry is born of the bitter realities of modern America. Prisons are going up all over the area. This growth industry in incarceration facilities is bringing renewed vigor to the regional economy.

On a cheerier note, the resurgence of interest in Route 66 has also brought tourist dollars to Grants—the highway celebrated its 66th anniversary in 1991, and, with a new signage program marking the old route and state historical societies (including one in New Mexico) promoting it, nostalgic road-trippers from around the world have been traveling the long lost patch of pavement, part of which still runs through Grants.

Uranium has not completely expended its half-life here either; in fact, Grants boasts the world's only uranium mining museum. The New Mexico Mining Museum and Visitor Center is a graceful stone and glass building that shimmers in the distance like a mirage. Go inside and you will discover that the facility not only rises above the ground but also delves beneath it, taking visitors on a self-guided tour of a typical uranium mine.

After descending the "mine shaft" in an elevator, you start at the station, the staging area where miners, equipment, and ore entered and left the mine. Mines with more than one level had a station at each level, each equipped with ore loading and unloading areas, a repair shop, and a common room where the miners ate lunch and held meetings. After leaving the station, you enter the mine itself to see examples of the mining areas and equipment, such as blasting caps and a long-hold drilling machine, which was used to extract the uranium from the tunnels.

The museum, which doubles as the local visitor's center (it even shares a phone number with the Chamber of Commerce), also has informational videos and exhibits on other area attractions and industries, as well as a fine collection of Anasazi Indian weaving, baskets, pottery, and other crafts.

But the main attraction is the underground uranium mine; it's a rare and unique glimpse of a workplace that few Americans will ever see firsthand. And with a little luck and world of peace, one that few Americans will ever work in again.

## FOR FURTHER INFORMATION

**Grants/Cibola County Chamber of Commerce**
P.O. Box 297
Grants, NM 87020
(505) 287-4802 or (800) 748-2142

**New Mexico Mining Museum and Visitor Center**
Business Loop 40
Grants, NM 87020
(505) 287-4802 or (800) 748-2142

CHAPTER

# OUT OF THIS WORLD

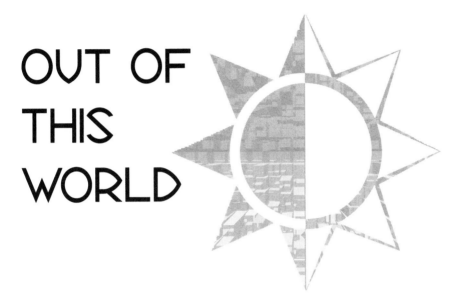

hings that go bump in the night aren't usually good omens for the tourist trade. But some communities have turned local legends and offbeat habits into capital claims, welcoming visitors to explore the spooky or silly heritage that is uniquely their own.

**ANOKA, MINNESOTA,** for instance, though it has gained more fame as the hometown of that companionable prairie radio host Garrison Keillor, also promotes its goosebump-inducing title of Halloween Capital of the World. But you'll find few, if any, satanic goings on there come October; indeed, the community's claim was created by local officials who were spooked by the naughty antics of youngsters. To put a stop to tricks such as knocking over occupied outhouses (this was back in 1920, mind you), the town leaders decided to make the holiday a hometown celebration. The town believes its Halloween happenings, which fill the month of October with orange and black events, are the longest-running, officially sanctioned Halloween festivities in the country — hence the Halloween Capital claim.

225

Another town famous for its spellbinding Halloween celebration is Salem, Massachusetts, a.k.a., the Witch City. Salem's Halloween events draw thousands of visitors who come for a parade, witches ball, and other eerie events. Long held in contempt for the infamous witch trials of 1692, Salem has finally turned its tragedy into a triumphant tourist treat.

It's home to a multitude of bewitching attractions, including the Salem Witch Museum, the Salem Wax Museum of Witches & Seafarers (motto: "We're Dripping with History"), the Witch Dungeon Museum (where the trials are reenacted), and the Witch House (home of one of the judges). Clearly, the legacy of Salem, or at least its name, still casts a powerful spell over tourists.

And nearby, visitors to the original Salem Village (now called Danvers) can spend their time touring the Rebecca Nurse Homestead (Nurse was executed as a witch), the Witchcraft Victims Memorial, and the Danvers Archival Center, which houses the largest collection of printed materials about the infamous witch trials.

Another place with a spooky slogan is Georgetown, South Carolina, the Ghost Capital of the South. Visitors can take ghost tours and even a ghost cruise of the local haunts, or enjoy the spooky production "Ghosts of the Coast" at the beautifully restored Strand Theater — a show that gives the term stage fright a whole new meaning.

If ghosts aren't quite your fright of choice, how about a monster or two? Eons before Steven Spielberg resurrected T-Rex, the state of Utah was a playground for ancient behemoths. Vernal, Utah, enjoys

In the Ghost Capital of the South, Georgetown, South Carolina, the buildings have a haunting history. *Photo by Robert Clark, copyright 1995, courtesy Georgetown County Chamber of Commerce*

The Utah Field House of Natural History (in Vernal, Dinosaur Capital of the World) has an impressive collection of dinosaur bones, rocks, fossils, and wildlife. *Photo by Frank Jensen, copyright 1995, courtesy Dinosaurland Travel Board*

the creature claim of Dinosaur Capital of the World. Visitors can tour Dinosaur Gardens, a Jurassic Park of dino-repros adjacent to the Utah Field House Museum. Inside the museum are the real relics. And throughout the area, dinosaur digs and discoveries are a way of prehistoric life.

Modern monster hunters can try tracking the ultimate American beast in **WILLOW CREEK, CALIFORNIA,** the Big Foot Capital of the World. Situated at the Gateway to Big Foot Country, Willow Creek attracts everyone from documentary filmmakers to curious campers, who use the town as a jumping-off point for wilderness journeys in search of the supersized pedestrian. Willow Creek honors its native monster at Big Foot Days, held Labor Day weekend.

Another creature is the featured attraction in **DOUGLAS, WYOMING,** the Home of the Jackalope. With tongue planted firmly in furry cheek, Douglas celebrates the mythical horned bunny — part jackrabbit, part antelope — with a statue in the local park that also hosts the Douglas Jackalope Days festivities.

Douglas has a vested interest in this antlered animal; as far back as 1939, it got hooked on the bunny's tale after a local prankster put a "stuffed" jackalope on display in a local hotel. The legend grew, and

Douglas, Wyoming, Home of the Jackalope, celebrated its centennial in 1990 by dedicating a park to its hometown beast. *Deb Skalicky, The Douglas Budget*

the town proclaimed itself Home of the Jackalope, even issuing hunting licenses. Other towns tried to follow Douglas' lead, which made the governor so hopping mad he made an official proclamation in 1985 declaring Douglas the one and only jackalope hometown.

Jackalopes are a decidedly American myth, born of the prairie and a few drunken campfire stories. But some newcomers brought the creatures of their homeland with them, at least in spirit. The legendary "little people" of northern Europe immigrated to the Midwest, it seems, for they have taken up residence in two capital communities: Dawson, Minnesota, which calls itself the Gnome Capital of the U.S.A., and Mt. Horeb, Wisconsin, which claims the title of Troll Capital of the World.

Mt. Horeb even has a few examples of these Nordic nuisances scattered about town, in the form of

## DID YOU KNOW...

### Bigfoot's Scientific Stamp of Approval

Though most folks think Bigfoot, the Loch Ness Monster, and other mysterious creatures are more legend than likelihood, a scientific field called "cryptozoology" takes them as seriously as any known species. The term was coined by the science's founding father, Frenchman Dr. Bernard Heuvelmans, author of the 1955 book *On the Track of Unknown Animals*.

local statues. Mt. Horeb spreads it on thick in another way, too; according to Barry Levenson, proprietor of the Mt. Horeb Mustard Museum and Mustard Emporium, Mt. Horeb is also the Mustard Capital of the World. Levenson's museum sponsors the Mt. Horeb Mustard Day in August to celebrate this condimental claim.

Wisconsin is home to other capitals with overtones that are out of this world: Elmwood, Wisconsin, is the UFO Capital of the

CYBERSPACE CONTACTS

## UFO Links on the Web

http://paradise.net/~jose/ufo/ufo.html

Wisconsin may have the monopoly on UFO capitals, but the World Wide Web can't be beat for UFO sightings. To start your alien Internet hunt, visit UFO Links on the Web, a compendium of on-line resources, such as the UFO Resources Directory, that delve into space ships, ETs, and other out-there phenomena.

World. It got its alien affiliation because of the numerous UFO sightings experienced in and around Elmwood. And Elmwood is not alone, even in Wisconsin: The town of Bellville makes a similar UFO Capital of the World claim for its sightings.

Another UFO capital is Roswell, New Mexico. Like Salem, Massachusetts, Roswell has turned a disturbing event into a local tourist industry. Roswell was the setting for the infamous Roswell Incident in the late 1950s, in which an alien spacecraft may or may not have crashed in a field outside of town. Some locals claimed to have seen the wreckage, and the official statements out of Roswell Air Force Base, which recovered the mysterious craft, were contradictory at best. Considering that Roswell is a mecca for many a UFO buff, it's amazing that the town hasn't capitalized more on its legend. Indeed, driving into town, you expect to find a strip of Alien Inns and UFO Burger Huts. Instead, you discover two small museums devoted to UFOlogy, and a tour offered by the owners of the farm where the UFO supposedly hit town. In 1995, Roswell held its first annual UFO festival, however, so the alien attractions are on the rise.

UFOs may not be a modern phenomenon (ancient writings report similar sightings), but our scientific advancement in this century has made them all the more alluring to our collective psyche. With science as our tool, we have crafted the ultimate monster to destroy humankind: the atomic bomb.

**OAK RIDGE, TENNESSEE,** a.k.a. the Atomic City, was itself created by the government as a secret community where scientists could
complete their work. Afterwards, the town was eventually settled by
civilians, who have turned Oak Ridge into a thriving community. Born
of the bomb, it has become a triumph of the human social instinct. But
its history lingers on at such local attractions as the Oak Ridge National
Laboratory and the American Museum of Science and Energy.

Not all of America's offbeat capitals are filled with fright; some
are merely magical. Take **COLON, MICHIGAN**, the Magic Capital of
the World. The world-famous Abbott's Magic Manufacturing Co. is in
Colon, making the small western Michigan town a must-see for
magicians — especially during Abbott's Magic Get-together in early
August, when prestidigitators from around the world descend on the
town to pull some tricks. But year-round, visitors pack the factory
showroom and stroll the small town that charmed Harry Blackstone,
Sr., so much that he made it his home from 1926 to 1949.

And some capitals just like to party. Like Anoka and its Halloween
festivities, a number of other towns take a certain holiday and make it
their own. Anthony, Texas/New Mexico, only celebrates its claim
every four years, but when it does, the country gets an extra day to
enjoy itself. That's because Anthony is the Leap Year Capital of the
World. And why not? It leaps two states, straddling Texas and New
Mexico. The town's day-long bash held every February 29th includes
everything from skydiving exhibitions to a dominoes tournament.

Groundhog Day is another February tradition honored with a
capital celebration — actually, with two. Both Punxsutawney, Pennsylvania, and Sun Prairie, Wisconsin, are famous for their Groundhog Day
celebrations (Punxsutawney was the setting for the Bill Murray movie
named for the day). Sun Prairie calls itself the Groundhog Capital of
the World, while Punxsutawney calls itself the Weather Capital of
the World, but they both hold a big party on February 2 to witness the local groundhog offer up shadowy predictions
about the imminence of spring. For more about the
battles between these two towns to hog the spotlight, see Chapter 10.

Another big party, also held in February,
is Mardi Gras. You might assume that New
Orleans is the Mardi Gras Capital of the
World, but in fact, Mobile, Alabama, uses
that claim to promote the fact that it was the
site of the country's first Mardi Gras.

As for St. Paddy's Day, the place to be is O'Neill, Nebraska, the Irish Capital of the World (see Chapter 6). O'Neill was founded by Irish settlers, and continues to celebrate its Emerald Isle heritage with one of the nation's largest St. Patrick's Day parties. Some 20,000 attendees party on in O'Neill, where the big bash is capped off by painting the World's Largest Shamrock at the intersection of Highways 20 and 281.

Moving into the summer months, one of the biggest holidays is the Fourth of July. While tens of thousands visit the Mall in the Nation's Capital, another community, New Castle, Pennsylvania, celebrates its own booming business as the Fireworks Capital of the World, thanks to the presence of two internationally renowned pyrotechnics manufacturers.

While many communities would rather bask in the warmth of an endless summer, others embrace the change of season. Clarion County, Pennsylvania, promotes itself as the Autumn Leaf Capital of the World. And a number of places ring in the holiday season any-time of year. Perhaps most famous is Santa Claus, Indiana, in south-western Indiana. The townspeople originally wanted to call it Santa Fe when it was founded in 1846, but another community beat them to the filing office; so, since it was Christmastime, the citizens of the tiny town changed the Fe to Claus and a ho-ho-hometown was born. No matter what the holiday in this town, Santa Claus gets into the act. It's home to the Holiday World amusement park, which features themed areas celebrating such festive occasions as Halloween, the Fourth of July, and, of course, Christmas.

And then there's Berrien Springs, Michigan, the World's Christmas Pickle Capital, which hosts the Christmas Pickle Festival in early December, including a parade led by the Grand Dillmeister, featuring Rudolph the Red-Nosed Pickle and tractors decorated as pickles. It just proves that you can slice a holiday any way you want and still find new ways to serve it up.

From the Bigfoot Capital of the World to the Witch City, the Fireworks Capital of the World to Santa Claus, Indiana, America is home to a charming collection of com-munities where a sense of mystery or fun are the main attraction. Some-times, the inexplicable or the simply celebratory can hold a magnetic power that draws a town together and attracts visitors to listen for those bumps or laughs in the night.

## ⊕ Oak Ridge, Tennessee

THE ATOMIC CITY

The atomic age has come and — some optimists among us might even say, gone — taking with it our scientific innocence, that halcyon concept of technology as our friend. But the harnessing of nuclear power has had its benefits as well, in the form of an extraordinarily powerful energy source, which, if carefully controlled, could provide almost infinite power supplies.

Enter Oak Ridge, Tennessee, the Atomic City. The Oak Ridge Project was part of the Manhattan Project, which developed the technology for the world's first nuclear weapons (the actual bombs were assembled in Los Alamos, New Mexico). Though some communities might find this a dubious distinction, Oak Ridge has embraced its powerful place in history with a slogan that sums up its philosophy: "Born of War, Living for Peace, Growing through Science."

The Manhattan Project actually built Oak Ridge. The community did not exist as such until the federal government came to Bear

The overlook at the Oak Ridge National Laboratory (ORNL) gives a panoramic view of the U.S. Department of Energy's multi-program research laboratory. *Courtesy Oak Ridge Convention and Visitors Bureau*

Creek Valley in 1942 and cobbled together a community — originally known as the Clinton Engineering Works, for the nearby town of Clinton — where its scientists and support staff could work in absolute privacy and security. What they created was more than a weapon of mass destruction; they also constructed a city, that today continues to thrive, with a population of 28,000 and an economic and tourism base still grounded in energy, atomic and otherwise.

The U.S. Dept. of Energy now operates the Oak Ridge National Laboratory (ORNL), where it all began, as its largest multiuse energy laboratory. A visitor's center at the laboratory provides tourists a view of its current work in energy sciences and technologies as well as an historical perspective on the Manhattan Project and its aftermath. An overlook also offers a panoramic view of the ORNL complex.

Oak Ridge is an atomic tourist's dream: Many of the landmarks from the Manhattan Project have been preserved as historic sites and are open for viewing. Stop by the Welcome Center in the Energy House on Tulane Ave. to pick up area guides that map out the local sites.

Your first stop should be Jackson Square Historic Park, on Tennessee Ave., where the original Manhattan Project townsite was constructed. Now a retail area, this is the town's core; the park features displays on the area's development.

Another atomic attraction is the Graphite Reactor, on Bethel Valley Road, at ORNL. The world's first continuously operated reactor, it was built as a pilot facility for the larger plutonium production complex located in Hanford, Washington. The reactor was decommissioned in 1963. Now listed as a National Historic Landmark, it's open to the public, with a self-guided tour of the control room and other areas, and models and displays that relate the story of the essential task it performed.

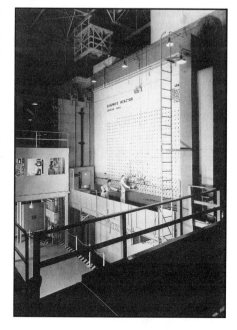

A National Historic Landmark, the Graphite Reactor can now be visited by tourists. *Courtesy Oak Ridge Convention and Visitors Bureau*

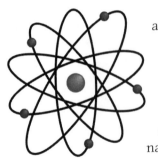

The Oak Ridge K-25 Site on Highway 58 is another important landmark: Formerly the Oak Ridge Gaseous Diffusion Plant, the K-25 plant was used for enrichment of uranium 235. The K-25 Site was one of several code-named facilities in the Oak Ridge area; Y-12 was another uranium enrichment plant, and X-10 was the code name for ORNL.

The K-25 Site can be toured or viewed from a visitor's overlook in a pleasant, wooded setting complete with picnic area. After your picnic, head for the massive American Museum of Science and Energy, with extensive, and often interactive, exhibits on the Manhattan Project, atomic power, and other kinds of energy, as well as fun sections on science and technology. Owned by the U.S. Dept. of Energy (and operated by a contractor), it's a free museum that offers some perspective on where Oak Ridge fits into the larger picture of technology, and the ways in which science, good or bad, has changed our world.

If you still have some energy, take one last excursion, this time to the Bull Run Steam Plant in nearby Claxton. Operated by the Tennessee Valley Authority (TVA), it's one of the world's largest coal-fired generating plants. Lobby exhibits on steam energy explain how the generation process works, and show how steam power is used in modern applications.

To see what the area was like before the feds moved in, visit the New Bethel Church on the ORNL grounds. It was one of the few structures left standing after the government bought up the 60,000 acres it needed for its top-secret complex. Built in 1924, it once served the farming community that disappeared beneath the Manhattan Project's mushroom shroud of secrecy. Today, the church has been restored, and displays artifacts on local life as it was before bomb research blew this area's rural existence off the map.

Oak Ridge may have its foundation in the Manhattan Project, but the city eventually outgrew its roots. In 1947, the Atomic Energy Commission took control of the Manhattan District, and two years later, the town was opened to the public for settling. In 1955, the Atomic Energy Commission sold the remaining government-owned buildings, including houses and industrial facilities, to the private citizens who were by then turning Oak Ridge into a real hometown.

The federal government never really left, though, as evidenced by ongoing Department of Energy projects; nevertheless, from this federal experiment sprang a real community. And the people of Oak Ridge aren't a bit bothered by their city's atomic past — after all, everything comes from the atom.

## FOR FURTHER INFORMATION

### General Information

**Oak Ridge Convention & Visitors Bureau**
302 S. Tulane Ave.
Oak Ridge, TN 37830
(423) 482-7821

### Attractions and Events

**American Museum of Science and Energy**
300 S. Tulane Ave.
Oak Ridge, TN 37830
(423) 576-3200

**Bull Run Steam Plant**
1265 Edgemoor Rd.
Claxton, TN 37116
(423) 945-7200

**Oak Ridge National Laboratory**
Office of Public Affairs
P.O. Box 2008
Oak Ridge, TN 37831
(423) 574-4160

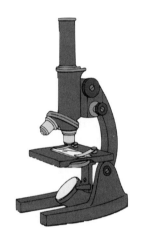

# ✪ Willow Creek, California

BIGFOOT CAPITAL OF THE WORLD

Though the monsters of the modern world are all too often human, we have a few creatures of epic proportions lingering in our collective closet, and few are as famous or frighteningly believable as Bigfoot. As recently as 1995, potentially significant sightings have made paranormal researchers once again wonder whether a manlike beast — perhaps a missing link in the chain of evolution — wanders the dense woodlands of the Pacific Coast.

At the gateway to one of Bigfoot's primary stomping grounds, the Salmon-Trinity Alps Wilderness area of Northern California, lies the town of Willow Creek — which proudly calls itself the Bigfoot Capital of the World. And it does more than just define itself by its proximity to this beast: Everywhere you turn in Willow Creek, you'll see evidence of Bigfoot's influence.

There's the Bigfoot Chevron: What better place to tank up before driving off onto those dark, narrow, isolated woodland roads for an idyllic camping trip? The Bigfoot Rafting Co. offers guided trips and raft rentals into the watery reaches of Bigfoot country. And Bigfoot Lumber where, one hopes, they sand the boards thoroughly to avoid those painful Bigfoot splinters.

Some businesses even use Bigfoot as a celebrity endorser: Cinnabar Sam's, a local eatery, proclaims

## DID YOU KNOW...

**Bigfoot Gets Around**
Willow Creek claims the title of world's Bigfoot capital, but the monster may have made tracks across America. According to the Geographic Database of Bigfoot/Sasquatch Sightings and Related Reports, potential Bigfoot evidence such as footprints, sightings, or eerie screams have been reported in spots ranging from Florida's Ocala National Forest to the woods of West Bath, Maine.

"Bigfoot Loves Our Fajitas." And Coast Central Credit Union advertises that "Even Bigfoot Saves with Us." But who would want to bump into him on a dark night at the ATM?

The town also has a Bigfoot statue that graces the town's Don Cave Memorial Park at the intersection of Highways 299 and 96; the statue looks more like a big ape than a hirsute man, but then maybe so does Bigfoot. The statue's builder, Jim McClarin, a Bigfoot booster, admired his subject so much that, when media attention heightened in the late 1960s and early 1970s, he openly feared the creature would be shot or captured. Like many in the area, his fascination with the mystery is a protective one; folks around here don't want Bigfoot caged or stuffed, autopsied or analyzed. As with any legend, once the absolute truth is known, something is diminished.

The Bigfoot Statue is in Willow Creek. *Photo courtesy Bill Lewinson*

Willow Creek celebrates its monster with a bestial blowout called Bigfoot Days, held over Labor Day weekend. It features a Bigfoot Parade (wear big shoes!), an ice cream social, softball and horseshoe tournaments, a barbecue, and craft and food booths. It's basically a hometown festival with a Bigfoot imprint.

Willow Creek's claim as the Bigfoot capital is more than fur deep. This region has seen a number of alleged Sasquatch sightings, some dating to the nineteenth century. The first reported sighting in California occurred in the logging town of Crescent City in 1886; over the next few years, there were reports of a seven- or eight-foot-tall beast in the area between Happy Camp and Willow Creek.

Bigfoot was not new to the region, however. Native American legend long included stories of a shy, giant manimal. And as towns and camps began sprouting up in the big guy's territory, settlers and mountainmen began reporting sightings. In the early 1800s, it was spotted in southern Oregon; by the middle of the century, the creature was reportedly spotted in Washington State as well. Some believers theorize that the 1840's gold rush and its attendant population explosion drove the critter deeper into the woods to escape encroaching civilization.

In this century, the wilderness areas bordering Willow Creek have been the source of numerous sightings and track discoveries. In 1958, humanlike footprints measuring between 16 and 17 inches were found in northeastern Humboldt County. Scientists determined that the creature that made them would have weighed between 600 and 800 pounds. The tracks were considered by many to have been hoaxes, but worldwide media attention resulted in a new name for Sasquatch: Bigfoot.

In the past 40 years, the region has become a favorite filming area for documentary teams in search of Bigfoot; so far, none of them has caught the critter on tape. The most famous Bigfoot film remains that of Roger Patterson, who claimed to have filmed the creature in 1967 as it lumbered through the woods near Yakima, Washington. The Patterson footage has been questioned because some experts say it looks like a guy in an ape suit on a camping trip.

According to Nita Rowley of the Willow Creek Chamber of Commerce, the most recent alleged sightings were "about two or three years ago, when a couple of boys told the Klamath newspaper they saw it." Klamath is northwest of Willow Creek. But lack of sightings doesn't stop the crowds; Rowley estimates that between 800 and 1,000 people stride into town for Bigfoot Days.

Whether Bigfoot exists, or is just in the minds of those who want to believe is irrelevant to the scores of visitors who come to Willow Creek in search of something they can't prove or explain. Like people buying lottery tickets, they know their chances of seeing the creature are slim; but every now and then, some say it does appear. And in that precious but tiny hope, they come to wander the wilderness in search of a missing link.

### FOR FURTHER INFORMATION

Willow Creek Chamber of Commerce
P.O. Box 704
Willow Creek, CA 95573
(916) 629-2693

# ❂ Anoka, Minnesota

HALLOWEEN CAPITAL OF THE WORLD

When things go bump in the night in most places, people dive under the covers. Not in Anoka, Minnesota. Here, they dance the night away. Anoka is the Halloween Capital of the World, and monsters and devils, ghouls and goblins are welcome in this spooky suburb of Minneapolis-St. Paul.

Anoka got its reputation by proclamation in 1920, when the town leaders were looking for a way to keep naughty kids off the streets during All Hallow's Eve. Things were getting out of hand, with kids soaping windows, turning cattle loose, and overturning occupied out-houses during the traditional evening of pranks. So George Green and other local business and civic leaders hit upon the idea of holding a full-scale Halloween celebration that could engage the whole town. To make it official, Anoka dubbed itself the world's Halloween capital.

Ever since — with the exception of 1942 and 1943, when World War II silenced the town festivities — Anoka has done Halloween big-ger and better than just about any community (with the possible exception of Salem, Massachusetts, a.k.a. Witch City).

Anoka at Halloween is like Rockefeller Center at Christmas. The houses are decorated as if by devilish elves, the townspeople don costumes worthy of a Broadway show, and every party is a black-and-orange fiesta. And collectors of valuable Halloween memorabil-ia know that Anoka is one of the best places in the country to hunt for vintage masks, trick-or-treat bags, and other scary-phernalia.

The last two weeks of October are given over to a full-throttle fright fest, with haunted houses, parades, and trick-or-treat walks for ghouls of all ages. Recent additions to the roster include the fancy dress Orange Tie Ball, where attendees receive orange bow ties.

Anoka's Big Parade of Little People brings out 3,000 local Halloween revelers the last Friday in October. *Photo by Jeff Perrin, Anoka County Union*

The festivities kick off with the Pumpkin Bowl, a big high-school football game that got its nickname from a *Minneapolis Star Tribune* writer when the game fell on Halloween in 1948. There's even a pumpkin-shaped trophy that goes to the game winner every year. Events continue almost daily until the Saturday before (or of) Halloween, when the celebration culminates with a full day of festivities, from the Grand Day Parade to a children's carnival. Then it's time for the biggest event of all, the coronation of Miss Anoka at the Anoka High School.

All this happy haunting does not happen overnight; the Anoka Halloween Committee works year-round planning for October. The all-volunteer organization meets to choose the schedule of events, plan the parties, and generally steer the course for the coming year's spirited celebration.

But Anoka is more than just a Halloween haven. It's also the hometown of two American heroes. The first, though perhaps little known outside the area, is Aaron Greenwald, believed to have been the first man to answer President Lincoln's call to arms when he enlisted in the Union Army. A native Pennsylvanian, Greenwald settled in Anoka in 1854, working in the local flour mills. He died on the soil of his home state, shot at Gettysburg as he knelt to load his musket. Anoka honors his memory with a park in his name.

Anoka's other favorite son is a modern cultural icon: Garrison Keillor, the loquacious bard of public broadcasting, grew up here. "But we're not Lake Wobegon," insists Chamber of Commerce president Peter Turok, warding off the inevitable comparisons between Keillor's make-believe town, reports of which are the highlights of his weekly Prairie Home Companion radio show broadcast from St. Paul. "People call all the time, expecting to find the stores and restaurants mentioned

## DID YOU KNOW...

**Halloween's Haunting History**
It's a bit tricky unearthing the dark roots of Halloween, but the holiday is often traced to an ancient Celtic festival called "Samhain," held the last day of October to herald the end of the Celtic year. The event honored the Lord of Death, and celebrants built bonfires and sacrificed animals (perhaps even humans) to pacify the spirits of the dead who were said to return to Earth the first day of November.

on Prairie Home Companion, but they're not here."

Still, Turok admits that Anoka bears some resemblance to Keillor's fictitious hometown. The kindness and humanity of the people are the same, for instance. When asked whether it could be said that Anoka is a "breath" of Lake Wobegon, Turok declares, "Yes, that's a perfect term for it. We're a breath of Lake Wobegon. We have the essence, but we're not actually the place."

Keillor does go back now and then, and no doubt the ghost of Anoka lingers within him in that delicate, indelible way of all hometowns. So when he tells his millions of listeners the latest news from Lake Wobegon, you can bet there's a breath of Anoka haunting the mist of his imagination.

## FOR FURTHER INFORMATION

**Anoka Area Chamber of Commerce**
222 E. Main St.
Anoka, MN 55303
(612) 421-7130

**Anoka Halloween Committee**
P.O. Box 385
Anoka, MN 55303

# ✪ Douglas, Wyoming

HOME OF THE JACKALOPE

Home, home on the strange, where the deer and the jackalope play? Yep, those long western nights could play tricks on lonesome cowpokes. Some even invented mythical beasties of the prairies to ease the boredom, and none of these whimsical critters is as revered or amusingly admired as the jackalope, a weird synthesis of jackrabbit and antelope.

This mythological hybrid is the subject of a plethora of Wild West T-shirts, bumperstickers, postcards, and even a few artfully assembled stuffed models. And nowhere is the myth more fondly preserved than in Douglas, Wyoming, the official Home of the Jackalope.

According to the cheeky description served up on the menu of Madame Clementine's, a local restaurant, the first jackalope was seen in 1829, when "an occasionally sober trapper, named Roy Ball, observed one in what is now the area of Douglas." The story goes that the animals were also known to Native Americans, who called them "dust devils" for the swirls of dirt the fast furballs kicked up. As the menu notes, jackalopes are still known for creating dust storms; however, "It is not true that the larger jackalopes cause tornadoes, but their speed and quickness is verified by the fact that they do mate during lightning flashes."

According to legend, pioneers even ate jackalope as game, though how they could catch this hurried hybrid is questionable. As the menu explains, "It was early known the animals could be quick-

ly disoriented by baiting them with alcoholic beverages, following which they became giddy and would often attempt to catch bullets with their mouths." Oddly, this was also true of the people who reported seeing jackalopes.

Jackalopes come in all sizes, from frisky little babies to monstrous carnivores. Luckily, few if any are left, since, as the menu explains, they were nearly wiped out by harsh winters in the 1880s, mild summers in the 1890s (lack of thunderstorms reduced mating), and "Prohibition.... and Daylight Savings Time."

The jackalope statue is the centerpiece for the Jackalope Day festivities. *Deb Skalicky, The Douglas Budget*

Despite this apparent population plummet, in 1939, Douglas taxidermist Doug Herrick prepared a jackalope for public display; it was, according to a 1985 proclamation by Wyoming Governor Ed Herschler, the "first Jackalope to appear in our fabulous world." Thus implying, perhaps, that the jackalope was a twentieth-century invention? Ahh, what a tangled web of wabbit.

The legend began to grow. Roy Ball (no doubt descended from the fellow by the same name who spied the first jackalope) bought Herrick's stuffed wonder and displayed it in his LaBonte Hotel in Douglas. In the 1940s, local newspaper columnist Jack Ward, who also served as the Douglas Chamber of Commerce secretary-manager, began publicizing the jackalope tale. Then the chamber began issuing jackalope hunting licenses, and soon media around the country were hopping all over the story. Douglas had established itself as jackalope central.

In 1960, the state issued the Douglas Chamber of Commerce a trademark on the word Jackalope; in 1970, the state issued the chamber a trademark on its claim as Home of the Jackalope.

Protecting the title hasn't been easy. Indeed, there have been so many interloping communities that the governor's 1985 proclamation put it bluntly: "WHEREAS, there is evidence that other towns, states, and organizations are claiming to have originated and promoted the jackalope; NOW, THEREFORE, I, ED HERSCHLER, Governor of the State of Wyoming, do hereby proclaim Douglas, Wyoming to be the official HOME OF THE JACKALOPE.... I encourage those writers and organizations which have attempted to rustle the origin and home of the Jackalope away from Douglas...to cease and desist from this misbegotten activity." Indeed!

Douglas celebrates its big bad bunny with more than words: Every June, it holds the raucous Jackalope Days, where locals gather for food and fun around the town's jackalope statue, the original of which was erected in 1965.

Douglas has more than a rabbit's foot in the door of history. It is a classic pioneer town, and the deep wagon wheel ruts from such major westward routes as the Oregon, Emigrant, Bozeman, and Mormon trails can still be found in the Douglas area. Along these trails, you'll also find the scattered graves of pioneers who died on the journey. Douglas's cemetery is also the final resting place for several notorious Wild West outlaws, including Doc Middleton and George Pike.

Much of the pioneer traffic took place before the town was established in 1886; like many communities, it was born of the railroad, and grew rapidly as settlers moved down track from Ft. Fetterman, an army outpost eight miles from Douglas that was heavily manned during the Indian uprisings. The fort still stands, and many of its buildings have been restored; it's the site for annual frontier reenactments during Ft. Fetterman Days, held in mid-June.

Another taste of the old West can be found in the Wyoming Pioneer Memorial Museum, home to a fine collection of Native American and pioneer artifacts. The museum even has one of the first schoolhouses built in Wyoming.

Though Douglas's pioneer spirit lives, it's a modern community with an economy based on power and agriculture. And then there's that jackalope tourism industry — it may not keep the town afloat, but it's helped put it on the map of modern mythology.

## FOR FURTHER INFORMATION

### General Information

**Douglas Area Chamber of Commerce**
121 Brownfield Rd.
Douglas, WY 82633
(307) 358-2950

## Attractions and Events

**Fort Fetterman**
c/o Fort Phil Kearny State Historic Site
P.O. Box 520
Story, WY 82842
(307) 358-2864

**Madame Clementine's Restaurant**
1199 Mesa Drive
Douglas, WY 82633
(307) 358-5554

**The Wyoming Pioneeer Memorial Museum**
P.O. Drawer 10
Douglas, WY 82633
(307) 358-9288

# ❀ Colon, Michigan

MAGIC CAPITAL OF THE WORLD

One of the first signs that childhood innocence is fading comes when a child watches a magician pull a rabbit out of a hat, and asks not where the rabbit came from but where the hat came from. This signals an understanding that the trick is about the hat, not the rabbit.

Chances are, that hat came from Abbott's Magic Manufacturing Co., the world's largest such factory, in Colon, Michigan, the Magic Capital of the World. Abbott's has been around since 1934, but Colon was a magical town even before its famous factory appeared on the scene. In 1926, the tiny town in southwestern Michigan became the home base for a troupe of performers headed by Harry Blackstone, Sr. He turned Angel Island on Colon's Sturgeon Lake into Blackstone Island, and he lived there until 1949 when health problems forced him to relocate to California.

The magical mayhem of Blackstone Island attracted magicians from around the globe to visit the leading magician of their time; Percy Abbott, an Australian by birth and magician by trade, was among these followers. He arrived at Blackstone Island in 1927 and

Abbott's showroom is a visual treat, with tricks galore and old magic show posters as decoration. *Laura Bergheim*

promptly fell for local lovely Gladys Goodrich and decided to stick around. Abbott, who had run a magic shop back home in Sydney, formed a partnership with the renowned Colon magician, and the pair opened the Blackstone Magic Company.

Unfortunately, a misunderstanding between the two caused the partnership to go "poof" after only 18 months, and Abbott went back on the road as a performer. But he didn't forget Gladys; he returned to marry her in 1929, and she joined him on the road. In 1934, with a baby on the way, they resettled in Colon, where Percy opened his Abbott's Magic Co. A partner, Recil Bordner, joined Abbott later that year (he would eventually buy out Abbott altogether in 1959), and what started as a tiny catalog company above the local grocery store was slowly transformed into the world's largest supplier of tricks and treats.

Today, there's no mistaking that Colon is the world's magic capital. Even the street signs are decorated with top hat symbols. Visitors stop first at the factory, of course; then it's on to other magical establishments throughout town — places such as Memory Lane Antiques, which specializes in old magic collectibles, and the "world famous" M & M Grill, with its autograph board featuring the signatures of magical legends (no doubt they're asked not to sign in disappearing ink).

But Abbott's is the top treat in town, and visitors from all over come to browse the marvelous showroom, where trained staff pull tricks on wide-eyed customers all day long. The showroom is decorated with antique post-ers from magic shows and during the summer it hosts magic shows featuring visiting magicians. They know their audience may be more knowledgeable than the average magic fan, but that only makes their job more challenging.

For those who want even more magical moments, visit Colon during the first week in August, when Abbott's hosts the Magic Get-together, an event dating back to 1935. It was at that first gathering of illusionists that Lester Lake, a.k.a., Marvelo, dubbed Colon the Magic Capital of

Abbott's Magic Manufacturing Co. enchants visitors in the summer with live performances. *Laura Bergheim*

the World. Subsequent Get-togethers were held in other locations every now and then, but the event is now firmly planted on its home turf of Colon.

Today, the Magic Get-together draws hundreds of magicians and thousands of spectators from around the world, who descend on the tiny town for this sleight-of-hand Superbowl during which participants share tricks of the trade. Colon during the Get-together is an enchanted city. Every sidewalk, it seems, has a magician or two practicing tricks. The stores are filled with performers, and every available venue, from Abbott's showroom to the Colon High School auditorium, hosts lectures and performances by world-class talent. The event even features specialty subevents such as the Vent-o-Rama, a ventriloquists' gabfest.

Colon's peculiar claim to fame makes it one of the country's most endearing capital communities. And one that could well serve as a lesson in the power of belief. There's magic in the explicable, and hidden truths are sometimes best left unknown. So sit back and enjoy the show.

## FOR FURTHER INFORMATION

**Abbott's Magic Manufacturing Co.**
124 St. Joseph St.
Colon, MI 49040
(616) 432-3235

# CHAPTER 10

# (NOT SO) BITTER BATTLES

ometimes capital communities find they must defend their sloganeering supremacy for the number one spot in an industry or crop, sport or celebration. How high are the stakes? If you call your town the watermelon capital of the world — as do at least a half-dozen communities — and hold a big watermelon festival that helps attract major tourist dollars and media attention, it can take the juice out of your fruit if a town just across the state line is making the same claim.

So what's a world capital to do if it's not all alone in the world, as is the case in **CRYSTAL CITY, TEXAS,** and **ALMA, ARKANSAS,** both of which go for the green as the Spinach Capital of the World. Both are known for their spinach-canning facilities, their spinach festivals, and their Popeye statues. Crystal City canned its title first, taking on its capital status in the 1930s when it started the Crystal City Spinach Festival. Popeye creator Elzie Segar even blessed Crystal City's spinach capital moniker with a special cartoon strip. Alma didn't join the fray until the late 1980s, when, in search of a way to promote the town, the locals decided their town was the true spinach capital and began holding their own spinach festival.

From a production perspective, Alma's claim seems reasonable — the local Allen Canning plant produces 56 percent of the world's canned spinach, and its Popeye brand, with the character officially licensed from King Features Syndicate, seems to bear the implicit stamp of approval from the brawny sailor man himself. Still, Crystal City got there first, and its spinach festival is better known. So the two spinach capitals remain in a stalemate, with neither showing evidence of wilting away.

Some face-offs aren't about the semantics of a capital title but rather about the cause of the community's claim to fame: Take **PUNXSUTAWNEY, PENNSYLVANIA,** and **SUN PRAIRIE, WISCONSIN,** both of which celebrate Groundhog Day by honoring their hometown's famously furry forecasters, Punxsutawney Phil and Jimmy the Groundhog. Sun Prairie holds the actual title of Groundhog Capital of the World, while Punxsutawney makes the more predictable claim of being the Weather Capital of the World (though it also goes by Home of the Groundhog). Both towns have been waging a good-natured groundhog war for decades, and the continuing conflict is sure to shadow the communities for years to come.

When a cadre of contenders lines up for a title — as in the Watermelon Capitals that range from **CORDELE, GEORGIA,** to **HOPE, ARKANSAS, SHARTLESVILLE, PENNSYLVANIA,** to **HERMISTON, OREGON, HEMPSTEAD, TEXAS,** to **RUSH SPRINGS, OKLAHOMA** — often the participants on this crowded field will just try to ignore each other and hope the others will go away. Still, the citizens in Cordele, Georgia, are fond of pointing out that their community won the title fair and round in 1991, at a competition designed to lay the capital claim dispute to rest; but Hope and Hempstead were the only other participants, representing a mere patch in the field of claimants.

Hope, Arkansas, is famous for its president (Bill Clinton) and its watermelons.
*Illustration by Michael Arnold, courtesy Hope Chamber of Commerce*

Another fruit that has inspired multiple capitalizations is the succulent strawberry; Plant City, Florida, calls itself the Winter Strawberry Capital of the World, while both Watsonville, California, and Ponchatoula, Louisiana, go for the whole hull as the Strawberry Capital of the World. Apples, meanwhile, are at the core of the dispute between Wenatchee, Washington, and Winchester, Virginia, both of which call themselves the Apple Capital of the World.

And peanuts are the subject of shell seekers in Dothan, Alabama, Sylvester, Georgia, and Blakely, Georgia, all of which call themselves the Peanut Capital of the World. They hold big peanut festivals and other events to butter up the local tourist trade and celebrate the crop. Ashburn, Georgia, meanwhile, calls itself the Center of the Peanut Belt, and boasts The World's Largest Peanut, which looms 10 feet high.

Even the ramp, a pungent wild leek popular in Appalachia, gets a rise out of Flanagan Hill, West Virginia, and Cosby, Tennessee, both of which call themselves world ramp capitals and hold festivals to honor their homegrown plant.

Prepared foods also can spark multiple capitals. Both Corsicana, Texas, and Claxton, Georgia, proudly bear the title of Fruit Cake Capital of the World. Claxton, Georgia, is the home of the Georgia Fruit Cake Co., founded by Ira S. Womble, who began his baking career in 1917, and, as the company's brochure proudly notes, "No one other than a direct descendant of the founder has ever mixed a batch of our cake." Corsicana, Texas, meanwhile, is home base for the Collin Street Bakery, which has been making its famous Christmas fruit cakes since 1896; it sells its cakes exclusively by mail order.

Now you might think that the world isn't big enough for two fruit cake capitals, but Claxton and Corsicana make a sincere effort to ignore each other. A call to the Corsicana

## CYBERSPACE CONTACTS

### Collin Street Bakery

http://www.collinstreetbakery.com/

Cyber-shoppers can order their capital fruitcakes on-line at Collin Street Bakery Web site. The company history page from this Corsicana, Texas, establishment reveals that "the grand-tasting DeLuxe [fruitcake], whose recipe had traveled six thousand miles from Wiesbaden, was introduced to the little town of Corsicana by a gentle German baker named Gus Weidmann."

Chamber of Commerce elicited a surprised response that Claxton and its bakery even existed, let alone that the communities share a common capital claim.

There's also a title tug-of-war over the all-American tradition of barbecue. Towns and cities taking on the tangy title of Barbecue Capital of the World range from urban legends such as **KANSAS CITY, MISSOURI,** and **MEMPHIS, TENNESSEE,** to smokey small towns such as **LEXINGTON, NORTH CAROLINA, LOCKHART, TEXAS,** and **OWENSBORO, KENTUCKY.** The regional differences in preparation and meats make it impossible to choose or prove a true 'cue capital, so this is more a companionable competition. Many of the capitals hold major cook-offs, and barbecue aficionados from around the country travel from event to event, smoking and saucing and ribbing together in celebration of this classic cooking style.

Among sports-related communities, golf is the major contender for capital competition, with numerous towns and cities claiming to be holey-er than their rivals. Though you could hardly call the competition a golf war, sometimes it seems as though every community with a good course has joined the capital club.

Neon barbecue signs are a colorful advertisement for Kansas City, Missouri's locally famed food. *Courtesy Convention & Visitors Bureau of Greater Kansas City*

Some golf communities literally stand out in their field. Orland Park, Illinois, a.k.a. the Golf Capital of the World, has a water tower that resembles a teed-up golf ball. It's an appropriate symbol: Within a 15-mile radius of the town, which was built by wealthy industrialists, duffers can play some 800 holes of golf.

Carmel, California, home to the world-famous (and now, Japanese-owned) Pebble Beach golf course, also calls itself the Golf Capital of the World. On the other coast, Myrtle Beach, South Carolina, calls itself the Seaside Golf Capital of the World.

The entire state of Ohio is the Golf Capital of the World—at least that's how governor Richard Celeste promoted the state in the 1980s. And Pinehurst, North Carolina, had its title of Golf Capital of the World officially proclaimed by the North Carolina General Assembly in a 1993 joint resolution bill, which states "the roots of American resort golf can be traced to the construction of the first nine holes at Pinehurst in 1896." The bill also notes that "the Pinehurst Resort and Country Club's No. 2 golf course is recognized as one of the top 10 golf courses in the world," and honors that course's designer, Donald Ross, as the "Father of American Golf Course Architecture."

Other competitive sports capitals include the windsurfing capitals of Hood River, Oregon, and the Outer Banks of North Carolina. And then there are the yachting capitals — Marblehead, Massachusetts, calls itself the yachting capital of America, while Newport, Rhode Island, is the Yachting Capital of the World. Marblehead had the capital claim first, thanks to the America's Cup, which was raced off the coastal town's shores; and Marblehead still has three major yacht clubs and several sailing schools. But when the famous race migrated south to Newport, that city claimed the title of world's yachting capital; Newport, too, has major yachting clubs and schools. It's also home to the Museum of Yachting, which includes the America's Cup Gallery, as well as the Hall of Fame for Single-Handed Sailors (honoring not handicapped, but solo, sailors).

But nearby Bristol, Rhode Island, boasts the actual America's Cup Hall of Fame, at the Herreshoff Marine Museum on Narragansett Bay. And it's there that you'll learn such trivia as the fact that the world-famous yachting event wasn't named for the United States, but rather for the yacht, *America*, which won the first race in 1851. If it had lost to its competition, the *Aurora*, we'd be call-

ing the event the Aurora's Cup. The race was actually started by the British, anyway.

Though there's always a tinge of competition when more than one town takes on the same title, more often than not, such contretemps are good-natured, witty, and sometimes downright delightful. There's nothing like a little pressure to bring out the best in a place; it can often result in bigger and better festivals and other creative efforts for attracting visitors. In the end, tourists are the winners. And, besides, America's a big country, and there's plenty of room for all the capitals in the world.

## *Right on 'Cue: The Search for the True*
## BARBECUE CAPITAL OF THE WORLD

Make no bones about it: Barbecue is an American culinary tradition that ranks among the country's most provocative and divisive diversions. Wherever you go in this country, you find local barbecue joints and their devoted denizens who swear by their homemade sauces and smokey meats, and swear at any other place that deigns to call itself better. And, as you might expect in such a competitive field, the number of Barbecue Capitals of the World seems to rival the number of ribs on a rack.

You'll find big cities, such as Memphis, Tennessee, and Kansas City, Missouri, laying claim to the Barbecue Capital crown; and you'll also find small towns such as Owensboro, Kentucky, Lockhart, Texas, and Lexington, North Carolina, calling themselves the Barbecue Capital.

Most capital claimants host barbecue cook-offs where cooks queue up from around the country (sometimes the world) to show their stuff. Entrants from one capital usually travel to the competitions in the other capitals in hopes of proving that their method of barbecue is the best.

Despite the ribbing among these rivals, their battles are better fought in the pits than in the public relations arena. The head-to-head competition is among the hundreds of barbecue teams (from capital cities and nontitled towns alike) that travel from cook-off to cook-off across the country and sometimes even around the world.

The regional differences in barbecue are so great as to make declaring the one true barbecue capital a bit like comparing the Apple Capital of the World with the Orange Capital of the World. Though the tasty dish may have the same name nationwide, and even the same basic cooking concept (smoked and seasoned or sauced meat), the preparation methods are so diverse that every barbecue capital could actually live up to its own local claim without putting a dent in the business of the other capitals.

Take Kansas City: It has so many barbecue eateries you could dine out every day for a month and still be taste-testing new joints. Local landmarks such as Arthur Bryant's Barbeque (whose ads proclaim "Famous throughout the world...but available only in Kansas City..."), Gates & Sons, and the brand-named K.C. Masterpiece (operated by the famous sauce maker of the same name), serve up a mouth-watering smoked meat that has been basted with a tomato-based sauce before cooking.

But down south in, say, Memphis, the sauce is slathered on after cooking. The city, which clarifies its capital claim by calling itself the Pork Barbecue Capital of the World, has more than 100 barbecue joints that showcase the local dish. Memphis' star attraction may be Graceland, but you're likely to enjoy the delights of such greaseland landmarks as Corky's Ribs and BBQ (which has so many fans nationwide they even ship their 'cue out Federal Express) and the ultimate blues brothers' joint, B. B. King's on Beale Street.

In Texas, the sauce is not the thing. They prefer their 'cue clean and simple, though some folks may slather on a bit of spicy sauce as an afterthought. And in central Texas, an area sometimes referred to as the Barbecue Belt, the town of Lockhart, about 30 miles south of Austin, is considered the top 'cue contender.

Lockhart is home to two of the state's most renowned barbecue joints, Kreuz (pronounced Krites) Market and Black's. At Kreuz, the dining experience is minimalist and meaty; you order your barbecue (beef or sausage) by the pound, and it's served up, blackened from the pit, on brown butcher paper. Black's, meanwhile, is a little more traditional — you eat your 'cue off of paper, but at least it's a paper plate. And at Black's, they break with Texas beef and sausage barbecue tradition by also smoking up chicken, and serving sandwiches and other foods as well.

In Kentucky, meanwhile, the southern rub and vinegar mix is popular, and they like their barbecue as fiery as a long summer's day. In Owensboro, joints such as the Moonlite Bar-B-Q Inn (which also sells its sauces bottled) serve up spicy Kentucky 'cue.

In the Carolinas, dry rubs — spices massaged into the meat to help seal in the juices — are popular these days, though they're also big on vinegar-based sauces. Lexington, North Carolina's barbecue is sold at its famous stands, run by longtime 'cue clans, and at its 16 or so restaurants, the most famous of which is the Lexington Barbecue No. 1. When you grab a pork sandwich or ribs from one of these places, you're likely to come back for seconds or thirds before you decipher the ingredients of the vinegary tomato sauce for which the locals are renowned.

It's not just the way these capitals sauce or spice their meats that's so different. It's the way they cook 'em that veers wildly from region to region. In the Midwest (especially in barbecue states like Missouri and Oklahoma) and Texas, closed-pit cooking seals in the flavor. But down in Memphis, the meat gets roasted over an open flame. In the Carolinas, there's no open flame (they use hot coals), but no closed pit, either. And in California, they tend to cook it up cowboy campfire style.

Once the cooking and seasoning methods have been smoked out, it's on to the meats themselves, which also vary from capital to capital. In Kansas City, anything that stops moving long enough to be tossed into the smoker is called barbecue. From beef brisket to pork butt, goat to squirrel, if you can cook it, it's barbecue in K.C. In

Memphis, it's pork ribs all the way. Texans love beef brisket, though barbecued pork sausage is another Lone Star specialty.

And Lexington, North Carolina? "What sets us apart is our mutton," explains a Chamber of Commerce booster. And the town can trace its barbecue background to 1700, when the Carolina's surveyor general John Lawson visited an Indian village near where Lexington now stands, and described a scene of native women tending their cooking fire. "The fire was surrounded with Roast Meat, or Barbakus, and the Pots continually boiling full of meat, from Morning to Night," Lawson reported.

One thing these capitals will agree on is that what amateurs on either coast call "barbecue" isn't. None of that backyard cook-out stuff counts. If you go to one of the capital cook-offs, you'll find hundreds of serious barbecuers who can expound on the do's and don'ts of 'cue. Sometimes they disagree with each other on the methods, but rarely on the basics.

For the uninitiated, attending the biggest barbecue events — notably, the Memphis in May International Festival World Championship Barbecue Cooking Contest and the American Royal International Barbecue Contest in Kansas City in early October — is like your first day of high school. Everyone you meet seems to know more than you do. That's because they do. A whole barbecue subculture exists in which serious hobbyists devote as much time to perfecting their secret sauces as golfers do to perfecting their swings.

Kansas City's American Royal International Barbecue Cook-off fills the fairgrounds with the smell of smoke and sauce. *Courtesy Convention & Visitors Bureau of Greater Kansas City*

Competitors at such events often have elaborate cookers shaped like everything from antique cars to giant pigs; and they often work in teams, with names like High on the Hog, the Rib Ticklers, the Bone Pickers, and the Holy Smokers. They wear T-shirts or uniforms with team logos, and set up tented areas where their entourage of friends and family hang out during the long process of cooking and judging. Some teams even hire bands and other entertainers to party the night away with the pit crew as they tend the smokers the night before the big judging.

Hardcore 'cue culture is surprisingly upscale. Walk through the parking area during one of these competitions and you'll see as many Mercedes as pick-up trucks. Barbecue may once have been a blue collar meal, but it has become a white collar obsession, with devoted cooks who spend their leisure time and money perfecting their skills and traveling the competition circuit.

To the cookers who come to the American Royal (which claims to be the world's largest barbecue contest) and other big events to smoke out the competition, this is serious business. Many have even attended barbecue school — Cue U as it's sometimes called — to bone up on the basics. And judges for the American Royal and other competitions are expected to take a judging class where they learn to look for such important elements as the smoke ring (it shows how deeply smoked the meat is), tenderness, and texture.

Judges learn that the meat is also to be judged on presentation. No garnishes are allowed except for parsley (those are American Royal rules, though some competitions allow more decoration), and the meat should look appetizing but be easily divided for serving. Toothpicks are a definite no-no at the American Royal — you'll get a zero grade for presentation if you stick it to your entry.

The judging at the American Royal goes on for two days. The first day's competition is the invitational, where winners from other events compete. The next day is the open judging. Anyone who pays a small entry fee can enter; all day long, golf carts troll the fair grounds picking up the standard-issue styrofoam containers from the barbecuers and delivering them to the judging area. There, hundreds of volunteer judges sit at tables, nibbling at numbered entries, grading them for taste, presentation, and tenderness. They mark their scores on computer cards as if taking a saucy SAT test. Time and again, the table captains who deliver the meat to the judges and watch over them as they taste caution against getting grease spots on the cards, which can cause the computer to misread the scores.

The American Royal is just one of hundreds of barbecue competitions around the country, and many entrants spend their free time traveling from one to another. Judges, too, travel from contest to contest. Many are certified. Jim "Trim" Tabb, a retired TWA pilot, has a fold-out business card that lists the competitions he has judged, including the American Royal, Memphis in May, the Pigs-N-Pepper in Carlisle, Massachusetts, and the World BBQ Championship in Lisdoonvarna, Ireland. "The toughest one was in Estonia," Tabb recalls, of the World BBQ Championship he judged in Tallinn a few years back. "They don't have much meat over there. The locals were going crazy, smelling all that meat they couldn't eat."

The other really big barbecue capital competition is the Memphis in May. Like the American Royal, this competition draws hundreds of cookers from around the country and the world. The barbecue contest is part of the city's month-long Memphis in May International Festival, which draws over a million visitors to events honoring a different nation every year. To celebrate the festival's 20th anniversary in 1996, the event honored all 18 previously fêted nations. The Championship Barbecue Cooking Contest during Memphis in May is held in the middle of the month and is one of the festival's tastiest highlights.

The Memphis in May barbecue competition draws an international crowd to cook, taste, and visit. *Courtesy Memphis Convention & Visitors Bureau*

Owensboro, Kentucky, holds its International Barbecue Festival in May, drawing cooks from around the world. Owensboro is such a party town, it has another nickname — Kentucky's Festival City — a title it earned from its barbecue festival and other events such as the Summer Festival and the International Blue Grass Music Association Fan Fest. And at Lexington, North Carolina's Barbecue Festival held in late October (a few weeks after the American Royal), the whole town gets into the act at events such as the Parade of Pigs.

The battle over the title of barbecue capital rages on, but only in a rib-tickling fashion. Everyone believes his or her barbecue is the best; but the pros also know there's no accounting for taste. And when it comes to barbecue, where there's smoke, there's fire, and these barbecue capitals are really cooking.

## FOR FURTHER INFORMATION

### General Information

**Convention and Visitors Bureau of Greater Kansas City**
1100 Main, Suite 2550
Kansas City, MO 64105
(816) 221-5242 or (800) 767-7700

**Lexington Area Chamber of Commerce**
16 East Center St.
P.O. Drawer C
Lexington, NC 27293
(910) 248-5929

**Lockhart Chamber of Commerce**
P.O. Drawer 840
Lockhart, TX 78644
(512) 398-2818

**Memphis Convention & Visitors Bureau**
47 Union St.
Memphis, TN 38103
(901) 543-5300

**Owensboro-Daviess County Chamber of Commerce**
P.O. Box 825
Owensboro, KY 42302
(502) 926-1860

## *Attractions and Events*

### American Royal International Barbecue Contest
1701 American Royal Court
Kansas City, MO 64102
(816) 221-9800

### Lexington Barbecue Festival
Contact the Lexington Area Chamber of Commerce

### Memphis in May World Championship Barbecue Cooking Contest
245 Wagner Place, Suite 220
Memphis, TN 38103
(901) 525-4611, ext. 104

### (Owensboro's) International Barbecue Festival
Contact the Owensboro-Daviess County Chamber of Commerce

## *Shadow Boxing: Sun Prairie, Wisconsin vs. Punxsutawney, Pennsylvania*
## FOR GROUNDHOG BRAGGING RIGHTS

Come February 2, as the frozen soul longs for the first signs of spring, weather forecasters and farmers and snow-bound hibernators look to two towns for a hint of warmer things to come.

On Groundhog Day, Punxsutawney, Pennsylvania, and Sun Prairie, Wisconsin, make a grand show of using their resident rodents as a barometer of the near future. After the critters have been pulled ceremoniously from their homes, the world waits to discover whether the burly beasts will see their own shadows. If so, the chilly prediction is for another six weeks of winter; if it doesn't, then spring is said to be just around the corner.

These competing Groundhog Days spawned a battle for groundhog dominance. Sun Prairie proclaimed itself Groundhog Capital of the World in 1952; Punxsutawney, whose fame was recently enhanced by the 1993 Bill Murray movie *Groundhog Day* (set, but not filmed, there), calls itself the Weather Capital of the World and Home of the Groundhog.

Crowds gather in Punxsutawney, Pennsylvania, on February 2, to see whether Phil will predict a shadowy future for spring. *Courtesy the Groundhog Club*

Groundhog Day evolved from a traditional German legend that said that if the sun was strong enough to cast a shadow on February 2, it meant nearly two more months of winter. And the highly revered woodchuck — groundhog — thought to be the most sensible of creatures, was trusted to see its shadow if there was one to be seen. From this idea evolved the celebration of Groundhog Day, a tradition brought to America by German immigrants in the nineteenth century.

Sun Prairie, a community of about 15,500 just east of Madison, Wisconsin, dates its Groundhog festivities to 1948 at the suggestion of local booster Margaret McGonigle, who got the idea from Ira Bennett of Eau Claire. The following year, the Groundhog Club was formed with Mrs. McGonigle as president. In 1950, the event expanded to include a carnival dance, held at the Tropical Gardens dance hall. And in 1951, despite the death of one of the groundhogs (a formal funeral was held at Angell Park), the festival went on as planned.

A published timeline of Sun Prairie's groundhog events traces these and other happenings, sometimes with weird results. A sampling: "1953 — An albino offspring of Sir No-Talk-in-Sleep and Miss Sleep-All-Winter [resident groundhogs] was crowned as Dauphin

King of the world's groundhogs at Sacred Heart's Parish Hall...1959: Prince Dauphine [sic], head of the groundhog clan, was stuffed...1961: Ray Patt picketed the *Sun Prairie Star Countrymen* for printing a prediction by the groundhog which contradicted the Groundhog Club's forecast...1962: Prince Dauphine [now stuffed] is launched on a trip to the moon with George Farwell and Carl Farwell manning the launch controls."

As you can imagine, Sun Prairie made quite a name for itself, and Punxsutawney, which had stood alone in the field since its first official Groundhog Day celebration in 1887, soon caught wind of the interloper. In 1952, a Punxsutawney newspaper sniffed that Sun Prairie was a "remote two-cow town buried somewhere in the wilderness." The line was drawn in the snow. That same year, Sun Prairie declared itself the Groundhog Capital of the World, throwing down the groundhog gauntlet. Punxsutawney was not amused.

Luckily, lots of geography separates the two towns, so, despite barbed references in the local papers, little meaningful conflict has taken place. But the rhetoric keeps the contention keen. In the 1980s, Wisconsin Attorney General Bronson C. La Follette declared Sun Prairie's resident groundhog, Jimmy, to be the official groundhog of the United States.

A press release, printed on Wisconsin Department of Justice letterhead, quotes La Follette as saying, "My research indicates that one Punxsutawney Phil, a groundhog residing in Punxsutawney, Pennsylvania, has attempted to establish himself as a national groundhog...In doing so, he has perpetrated a colossal fraud on the people of America. He has

## CYBERSPACE CONTACTS

### Groundhogs@Sun Prairie

http://tmcweb.com/sprairie/ghog.htm

### Punxsutawney's Groundhog Day Page

http://www.groundhog.org/

Can a groundhog see his shadow in cyberspace? Both Punxsutawney Phil and Sun Prairie's Jimmy the Groundhog have their own little hidey holes on the Web. Groundhogs@Sun Prairie offers Jimmy stories and related links, while Punxsutawney's glossy Groundhog Day site includes a local history page, events calendar, map, and souvenir catalog (fluorescent Phil stickers, anyone?).

had considerable exposure in the news media, primarily because the sun rises earlier in Pennsylvania than it does in Wisconsin."

La Follette went on to claim that "For several years, his sponsors saw fit to utilize a stuffed animal resembling a groundhog to make the annual weather prediction.... Obviously, he never saw his shadow or anything else because he wasn't real."

Then, as the kicker, La Follette pointed out that Jimmy was simply a better forecaster than Phil: "Jimmy has been making an annual appearance in Sun Prairie since 1948, with a remarkable record of 90 percent accuracy in his predictions. Punxsutawney Phil, the pretender to the title, has a dismal 17 percent record."

Therefore, La Follette concluded, "Clearly, Jimmy is the official state groundhog, but he is more than that. He is the official groundhog of the U.S.A.... I hope this clears up the matter beyond the shadow of a doubt."

Still, Sun Prairie has to deal with the pesky fact that Punxsutawney is more famous for its groundhog. The movie — which, Carolyn Rusk, executive director of the Sun Prairie Chamber of Commerce points out, was filmed just over the Wisconsin border in Woodstock, Illinois, and therefore closer to the Groundhog Capital than to the Weather Capital — didn't help any. Then again, she insists, it didn't hurt much either. "*Groundhog Day* was all about trying to get out of Punxsutawney," Rusk laughs. "Nobody has ever made a film about trying to leave Sun Prairie!"

Geography is destiny, so because the sun does rise earlier in Pennsylvania than it does in Wisconsin, most people have heard more about Phil than about Jimmy. Make that Jimmy, Jr., who has followed in his father's pawprints since Jimmy, Sr., went to groundhog heaven.

Punxsutawney is situated about 90 miles northeast of Pittsburgh, in the Cooks Forest region. It was settled mainly by Germans, who brought the groundhog legend from Europe; when they found an abundant supply of these varmints in the woodlands here, they kept the legend alive. The Punxsutawney Groundhog Day celebration began back in the 1880s, at first as a small party to break the winter blaahs. By 1887, it was an established annual event starring Punxsutawney Phil.

You'd assume that the first Phil was today's Phil's great, great, grand-groundhog — but not so, insists Nanci Puchy, executive director of Punxsutawney's chamber of commerce. Puchy says it's the very same groundhog; he's given a "magic elixir" every summer at

Punxsutawney's official groundhog handler and Groundhog Club president make a great show of Phil's forecasting skills. *Courtesy the Groundhog Club*

the annual Groundhog Picnic which keeps him forever young. No one knows what's in the secret potion, she says — it's mixed up by his handler, a veritable Ponce de Leon of groundhog youth.

And that accusation that a stuffed animal has sometimes been used in place of Phil? Groundhogwash! "Absolutely not!" exclaims Puchy in a mock huff. She admits that there may have been a stuffed groundhog somewhere in Punxsutawney's past, but that he was probably just "a relative of Phil's" who was so well loved his handlers kept him around past his mortal prime. The stuffed woodchuck may have been used for a few photos, but, Puchy assures, "It's the real Phil that comes out every year to predict the weather!"

Though Punxsutawney's festivities take place all over town, the big moment happens at Phil's longtime "official residence," Gobbler's Knob, just outside of town. Media from around the world converge for the event, though Sun Prairie gets the lion's share of midwestern coverage. Everyone gathers around the stump from which the official groundhog handler and the president of the local Groundhog Club pull Phil like a rabbit from a hat; then the crowd watches to see if he notices his shadow.

Though seemingly a small step up from watching the grass grow, it only happens once a year, so it's an exciting moment. And when the result is known, the news is flashed all over the world. It even gets faxed to Washington, DC, for inclusion in that day's *Congressional Record*.

Phil sees his shadow about 70 percent of the time, a ratio that, depending on who you ask, is "100 percent accurate" (Puchy) or "17 percent accurate" (La Follette). In this age of Doppler radar and computerized storm tracking, it doesn't much matter anyway. It's the tradition that counts.

Punxsutawney keeps its groundhog heritage going even after the snow has melted. The town also fêtes its fur-weather friend during the first week in July, at the Groundhog Festival, and again in August during the Groundhog Picnic. The festival, which dates to 1966, includes such events as a salad luncheon (eat like a groundhog, think like a groundhog), a stage play, a frog jumping contest, and the pet parade. The picnic, held at Gobbler's Knob, also includes that magic moment when Phil quaffs his elixir of life. "It's supposed to keep him going another seven years," Puchy explains.

One event that no longer takes place, however, is the annual summer Groundhog Hunt, an activity that started in the 1880s, but which wise locals soon ended when they realized the critters were better at predicting the weather than at eluding hunters.

Revelers can also visit Phil year-round at the Civic Complex library's Groundhog Zoo, a "showcase home" built so Phil's fans can see the "Seer" (as he's nicknamed) in person. Though Phil bears the heavy burden of his celebrity, he's not home alone. A bunch of his cousins, "hand-raised by the inner circle" of the Groundhog Club, Puchy says, shares his digs. One even seems to be auditioning for Phil's job: "We've got this crazy groundhog that loves to dance! When visitors show up, he runs right up and just dances and dances for them."

Nearby, Phil has been captured for posterity in a life-sized bronze statue created by sculptress Jimilu Mason. Another Phil statue, this one carved from a tree stump, is on display in Barclay Square, where Phil's annual appearance takes place. And Groundhog Day history and memorabilia is preserved at the Punxsutawney Area Historical and Genealogical Museum in the magnificent Bennis House, built in 1903 by renowned architect Stanford White.

Is America big enough for both Phil and Jimmy, Jr.? "Nobody's ever been hurt by this feud," explains Sun Prairie's Rusk. And as long as no fur flies and spring arrives eventually, it seems there's a place for both Punxsutawney and Sun Prairie.

## FOR FURTHER INFORMATION

### General Information

**Punxsutawney Chamber of Commerce**
124 W. Mahoning St.
Punxsutawney, PA 15767
(814) 938-7700 or (800) 752-PHIL

**Sun Prairie Chamber of Commerce**
109 E. Main St.
Sun Prairie, WI 53590
(608) 837-4547

### Attractions and Events

**Punxsutawney Area Historical and Genealogical Museum**
Bennis House
401 W. Mahoning St.
Punxsutawney, PA 15767
(814) 938-2555

**Punxsutawney Groundhog Club and Groundhog Festival**
124 W. Mahoning St.
Punxsutawney, PA 15767
(814) 938-7700 or (800) 752-PHIL

**Sun Prairie Historical Museum**
115 E. Main St.
Sun Prairie, WI 53590
(608) 837-2915

## Salad Wars: Crystal City, Texas vs. Alma, Arkansas for the Title of
# SPINACH CAPITAL OF THE WORLD

When Popeye and Bluto duke it out, the law of comics demands that the famous sailor man beat the bearded strongman. But what would happen if Popeye had to battle a mirror image of his fulsomely forearmed self? Just such a symbolic match-up has been going on for about a decade between the towns of Crystal City, Texas, and Alma, Arkansas, both of which proudly proclaim themselves the Spinach Capital of the World.

Popeye plays a key role in both capital claims, since both regard the spinach-loving character as their patron saint of agriculture, signified by Popeye statues — Crystal City's was built in 1937, Alma's in 1987.

Spinach is an important crop for both communities. Crystal City, situated in Zavala County in central Texas just off Highway 83, is at the heart of the state's most productive spinach-growing areas. And its claim to the Spinach Capital title is, at least in chronological age, a much more mature one.

Crystal City was established in 1907, when the Cross S Ranch was divided. Ten years later, the first four acres of spinach were planted as a test crop; by 1919, spinach had become the community's principal crop. The area economy experienced what was called the Spinach Boom as railcar after railcar loaded with fresh, leafy "green gold" left Crystal City bound for worldwide distribution. Canning plants, including one that later became a Del Monte facility, also opened. The Del Monte plant now turns out some 2.5 million cases of canned spinach a year.

The community's first Spinach Festival was held

### DID YOU KNOW...

**Popeye's Brawny Beginnings**
Popeye's first appearance was in Elzie Segar's daily comic strip "Thimble Theater," but his popularity soared after Max and Dave Fleischer produced the 1933 cartoon "Popeye the Sailor." And though spinach is Popeye's leafy vegetable of choice, one cartoon, set in ancient times, showed him eating *garlic* to build up his strength. Hear that, Gilroy?

in 1936, with much of the activity taking place around a ship-shaped platform surrounded by bushels of spinach. Participants dressed like Popeye or his pals; and the governor of Texas, in a Spinach Week proclamation, called Crystal City "The World's Largest Spinach Shipping Center." The locals also sent a note of appreciation to Popeye's creator, Elzie Segar, thanking him for promoting spinach. Segar responded with a kind note in kind, and the idea was hatched to build a Popeye statue, which was unveiled in 1937, dedicated "To All the Children of the World."

Segar was so delighted he even drew a special Popeye cartoon featuring his characters attending the Crystal City Spinach Festival. But he never had the opportunity to visit the statue in person. He died in 1938 of Hodgkins Disease at the age of 44.

The Spinach Festival was also short-lived, at least for a while. In 1941, when all sailors went to war, the festival was canceled; in fact, the war washed away the community's taste for spinach celebrations for 40 years. But in 1982, Reverend Efraim Espinoza led the charge to bring back the event. It quickly grew into a major regional festival; today, it's still held in mid-November, and draws more than 50,000 to the community of 8,000 for the three-day event which features a parade, carnival, spinach cook-offs, gala dance, and the crowning of the Spinach Festival Queen.

And Popeye stood watch over the town all those years from his post in front of City Hall. During the 50th anniversary celebration for the statue, Joe D'Angelo, president of King Features Syndicate, sent a proclamation declaring Crystal City the Spinach Capital of the World, and anointing the locals as honorary captains in Popeye's crew.

Alma, situated in northwest Arkansas at the intersection of I-40 and Highway 71 North, in fact grows and cans more spinach than its Texas rival. "Alma has 3,000 people, and our Main Street is about four blocks long. The downtown is like in most small cities," notes George Bowles, owner of the local Kustom Kaps silkscreening company and spinach capital concept co-conspirator.

As Bowles recalls it, "There was this coffeeshop, and we were all sitting around trying to come up with a way to help promote Alma, and at that point a spinach truck drove by. So we said, 'hey, why not call ourselves the Spinach Capital of the World?'" So the mayor passed a proclamation declaring Alma's newly minted title, and newspapers around the country picked up the story from the wire services.

Alma, Arkansas's Popeye statue is a reminder of the town's Spinach Capital claim (though Crystal City has one, too). *Courtesy George B. Bowles, Kustom Kaps*

When news reached Crystal City, the spinach started to fly. And at first Alma was cowed by all the rancor. But, Bowles notes, "Alma grows 60 million pounds of spinach a year, and Allen Canning [the local cannery] cans 56 percent of all the spinach in the world. Well, 56 percent is a lot more than 44 percent, so we just felt we had more of a claim."

Alma launched its own spinach festival, held the third weekend in April, and even put up its own Popeye statue. Alma also boasts an original monument: the World's Largest Spinach Can, on Mountain Grove Road.

"This rivalry has gone on for quite some time," Bowles says, pointing out that, while Crystal City gained the endorsement of Popeye creator Elzie Segar years ago, it's Alma's own Allen Cannery that produces the official, King Features–sanctioned Popeye Spinach brand. "How much more do they need to know [in Crystal City]?" demands Bowles. "We've got 56 percent of the canning *and* Popeye Spinach." Visitors to Bowles' shop can see a small collection — "It's not quite a museum" — of news clippings and memorabilia relating to the spinach capital claim and the spinach festivals.

Naturally, Crystal City feels it still has the right to the title, regardless of Alma's claims of greater productivity or name-brand label. Asked about Alma's claim, Maria Rivera, of Crystal City's International (Spinach) Festival office, exclaims with a chortle, "That's a fake! That's a wannabe. They don't compare to our [claim].

They probably produce more spinach there, but Elzie Segar proclaimed us the Spinach Capital!"

Miguel Delgado, Crystal City's city manager and former Spinach Festival associate director, concurs. "We're the real spinach capital!" As a case in point, he provides a copy of a 1993 Texas Senate proclamation, which aimed a direct volley at Alma. It reads in part, "WHEREAS, thwarting the claim of its spinach rival, Alma, Arkansas, Crystal City's dominance as 'Spinach Capital of the World' has been proclaimed by authorities such as former President Ronald Reagan and Joseph F. D'Angelo, Board President of King Features Syndicate, Inc....therefore, be it PROCLAIMED, that the Senate of the State of Texas hereby joins the citizens of Texas in affirming Crystal City's unchanged position of Spinach Capital of the World...."

Historically, it might seem that the first Spinach Capital is the true Spinach Capital. But taking into account actual productivity, well, Alma seems to have the title in the can. So, for the moment, it's a draw, since neither town will back down from the claim, and both hold their festivals and crown their Spinach Queens with the self-righteous spirit of royalty done wrong.

## FOR FURTHER INFORMATION

### General Information

**Alma Area Chamber of Commerce**
825 Fayetteville Ave.
P.O. Box 2607
Alma, AR 72921
(501) 632-4127

**City of Crystal City**
101 E. Dimmit St.
Crystal City, TX 78839
(210) 374-3477

### Attractions and Events

**Alma Spinach Festival**
Contact the Alma Area Chamber of Commerce

**Crystal City Spinach Festival Association**
P.O. Box 100
Crystal City, TX 78839
(210) 374-3161

## Seed-Spitting Mad: Will the Real
# WATERMELON CAPITAL OF THE WORLD
## Please Stand Up?

What is it about the watermelon that makes it so universally appealing, so summer fresh and thirst-quenching? It's more sugar water than meat, so seedy you could practically plant a farm in your mouth, and, boy, when you drop one from the roof, how it explodes. But those aren't bad things — not when you're talking watermelon.

The watermelon is so loved, and grows so easily that towns all over America proudly proclaim themselves the Watermelon Capital of the World. Hope, Arkansas, as hometown to President Clinton, has recently gained fame that extends beyond its fruit-flavored festival, but others, such as Cordele, Georgia, grip the title with gusto and challenge all comers to snatch it away.

In researching this book, I contacted the U.S. Chamber of Commerce, which put a mention in its newsletter noting that I wanted to hear from capitals of the world. As an example, I had used Hope, Arkansas, not realizing just how many contenders dotted the map.

In April 1993, I received the following response from Sally Dunn, president of the Cordele-Crisp Chamber of Commerce, Inc.: "The challenge to determine the 'true'

Hope, Arkansas, is just one of many watermelon-growing towns that lay claim to the world capital title. *Courtesy Hope Chamber of Commerce*

Watermelon Capital of the World was held in Atlanta, Georgia, in July of 1991. Hope, Arkansas, Hempstead, Texas, and Cordele, Georgia, all competed in a taste-off, judged by such notables as [former Georgia Supreme Court] Chief Justice Thomas Marshall. Cordele won the challenge singlehandedly and has received attention all over the world."

That taste-off was the first (and so far only) MelonFest — none has since been undertaken. Sponsored by the International Watermelon Society, it was held to settle a longstanding dispute among the competing capitals (other melon growers, such as those in Ocala, Florida, were also invited, but didn't enter). The judges rated the melons for taste, texture, and color, and ranked Cordele's watermelons first, with Hope and Hempstead coming in second and third. So Cordele won the title, and Cordele's Watermelon Capital Queen (crowned at the town's annual festival) got the honor of bringing home the watermelon slice–shaped trophy.

Despite the promise that this contest would determine the "true" watermelon capital, neither Hope nor Hempstead threw their capital claims away like rotten rinds; they continued to insist on their delicious dominance, though they declined future invitations to similar events.

And the taste-off didn't address the claims of numerous other communities to the capital title. Among the other towns and areas that call themselves watermelon capitals are Hermiston, Oregon, Luling, Texas, Hampton County, South Carolina, Shartlesville, Pennsylvania, and Rush Springs, Oklahoma. Rocky Ford, Colorado, and Green River, Utah, go for the more generic title of Melon Capital of the World, though both are well known for their watermelons. And since these towns are sprinkled so liberally around the country, they coexist in relative peace, each celebrating in its own way its favorite fruit.

Each has a watermelon festival, as do many other places that make no capital claims but simply want to spend a warm weekend drooling sweet juice and spitting seeds. Watermelon festivals are as ubiquitous as summer picnics in America. But when a watermelon capital throws a festival, it's a biggie.

Cordele, having established itself in the books as the official watermelon capital, holds its annual Watermelon Days Festival the first two weeks of July, one of the longest festivals in the country. Cooking, eating, carving, and seed-spitting contests are major highlights, as are the parade and the crowning of the Watermelon Capital

Queen. Cordele's watermelon farms grow more than 200 million pounds of watermelon annually, making it one of the nation's most productive areas.

And is there something about watermelon country that breeds presidents?

Cordele is situated in central Georgia, just 35 miles east of Jimmy Carter's hometown of Plains (which is known for peanuts). The town that bred Bill Clinton, the "Man from Hope," is in south-western Arkansas, not far from the Texas border. Hope's watermelon festival, which takes place in mid-August, dates back to 1926. It ceased in 1930, from lack of interest, but was revived in 1976. More than 1,000 watermelons, both red and yellow, are donated by area growers and devoured by the 50,000 attendees who crowd the community of 11,000 for the event.

Though the festival has such ubiquitous events as watermelon eating and seed-spitting competitions, concerts and cakewalks, it's the weigh-ins that people come to oooh and aaah over. Hope has a reputation for growing the biggest watermelons in the world. In 1979, it first grabbed a place in the *Guinness Book of World Records* with a 200-pound melon. And in 1985, a Hope grower took the annual record again, this time with a melon that tipped the scales at 260 pounds. How do they do it? Wanda Hayes of the Hope Chamber of Commerce says, "We've got a special soil. And of course a lot of tender loving care for the watermelons. They're treated very special. [The farmers] put little sheds over them to protect them from the sun." The sun can damage the melon skins, Hayes explains.

The Lone Star State's entrant into the 1991 competition, Hempstead, is not even Texas' only watermelon capital. Another Texas town with a major melon reputation is Luling, host of the renowned Watermelon Thump, held the last weekend in June. One of the nation's most famous watermelon festivals — perhaps because of its unforgettable name — the Thump draws some 35,000 attendees, many of whom come to witness (at some distance), the World Championship Seed-Spitting Contest. The current record is 68 feet, 9 and 1/8 inches. A champion melon auction, huge parade, and Beer Garden with live performances also keep the crowds coming back every year.

Out west in another fruitful part of the nation, Hermiston, Oregon, doesn't host the kind of regional competition that drives those in the south and southwest a little mad during the festival sea-

### CYBERSPACE CONTACTS

# National Watermelon Promotion Board

### http://www.watermelon.org/

Got a juicy question about watermelon? The Web site for the National Watermelon Promotion Board has all the answers, plus plenty of recipes, industry stats, and articles from "The Melon Report." There's even a Kid's Stuff page with games and instructions on growing a watermelon with "seeds right from your own melon slice...."

son, but it doesn't mean that Hermiston isn't bothered by what it sees as a pack of pretenders. Kenneth Oplinger, executive director of the Greater Hermiston Chamber of Commerce, wrote: "The Hermiston watermelon is known throughout the United States as one of the best melons in the world." Oplinger added that, in the summer, "thousands of Amer-icans follow the Oregon Trail, and happen upon the true Watermelon Capital of the World, Hermiston, Oregon."

But unlike Cordele or Hope, Hermiston's claim is relatively low-key. Nearby Irrigon hosts a small Watermelon Festival in July, while Hermiston's big events include the Spud Festival (in July) and the Chamber of Commerce Wine and Cheese Festival (in October).

Back east, Shartlesville, Pennsylvania, is the new kid on the melon cart, having only recently taken up the Watermelon Capital of the World title. Shartlesville's Watermelon Festival, held in August, is as fresh as its capital claim. The fun and funny event lives up to its slogan, "If you can do it with a watermelon, you can do it here," by putting a new spin on the standard eating and seed-spitting contests with events such as the watermelon rolling relay races and the watermelon and spoon races (the bigger the spoon, the better). And a watermelon fashion show features locals modeling melon-themed finery.

Watermelon artistry is also on display during the two-day event, with exhibits of watermelon sculpture, carving, and related crafts. The local American Museum of the Watermelon shows off some of its collection of watermelon artifacts during the festival as well. The town's Painted Ladies retail district, a colorful Victorian collection of shops and businesses, is up to its elbows in the event, with stores hosting watermelon events and offering discounts to festival-goers.

Karen Kinnane's American Museum of the Watermelon in Shartlesville, Pennsylvania, exhibits colorful and quirky melonabilia. *Photo courtesy Karen Kinnane*

Local artist Karen Kinnane is the driving force behind the town's capital claim and its attendant melon mania; not only is she integral in running the festival, which she got off the ground in 1989, but she's also the curator of the watermelon museum and does some nifty watermelon crafts and carvings herself.

Farther south, Hampton County, South Carolina, is another watermelon capital with its own take on the subject. Though this Low Country county is a productive watermelon growing area, its capital claim comes from its pride in the Hampton County Watermelon Festival, the state's oldest continually celebrated festival, dating back to 1939. The town of Hampton, the county seat, along with its sister city of Varnville, hosts the late June festival, which draws more than 60,000 visitors. The festival, presided over by King Melon, naturally features seed-spitting and watermelon-eating contests, as well as food booths and local crafters. When night falls, everyone gets dressed up to dance that fructose off at the big Melon Ball.

The festival is also known for its beauty queens; young lovelies from around the region compete for the title of Miss Coastal Empire. It's one of the South's most prestigious pageants; some contestants have come from famous families (Miss Coastal Empire 1964 was

Ellen Thurmond Senter, sister of Senator Strom Thurmond) while others have married into them (Nancy Moore, who attended the 1966 pageant as Miss Aiken, later became Mrs. Strom Thurmond).

Of the merely melon capitals, Rocky Ford, Colorado — also sometimes called the Sweet Melon Capital of the World — is in southeast Colorado, a rich agricultural area that grows everything from asparagus in April to pumpkins in September. Its melon crop, grown August through September, includes honeydew and cantaloupe, but it's particularly renowned for its local watermelons. One highlight of Colorado's Arkansas Valley Fair, held the third week of August, is the Rotary Club watermelon giveaway, when some 30,000 pounds of watermelons are handed over to eager festival-goers. Likewise, Green River, Utah, another Melon Capital, is most famous for its watermelons. The annual Green River Melon Days festival, held the third weekend in September, draws some 2,000 melon lovers. But all through the summer and into the fall, you'll see carts along the road selling fresh melons as well as jams and jellies and other melon-made goodies.

No matter where you live, chances are there's a watermelon capital near you. And they all have fun festivals and great souvenirs to celebrate their melon calling. But don't forget: Cordele, backed by the results of the 1991 taste-off, insists that it's the only true watermelon capital. If you beg to differ, you'll have a tasty time trying to prove otherwise.

## FOR FURTHER INFORMATION

**Cordele-Crisp Chamber of Commerce**
P.O. Box 158
Cordele, GA 31015
(912) 273-1668

**Greater Hermiston Chamber of Commerce**
415 South Hwy. 395
P.O. Box 185
Hermiston, OR 97838
(541) 567-6151

**Green River Melon Days**
Green River Trade Council
John Wesley Powell Museum
885 E Main St.
Green River, UT 84525
(801) 564-3526

Hampton County Chamber of Commerce
Courthouse Annex
P.O. Box 122
Hampton, SC 29924
(803) 943-3784

Hempstead Chamber of Commerce
1250 Austin St.
Hempstead, TX 77445
(409) 826-8217

Hope Chamber of Commerce
P.O. Box 250
Hope, AR 71801
(501) 777-3640

Luling Chamber of Commerce and
Watermelon Thump Headquarters
P.O. Box 710
Luling, TX 78648
(210) 875-3214

Rocky Ford Chamber of Commerce
105 N. Main St.
Rocky Ford, CO 81067
(719) 254-7483

Shartlesville Watermelon Festival and
American Museum of the Watermelon
P.O. Box 212
Shartlesville, PA 19554
(610) 488-7792

# APPENDIX

## CAPITAL HAPPENINGS — A MONTHLY LISTING OF SPECIAL EVENTS

---

### SPRING

---

#### — March —

**O'Neill St. Patrick's Day Celebration**
(O'Neill, NE): Annually on or around St. Patrick's Day (March 17th). Nebraska's Irish Capital goes for the green. Contact: O'Neill Area Chamber of Commerce, 315 E. Douglas St., O'Neill, NE 68763; (402) 336-2355.

**Taste of Solvang**
(Solvang, CA): Mid-March. Danish-filled dessert fest. Contact: Solvang Conference & Visitor's Bureau, 1511-A Mission Dr., Solvang, CA 93463; (800) GO-SOLVANG.

#### — April —

**Alma Spinach Festival**
(Alma, AR): Third weekend in April. Spinach capital festival, with Popeye and the gang. Contact: Alma Area Chamber of Commerce, 825 Fayetteville Ave., P.O. Box 2607, Alma, AR 72921; (501) 632-4127.

**Dandelion Festival**
(Vineland, NJ): April. Weeds are our friends. Contact: Greater Vineland Chamber of Commerce, City Hall, 7th and Wood Sts., P.O. Box 489, Vineland, NJ 08360; (609) 691-7400 or (800) 309-0019.

**Mule Day**
(Columbia, TN): First weekend in April. Celebration of town's mule-trading heritage. Mule Day Office, P.O. Box 66, Columbia, TN 38402; (615) 381-9557.

## — May —

### Blessing of the Shrimp Fleet

(Brunswick, GA): Mother's Day. Shrimp boats on parade. Contact: Brunswick & the Golden Isles of Georgia Visitor's Bureau, 4 Glynn Ave., Brunswick, GA 31520; (912) 265-0620 or (800) 933-COAST.

### Breaux Bridge Crawfish Festival

(Breaux Bridge, LA): First weekend in May. Zydeco crawdad feastathon. Contact: Breaux Bridge Crawfish Festival Association, P.O. Box 25, Breaux Bridge, LA 70517; (318) 332-6655 or (800) 346-1958.

### Decoy, Wildlife Art & Sportsman Festival

(Havre de Grace, MD): First weekend in May. Ducky festival honoring decoys and related activities. Contact: Havre de Grace Decoy Museum, 100 Giles St., Havre de Grace, MD 21078; (410) 939-3739

### International Barbecue Festival

(Owensboro, KY): May. Barbecue battle for smoked meat supremacy. Contact: Owensboro-Daviess County Chamber of Commerce, P.O. Box 825, Owensboro, KY 42302; (502) 926-1860.

### Memphis in May World Championship Barbecue Cooking Contest

(Memphis, TN): Mid-May. Big barbecue cook-off. Contact: Memphis in May, 245 Wagner Place, Suite 220, Memphis, TN 38103; (901) 525-4611.

## SUMMER

## — June —

### Battle Creek Cereal Festival

(Battle Creek, MI): Second weekend in June. World's longest breakfast table — eat all you want, they'll make more. Contact: Greater Battle Creek/Calhoun County Visitor and Convention Bureau, 34 W. Jackson St., Suite 4-B, Battle Creek, MI 49017; (616) 962-2240.

### Bradley County Pink Tomato Festival

(Warren, AR): Mid-June. Tomatoes in the pink are cause for partying. Contact: Bradley County Chamber of Commerce, 104 N. Myrtle, Warren, AR 71671; (501) 226-5225.

### Elkhart Jazz Festival

(Elkhart, IN): Mid-June. Jazz and blues fest in Band Instrument Capital of the World. Contact: Elkhart Jazz Festival, Elkhart Centre, P.O. Box 1284, Elkhart, IN 46515; (219) 295-8701 or (800) 597-7627.

### Firefly Festival

(Boone, NC): Mid-June (usually the second weekend). Light-hearted celebration. Contact: Firefly Festival Association/Boone Convention and Visitors Bureau, 208 Howard St., Boone, NC 28607; (704) 262-3516.

### Hampton County Watermelon Festival

(Hampton, SC): Late June. Watermelon queens and seed-spitting contests reign supreme. Contact: Hampton County Chamber of Commerce, Courthouse Annex, P.O. Box 122, Hampton, SC 29924; (803) 943-3784.

### Jackalope Days

(Douglas, WY): June. Home of the Jackalope celebrates its bad bunny in a big way. Contact: Douglas Area Chamber of Commerce, 121 Brownfield Rd., Douglas, WY 82633; (307) 358-2950.

### Luling Watermelon Thump

(Luling, TX): Last weekend in June. Thump-a-thon for watermelon fans. Contact: Luling Chamber of Commerce and Watermelon Thump Headquarters, P.O. Box 710, Luling, TX 78648; (210) 875-3214.

— July —

### BagelFest

(Mattoon, IL): Last weekend in July. Big breakfast bash for good-for-you round breads. Contact: Mattoon Area Chamber of Commerce, 1701 Wabash, Mattoon, IL 61938; (217) 235-5661.

Mattoon, Illinois's BagelFest brings out bagels of all sizes.
*Courtesy Mattoon Chamber of Commerce*

### Gilroy Garlic Festival
(Gilroy, CA): Mid-July. Bad-breath fest. Contact: Gilroy Garlic Festival Association, P.O. Box 2311, Gilroy, CA 95020; (408) 842-1625.

### Kansas Wheat Festival
(Wellington, KS): Second week of July. Amber seas of grain celebration. Wellington Area Chamber of Commerce, 207 S. Washington, Wellington, KS 67152; (316) 326-7466.

### National Cherry Festival
(Traverse City, MI): Early July. Pit-filled party. Contact: National Cherry Festival, 108 Grandview Pkwy., Traverse City, MI 49684; (616) 947-4230.

### Punxsutawney Groundhog Festival
(Punxsutawney, PA): July. Woodchucks would chuck it all to attend this groundhog party. Contact: Punxsutawney Groundhog Club, 124 W. Mahoning St., Punxsutawney, PA 15767; (814) 938-7700 or (800) 752-PHIL.

### Steamboat Days
(Winona, MN): Early July. Riverfront town celebrates its steamy heritage. Contact: Winona Area Jaycees, P.O. Box 308, Winona, MN 55987.

### Watermelon Days Festival
(Cordele, GA): First two weeks of July. Watermelon Capital champ throws fortnight of festivities. Contact: Cordele-Crisp Chamber of Commerce, P.O. Box 158, Cordele, GA 31015; (912) 273-1668.

## — August —

### Abbott's Magic Get-Together
(Colon, MI): First week in August. Magic Capital hosts major magician's fun fest. Contact: Abbott's Magic Manufacturing Co., 124 St. Joseph St., Colon, MI 49040; (616) 432-3235.

### Arkansas Valley Fair
(Rocky Ford, CO): Third week of August. Melon capital fruit giveaway is a big hit at this country fair. Contact: Rocky Ford Chamber of Commerce, 105 N. Main St., Rocky Ford, CO 81067; (719) 254-7483.

### Hope Watermelon Festival
(Hope, AR): Mid-August. President Clinton's hometown celebrates its local melons. Contact: Hope Chamber of Commerce, P.O. Box 250, Hope, AR 71801; (501) 777-3640.

### Maine Lobster Festival

(Rockland, ME): First weekend in August. Crustacean chow-down, parade, and races. Contact: Maine Lobster Festival Committee, P.O. Box 552, Rockland, ME 04841; (207) 596-0376 or (800) LOB-CLAW.

### National Blueberry Festival

(South Haven, MI): Mid-August. Berry good festival. Contact: National Blueberry Festival, P.O. Box 469, South Haven, MI 49090; (616) 434-6791.

### Shartlesville Watermelon Festival

(Shartlesville, PA): August. Wild and silly melon fest. Contact: Shartlesville Watermelon Festival, P.O. Box 212, Shartlesville, PA 19554; (610) 488-7792.

### Waterfront Festival

(Gloucester, MA): Third week in August. Maritime history and culture in one of America's foremost seafaring communities. Contact: Cape Ann Chamber of Commerce, 33 Commercial St., Gloucester, MA 01930; (508) 283-1601.

## FALL

### — September —

### Annual Cranberry Festival

(Bandon, OR): Late September. Boogie down at bog fest. Contact: Cranberry Festival Association, P.O. Box 348, Bandon, OR 97411; (541) 347-2277.

### Annual Duck Fair

(Havre de Grace, MD): September. The real decoy festival. Contact: Havre de Grace Decoy Museum, 100 Giles St., Havre de Grace, MD 21078; (410) 939-3739.

### Annual Marigold Festival

(Pekin, IL): Weekend after Labor Day. Favorite flower festival. Contact: Pekin Chamber of Commerce/Marigold Festival Committee, P.O. Box 636, Pekin, IL 61555; (309) 346-2106.

### Bigfoot Days

(Willow Creek, CA): Labor Day weekend. Bigfoot capital stomps through a weekend of fun and games. Contact: Willow Creek Chamber of Commerce, P.O. Box 704, Willow Creek, CA 95573; (916) 629-2693.

### Danish Days

(Solvang, CA): Third week of September. Danish Capital of America shows its great Dane roots. Contact: Danish Days Foundation, P.O. Box 1474, Solvang, CA 93464; (805) 686-9386.

### Green River Melon Days

(Green River, UT): Third weekend in September. Melons, melons everywhere. Contact: Green River Travel Council, John Wesley Powell Museum, 885 E. Main St., Green River, UT 84525; (801) 564-3526.

### Kentucky Bourbon Festival

(Bardstown, KY): Third weekend in September. Drink up, but don't drive home. Contact: Bardstown–Nelson County Tourist and Convention Commission, Office of Special Events, 107 E. Stephen Foster Ave., P.O. Box 867, Bardstown, KY 40004; (502) 348-0255.

This prize-winning pumpkin tipped the scales at 600 pounds during the Morton Pumpkin Festival in 1995. *Courtesy Morton Chamber of Commerce*

### Morton Pumpkin Festival

(Morton, IL): Second week of September. Great pumpkin party. Contact: Morton Chamber of Commerce, 416 W. Jefferson St., Morton, IL 61550; (309) 263-2491.

### Mushroom Festival

(Kennett Square, PA): Mid-September. 'Shroom celebration. Contact: Chester County Tourist Bureau, 601 Westtown Rd., Suite 170, West Chester, PA 19382; (610) 344-6365 or (800) 228-9933.

### National Lentil Festival

(Pullman, WA): Third weekend in September. Legume-a-thon. Contact: Pullman Chamber of Commerce, N. 415 Grand Ave., Suite A, Pullman, WA 99160; (509) 334-3565.

### Schooner Festival

(Gloucester, MA): Early September. Set sail for old-fashioned fun. Contact: Cape Ann Chamber of Commerce, 33 Commercial St., Gloucester, MA 01930; (508) 283-1601.

## — October —

### American Royal International Barbecue Contest

(Kansas City, MO): Early October. World's largest barbecue competition smokes out top taste treats. Contact: American Royal International Barbecue Contest, 1701 American Royal Court, Kansas City, MO 64102; (816) 221-9800.

### Annual World's Championship Quartz Crystal Dig

(Mount Ida, AR): Mid-October. Crystal dig and rock show for new and old agers alike. Contact: Mount Ida Chamber of Commerce, P.O. Box 6, Mount Ida, AR 71957; (501) 867-2723.

### Anoka Halloween Events

(Anoka, MN): Throughout October. Halloween Capital scares up a month's worth of tricks and treats. Contact: Anoka Area Chamber of Commerce, 222 E. Main St., Anoka, MN 55303; (612) 421-7130.

### Kaolin Festival

(Sandersville, GA): Mid-October. Celebration honoring versatile white clay. Contact: Washington County Chamber of Commerce, 119 Jones St., P.O. Box 582, Sandersville, GA 31082; (912) 552-3288.

### Lexington Barbecue Festival

(Lexington, NC): Late October. Southern barbecue cook-off and celebration. Contact: Lexington Area Chamber of Commerce, 16 East Center St., P.O. Drawer C, Lexington, NC 27293; (910) 248-5929.

— November —

### Crystal City Spinach Festival

(Crystal City, TX): Early November. Leafy greens star at this iron-filled festival. Crystal City Spinach Festival Association, P.O. Box 100, Crystal City, TX 78839; (210) 374-3161.

### Norsefest/Lutefisk Fest

(Madison, MN): Second weekend in November. All-you-can-eat lye-soaked cod fest. Contact: Madison Area Chamber of Commerce, 404 6th Ave., Madison, MN 56256; (320) 598-7373, ext. 14.

### Salley Chitlin Strut

(Salley, SC): Weekend after Thanksgiving. Locals strut their chitlin stuff. Contact: Town of Salley, Office of the Mayor, P.O. Box 484, Salley, SC 29137; (803) 258-3485.

## WINTER

— February—

### Groundhog Day Festivities

(Sun Prairie, WI, and Punxsutawney, PA): Annually on Feb. 2. Will Phil and Jimmy see their shadows? Dueling groundhogs forecast the weather (maybe). Contact: Punxsutawney Chamber of Commerce, 124 W. Mahoning St., Punxsutawney, PA 15767; (814) 938-7700 or (800) 752-PHIL and Sun Prairie Chamber of Commerce, 109 E. Main St., Sun Prairie, WI 53590; (608) 837-4547.

### National Date Festival

(Indio, CA) February. Celebrates the great date (fruit, not romance). Contact: Riverside County Fair Grounds, 46-350 Arabia St., Indio, CA 92201; (619) 863-8247.

# APPENDIX

## RECOMMENDED READING

Bergheim, Laura A. *Weird, Wonderful America: The Nation's Most Offbeat and Off-the-Beaten Path Tourist Attractions.* New York: Collier Books, 1988.

Brumberg, Bruce and Karen Axelrod. *Watch It Made in the USA: A Visitors Guide to the Companies That Make Your Favorite Products.* Santa Fe, NM: John Muir, 1994.

Canton, George. *Pop Culture Landmarks: A Travelers Guide.* Detroit: Visible Ink, 1995.

Dickson, Paul and Robert Skole. *The Volvo Guide to Halls of Fame.* Washington, DC: Living Planet Press, 1995.

Geffen, Alice and Carole Berglie. *Food Festival: The Guidebook to America's Best Regional Food Celebrations,* second edition. Woodstock, VT: The Countryman Press, 1994.

Gurvis, Sandra. *The Cockroach Hall of Fame and 101 Other Off-the-Wall Museums.* New York: Citadel Press, 1994.

Johnson, Greg and Vince Staten. *Real Barbecue.* New York: Harper & Row, 1988.

Kennedy, Roger G. *Rediscovering America.* Boston: Houghton Mifflin, 1990.

Kuralt, Charles. *A Life on the Road.* New York: Ivy Books, 1991.

————*On the Road with Charles Kuralt.* New York: Fawcett, 1986.

# APPENDIX

# C

## A STATE INDEX OF WORLD CAPITALS

Featured entries are listed in italics.

### Alabama

Bass Capital of the World (Eufala), 126, 129

Butterfly Capital of Alabama (Selma), 45

Crappie Capital of the World (Weiss Lake), 129

Fire Hydrant Capital of the World (Albertville), 9

Helicopter Capital of the World (Ozark), 8

Mardi Gras Capital of the World (Mobile), 230

Peanut Capital of the World (Dothan), 65, 251

Piston Engine Manufacturing Capital of the World (Mobile), 8

Sock Capital of the World (Ft. Payne), 2–3

Soil Pipe Capital of the World (Anniston), 9

### Alaska

Canned Salmon Capital of the World (Ketchikan), 129

*Eagle Capital of America* (Haines), 43, 46–48

Hanging Basket Capital of the World (Anchorage), 66

Salmon Capital of the World (Ketchikan), 129

### Arizona

Dude Ranch Capital of the World (Wickenburg), 175

### Arkansas

Folk Music Capital of the World (Mountain View), 174

Goldfish Capital of the World (Paragould), 129

Minnow Capital of the World (Lonoke), 129

*Pink Tomato Capital of the World* (Bradley County), 67, 89–90

*Quartz Crystal Capital of the World* (Mount Ida), 202, 214–216

Rice and Duck Capital of the World (Stuttgart), 44

*Spinach Capital of the World* (Alma), 65, 249, 250, 268, 269–270, 271

*Watermelon Capital of the World* (Hope), 65, 250, 272, 273, 278

World Championship Duck Calling Competition (Stuttgart), 44

### California

Almond Capital of the World (Sacramento), 64

Artichoke Center of the World (Castroville), 64

Asparagus Capital of the World (Stockton), 64

Avocado Capital of the World (Fallbrook), 64

Bass Capital of the West (Clear Lake), 129

*Bigfoot Capital of the World* (Willow Creek), 227, 235–238

Blackberry Capital of the World (McCloud), 64

Broccoli Capital of the World (Greenfield), 64

Brussels Sprout Capital (Santa Cruz), 64

Butterfly Town (Pacific Grove), 45

Camellia Capital of the World (Sacramento), 65

Carrot Capital of America (Holtville), 64

Cherry Capital of the World (Linden), 64

*Danish Capital of America* (Solvang), 147, 149–152

*Date Capital of the World* (Indio), 65, 75–77

Egg Basket of the World (Petaluma), 101

Film Capital of the World (Hollywood), 174

Flower Capital of the World (Encinitas Leucadia), 65

288

# INDEX

| | DATE | | |
|---|---|---|---|
| | | | |
| | | | |
| | | | |
| | | | |
| | | | |
| | | | |
| | | | |
| | | | |
| | | | |

8-27-97